The Supply Side Revolution in Britain

To Margaret Thatcher

The Supply Side Revolution in Britain

Patrick Minford

Edward Gonner Professor of Applied Economics
University of Liverpool

Edward Elgar
Institute of Economic Affairs

The Institute of Economic Affairs was set up as a research and educational trust under a trust deed signed in 1955. It began regular publication in 1957 with specialised studies of markets and prices. It is a company limited by guarantee, controlled by Managing Trustees, and independent of any political party.

Published by
Edward Elgar Publishing Limited/Institute of Economic Affairs
Gower House
Croft Road
Aldershot
Hants GU11 3HR
England

Edward Elgar Publishing Company
Old Post Road
Brookfield
Vermont 05036
USA

British Library Cataloguing in Publication Data
Minford, Patrick
  The supply side revolution in Britain.
  1. Great Britain. Economic conditions. Policies of
  government, history
  I. Title II. Institute of Economic Affairs
  330.941

Library of Congress Cataloging in Publication Data
Minford, Patrick
  The supply side revolution in Britain / Patrick Minford.
    p. cm.
  Includes index.
    1.Great Britain – Economic policy – 1945– 2. Supply-side
  economics – Great Britain. 3. Thatcher, Margaret. I. Title.
  HC256.6.M56 1991
  338.941–dc20   90–20810
                                                                CIP

ISBN 1 85278 426 1
     1 85278 428 8 (paperback)

Printed in Great Britain by
Billing & Sons Ltd, Worcester

Contents

Figures and Tables

Figures

Tables

Preface

The essays in this book were written over more than a decade and bear the imprint of many influences, as the references in the text make clear.

There is of course the ubiquitous influence of the classical tradition in economics, revived in modern times by Milton Friedman, Karl Brunner and the New Classical economists, notably Robert Lucas and Thomas Sargent.

Closer to home, I own an enormous debt to my colleagues at Liverpool over these years, some of whom are co-authors of these essays; and in particular to Kent Matthews and David Peel who were co-founders of the Liverpool Research Group in Macro-economics. It was within this Group that the research programme drawn on in these pages took place. The names of fellow-researchers who at various times have helped in the programme are to be found throughout the book: I must thank especially Anupam Rastogi and Paul Ashton, who have been key collaborators for many years.

A programme of research like ours could not have taken place without considerable financial support. That has been provided continuously, though also with continuous probing and questioning to our undoubted benefit, by the Economic and Social Research Council since 1977, and from 1983 the ESRC Consortium for Forecasting and Modelling. There may seem to be an inconsistency between calling for free market discipline and receiving public money for research: I hope not, and argue as much later in these pages. The taxpayer must ultimately judge whether the money was well spent in obtaining a better understanding of the ways the economy is managed. At any rate I am most grateful to the ESRC, the Consortium, and through them to the taxpayer for their fourteen-odd years of support to date.

Three friends outside Liverpool have had particular influence on me: Michael Beenstock, Arthur Seldon and Alan Walters. All three have helped me enormously over the years in my intellectual efforts to integrate 'micro' with 'macro', the recurring theme of this book.

Arthur was also responsible for many of these pieces appearing in print, in the IEA's publications under his editorship; and from him I absorbed some elements of writing economics in plain English – how good that is both for one's writing and for one's economics!

The essays have been left in all essentials in their original form; I have corrected some grammatical and other infelicities. I am grateful to Jane Lucas for helping me to put the volume together, to Sylvia Allan for elegantly and accurately re-typesetting the essays, and to Julie Leppard and the efficient team at the IEA and Edward Elgar for bringing the book out so fast on two continents. My wife, Rosie, and the family have put up with much over the years as I struggled with research and writing; I am indebted to them for that and also for the improvements induced by our numerous family arguments on these matters.

Finally, I salute the peaceful revolutionary who carried out the supply side revolution in Britain. Margaret Thatcher has now stepped down as leader of her party but her example remains: she showed how it could be done. Thatcherism is now irreversibly in the British people's bloodstream, after decades of socialism had led them to forget how free markets had once been the basis of their rights and prosperity. This book is – inevitably – dedicated to her.

Introduction

Whether one likes it or not, the dozen years since Mrs Thatcher gained power in 1979 have constituted a peaceful revolution in the way the British economy is organised. Virtually no area of activity has remained untouched by the drive to instate market forces and reduce government intervention. Tax rates have been cut and restructured, labour laws have reduced union monopoly power, credit and exchange controls have been abolished and financial markets decartelised, monetarist policies for inflation have been substituted for wage and price controls, the transport industry has been deregulated, competition has been intensified in education (by, for example, schools opting out of the state sector), an internal market for hospital care and consumer choice of doctors, privatisation and contracting out in the public sector . . .

The list goes on and on, making this period of change probably the most radical in our history. In twelve short years Mrs Thatcher's governments have rolled back market obstacles that in some cases have taken a century or more to put in place, though admittedly not a few were the creation of Attlee's 1945 government, subsequently acquiesced in and even extended by later Conservative governments.

Much could be written about this period, has and certainly will be. It is not yet over, and the next election will decide whether there will be a fourth term to allow Mrs Thatcher's chosen successor, John Major to take the programme through to its full conclusion.

This book however is not for the most part directly about it. Rather, it gathers together, under one cover, the papers in which I have discussed these policies before (and while they were formed), together with the reasoning behind them. The papers are all written for people with an interest in, and possibly limited knowledge of, economics. The majority of them were published by the Institute of Economic Affairs, which has a fine tradition of such writing, and whose Research and Publications Director, Arthur Seldon, helped and stimulated me to write many of them. These papers draw on and, to some extent, develop in the British context the free market

1

ideas which both justify Mrs Thatcher's policy revolution and have
had a considerable influence on its development.

The papers were generally written in the heat of battle; they are
attempts to persuade. They draw on and explain in non-technical
terms a large programme of research into the British economy
which my colleagues and I have been pursuing at Liverpool
University. It is one thing to believe in free markets, quite another
to get them working in a particular economy without side-effects in
the course of introduction which causes a popular revulsion. As has
been remarked, the water at Niagara is calm one mile upstream and
one mile downstream, but the transition creates problems.

How can that transition be designed? What problems are suitable
for the Big Bang approach? Which must be tackled quickly, which
are second order and can be postponed? These, and similar
questions, require careful and, if possible, quantitative analysis.
Politicians about to run the gauntlet of reform need to be sure the
potential gains are worth it and that at least some gains from some
parts of it will show up before the next election.

Some essays also stand back from the fray and reflect on the
nature of political change and this episode in particular. What
creates popular coalitions for change? Why did Mrs Thatcher's
reforms become accepted, in spite of virulent opposition from
vested interest groups? Is there a moral justification for the
Thatcherite refusal to redistribute beyond the requirements of the
'deserving poor'? These are questions which the Supply Side
Revolution in Britain has brought into strong belief.

The book therefore naturally divides into two halves; the first
(and longest) consists of policy analysis and prescription, the second
of reflections on the policy process and the determinants of power.
In the rest of this introduction, I give an account of the ideas in these
papers and the context in which they were written.

Policy Analysis and Prescription

Monetarism

Monetarism, in the narrow sense of controlling the money supply in
order to bring down inflation, was the starting point of Mrs
Thatcher's policies and opens this book. In July 1980 Sir Geoffrey
Howe had just presented the first budget of this government in

which he had announced his plan to reduce the growth rate of the money supply (then measured by M3) and the Public Sector Borrowing Requirement. Having urged just such policies on him and Mrs Thatcher I wrote in support of them in *The Banker*, asking however for a further explicit commitment to a set of targets over several years.

The idea was to tie the government's prestige to the achievement of these targets, so that retreat would be embarrassing and their credibility would be correspondingly enhanced with the private sector. With rational expectations (which implies intelligent use by the public of such available information about policy and other relevant factors affecting the economy) the very belief that these policies would be followed would condition wage bargaining and price setting, so making it easier to bring down inflation without serious recession.

In his next Budget, Howe went ahead with this idea and the Medium-Term Financial Strategy was born. Shortly afterwards, I argued to the House of Commons Treasury Committee, that the MTFS would bring down inflation to 4.3% by 1983 at the cost of no growth in 1980 followed by a slow recovery (1.6% in 1981, 2.9% in 1982). This Liverpool inflation forecast which was widely derided turned out to be startlingly accurate: inflation in 1983 was 4.6%. However, the growth forecast was too optimistic by a long way: growth was -2% in 1980 and -1.1% in 1981, and only in 1982 did recovery begin with growth of 1.8%. This, I believe, was largely the result of poor credibility.

In April 1981 I wrote with David Peel about the state of the economic strategy, the next paper. We focused on the difficulties with creating credibility for the MTFS. There was little evidence to the public that the government would stick to its targets. The MTFS only appeared in the 1980 Budget, a year after monetarist policies were anounced; both the PSBR and the M3 targets were exceeded in the first year, and again in the second. We know now that the M3 overshoot was the result of deregulation and that the wider aggregates were no longer suitable targets; also that the PSBR was being badly affected by incipient recession, yet at the time there was confusion.

Credibility only began to be established when Howe's 1981 Budget raised taxes in order to reduce the PSBR, even though we were in recession. Because this flew against the conventional

Keynesian wisdom, the penny finally dropped with the public that policy had really changed – long term. There was less talk of the inevitable 'U-turn'.

Peel and I argued that credibility could have been guaranteed to be established by 'immediacy', a policy of cutting the PSBR and money supply growth at once on coming into government. I had advocated this in my evidence to the Treasury Committee (I returned to it periodically, as in the next paper giving a general account of rational expectations and the New Classical economics). Yet this course had been rejected from the start in favour of the 'gradualism' advocated by Professor Milton Friedman. Given that, we argued that at least it was essential to hit the targets from the start.

I returned to these issues much later (1988) in a review of monetary policy in the context of deregulation – the next paper. With the benefit of hindsight it can be seen that M3 should not have been used and that the policies which were actually followed were pretty 'immediate': the growth of M0, the most reliable monetary indicator, fell rapidly from 1979 and the PSBR was cut drastically when allowance was made for the effects of recession. In a rewriting of history with actual and announced immediacy in place of the unintended near-immediacy that took place, I found that policies would have delivered a still faster drop in inflation without such a prolonged rise in unemployment. If, in addition, other policies to bring down unemployment had been followed earlier, the early 1980s would have been a less painful experience.

Unemployment – The Supply Side in the Labour Market

In the 1981 paper, Peel and I had also spelt out more explicitly the reasons for rising unemployment and the policies which could reduce it. I had referred to this analysis briefly in the earlier Treasury Committee piece but by 1981, with unemployment reaching 2 million, it began to move to centre stage. Inflation was soon to fall steadily, and the problems of growth and unemployment accordingly took precedence in public attention.

The analysis was highly unpopular on the left and bitterly attacked. It stressed the crucial role of freely available unemployment benefits in keeping wages up and in discouraging the unemployed from taking low-paid jobs which either were, or could easily become, available. Taxes on labour of any sort exacerbated the problem by raising the pre-tax wage that must be achieved to equate with benefits. Union power worsened matters by raising wages in the union sector, so reducing jobs there and forcing more people to find low-paid jobs in the non-union sector; yet given the benefits available these would not be attractive, and those searching would go on the dole.

The analysis is set out more fully in the two articles that follow, the first provocatively entitled 'Trade Unions Destroy a Million Jobs', the second looking at unemployment internationally. In these, there is also some brief account of the policies that could cure the problem of unemployment which I saw as central to the efficient working of the economy. However, a full statement of the necessary policies did come out later in 1983 in *Unemployment – Cause and Cure*. It went into details of how benefits could be reformed by a 70% cap, loss of benefits on job refusal (including refusal of a public job on 'workfare'), and a negative income tax approach to in-work benefits. These last two were eventually implemented in the Restart programme from mid-1986 and the Fowler reforms of benefits which became law in 1987.

The book also set out proposals to eliminate the closed shop and reduce union immunities with the eventual aim of abolition. The government never accepted the idea of abolition, but in a series of four laws since 1982, have steadily cut back on immunities and finally eliminated the closed shop.

What the book did not do was go into how taxes might be reformed and cut, and with what concomitant cuts in public programmes. I set this out however in a long article for Economic Affairs in the Spring of 1984, 'State Expenditure – A Study in Waste'; I subsequently included this with revised figures in the second edition of *Unemployment – Cause and Cure* (Basil Blackwell, 1985). Two excerpts are included as Chapter 7. I argued that the objectives of most public programmes could be achieved by market forces combined with direct financial assistance to those in need; then taxes could be brought down and unemployment substantially reduced. This, in turn, of course, would eliminate much public spending devoted to the alleviation of unemployment: not just benefits but also policies, such as regional, inner city, training, indirectly caused by unemployment. There would be other benefits to the economy from lower taxes, including those conventionally measured by consumer surplus, but I argued that by far the greatest benefit would be the reduction of unemployment itself.

In a related recent article, 'The Poverty Trap after the Fowler Reforms' (Chapter 8), I considered how the tax and benefit system could be reformed to deal with the 'poverty trap': the condition where extra income is not worthwhile taking for someone in work because loss of benefits and extra tax eat deeply into it. It turns out that it is of most gain to the economy to devote available savings in public spending to lowering general taxation, such as the standard rate, rather than to lowering tax on the least well-off or to reducing the rate of benefit withdrawal. The reason is that it is extremely expensive to do the latter and the extra incentives so created for the least well-off are far more than offset by the worsening of incentives for the great majority.

It is worth mentioning in passing that cutting the high marginal tax rates on high earners is the opposite to this. Far from costing revenue, the evidence suggests that it will increase it. It is by now well known that the cuts in top tax rates from 83% to 60% in 1980 and again to 40% in 1988, raised the share of revenue contributed by top earners after both cuts. I include (Chapter 15) a note written in early 1987 setting out the facts then; subsequently, Paul Ashton and I published the results of research on the hours of work of top earners. We found that their response to higher marginal pay was strong: a 0.5% increase in hours for every 1% rise in it. The implication was that the hours response alone would yield a rise in revenue from the first cut in top rates while it would have made the second revenue – neutral. Add on the effects of tax avoidance and migration, and you have strong grounds for lowering the top marginal rate: not only does the economy gain in output and efficiency, but also the Exchequer receives more revenue, which allows the burdens on other taxpayers to be reduced, yielding still further gains to the economy.

The Supply Side in Other Markets

The work on public expenditure aroused my interest in the operation of the many other markets in which there were obstacles (or 'distortions') to free market forces and whose malfunctioning spilled over into the labour market, causing unemployment. In a number of papers I attempted to analyse, and if possible quantify, the direct losses of consumer welfare (as well as the indirect losses through unemployment) in some of these markets.

My colleagues and I began with housing where, after several years' work, we published in 1987 a book, *The Housing Morass*, discussing the effects primarily of the Rent Acts and other rented sector intervention on the mobility of manual workers. While we identified costs of other interventions, such as mortgage tax relief on owner-occupied housing, we found the overwhelming cost to come through immobility of these workers, who for the most part used rented housing. The immobility added to regional (and so also national) unemployment.

The next paper in this volume is an account of this work we wrote in *Economic Affairs*. By 1988 the government had brought forward a new law which substantially liberalised the rented sector for new landlords.

This work led naturally to work on the regional question, which is the topic of the next two papers. My argument is that a shift of advantage away from the North to the South will have two main impacts under our previous (now partly modified) institutions.

First, manual labour in the North will become unemployed and will not move. Their wages will fall in the North but not enough to make it attractive to rent whatever marginal accommodation can be found (effectively at high B & B rates) in the South. Meanwhile, in the South, manual wages will rise and unemployment will fall, but not as much as it will rise in the North, because already it is low in the South and extra labour correspondingly hard to come by.

Secondly, non-manual workers, because home-owning, will be freely mobile, in the sense that they can sell their homes at whatever price the market offers and buy another elsewhere. So, as Northern activity falls, reducing their wages, so these workers will attempt to migrate as long as wages (net of living costs) are higher in the South.

These workers will also not be unemployed for long, North or South, because their unemployment benefits are low relative to wages, so they will get a job even if lower paid than before. Thus, the shift of advantage from the North will not cause unemployment but will trigger emigration among these workers.

However, this migration to the South will put upward pressure on land prices there, because of limited land with planning permission. This rise in land prices will in turn raise the costs of doing business in the South relative to the North. High land prices in the South therefore become the Northerners' best friend. The migration pressure is largely frustrated by the shortage of land and, in turn, pushes business into migration Northward. In this non-manual part of the labour market, market forces are unleashed which restore the North-South balance. Unfortunately, in the manual part no such forces are released, only Northern unemployment results. This makes it essential to liberate the forces in this part too, both by facilitating migration through a liberalised rented sector and by improving the workings of the regional labour markets (through a less attractive benefit system, less powerful unions and the other measures discussed above).

These ideas are spelt out in rather more detail, with distinctions between different sectors and an analysis of the possible causes of the shift in advantage against the North, in the second of these two papers, written with Peter Stoney. Among the particular disadvantages of the North we identified transport and the operation of the Dock Labour Scheme, now thankfully no more.

'How to De-politicise Local Government' takes up the theme of the community charge (or poll tax) and other issues of local government. I argue that the poll tax will totally change local authorities' attitudes to charging for their services individually if they can. Only local services that the floating local voter actually wants to pay for will be funded by the poll tax, the rest will be paid for specifically by charging. Local governent will be depoliticised in the sense that it will attend purely to value for money, instead of being able to fund political causes ('nuclear free zones' and other matters of little value to its voters) secure in the knowledge that the floating voters will not have to bear the true cost.

During 1988, the question of NHS reform came to the fore: the government had intended to leave it for another term but its inability to handle the demands on it, in spite of steadily rising provision, brought the issue of reform forward. 'A Policy for the National Health Service' sets out a market alternative for the NHS in detail. It argues that the principle of the NHS is the support of those who cannot afford a minimum standard of health-care provision, for whatever reason, including lack of income or chronic illness. This principle is not compromised by giving the support directly and allowing the market to operate.

The paper deals with a range of arguments against this, special to the case of health care. Though there are difficulties, such as the tendency for private medical care to overcharge insurance companies, they can be dealt with by allowing the market to develop its own mechanisms: in this example the insurance companies buy into the medical business and refer their patients to their own firms, or otherwise refuse to pay more than what these firms would charge.

Health care is a service industry in which the providers know more than their customers – 'asymmetric information'. But, in this respect, it is not different in principle from many other service industries – airlines, legal services, dentistry, education – where we would not consider wholesale state provision. We should not for health care either.

'Higher Education – A Simple Solution' turns to my own patch and applies the same basic analysis to universities and polytechnics. The details differ but the essential argument is the same. There is no need for a panoply of state institutions: all that is necessary is for the state to support a scholarship system which channels payments directly to students worthy of support, either because of individual or subject need.

Power and the Political Economy of Reform

Why do revolutions, peaceful or bloody, take place? In these last essays I turned to the issue of power and, how in particular, the power to reform is acquired.

In the first, previously unpublished, piece I argue that power tends to a fundamental distribution, in which there is no capacity by any blocking coalition of the people to overthrow it. Such power can be thought of as 'legitimate' or in tune with 'natural rights'; people willingly submit to some power because it is generally cheaper to concentrate policing, defence and related public functions in a central body. The nature of this centralism depends on geography and technology, principally.

The tendency towards this power distribution is enforced by intermediaries, politicians acting in free competition, who offer their services to the people (in return for diverse rewards paid out of the proceeds of liberation) to restore to them their proper rights. These politicians will typically be fellow-countrymen but they need not be, nor need they be resident in the country (indeed often they can only survive if they are not!).

When power is disposed differently, it is still of course power (and actual rights are defined accordingly), but the discontent it creates produces the opportunity for the political entrepreneur and for revolution.

This paper was written in 1987, well before the recent events in Eastern Europe and South Africa. I have, as with all the other papers in this volume, left it essentially as I wrote it originally. In this case, it allows an empirical test of the thesis to be unfolded by events which have, by and large, confirmed it.

It is also no accident or politeness between politicians that has led so many Eastern European revolutionaries or reformers and in South Africa, Mr De Klerk, to look repeatedly to Mrs Thatcher and Britain's experience under her reform programme for lessons and guidance. In the next and last two articles, I discussed Mrs Thatcher's reform programme primarily in political terms, that is looking at it as an exercise in permitting a blocking coalition to become effective.

In 1983, Sir Geoffrey Howe set out his vision of Conservative government. My comments attempt to turn his somewhat vague remarks into a more precise vision of the reforming programme he and Mrs Thatcher seemed to be groping towards (later, I went into much greater detail in 'State Expenditure – A Study in Waste', included in part as Chapter 7 of this volume). I also raised the question of political tactics: a reform programme must be sustained by regular overt rewards to the coalition. It must be popular as well as having a theoretical long-term payoff.

Much later, in 1988 and 1989, in the last paper, it was possible to look back on the first eight years and discern the outline of how Mrs Thatcher's revolution was sold to and embraced by the British people. The people were, of course, discontented at the start (in 1978–9 there was indeed the famous 'winter of discontent' consisting mainly of public service strikes) but that by no means implied that they would accept the specific diagnosis of their malaise.

In retrospect, it seems obvious that they should wish to have greater economic freedom and control over their own lives (therefore political freedom too), as well as the fruits of a more successful economy based on free enterprise. But this assessment obscures the process of persuading them that the turmoil in transition was worth the end-state, and perhaps even of discovering their preferences for greater freedom relative to centralised protection and control.

Presumably, all revolutions in their various ways involve such processes of persuasion and discovery.

It is here that we can see the much-disputed power of ideas. People will only agree to revolutionary programmes on the basis of ideas about their effect, no-one, let alone a disparate group of people, will throw over even an uncomfortable state for an unknown alternative without an idea of what it might contain. Marx and Lenin described to an earlier generation of discontents what the Communist state might contain, so inspiring the Communist revolutions of this century. When people accepted their descriptions, then the fundamental distribution of power among those people was the Communist state. However, their analysis of the fruits of a Communist state turned out to be wrong. Even now, we do not know what difficulties our free market systems will throw up which could upset their legitimacy. But the balance of ideas, including the empirical evidence we have accumulated, at present sustains a fundamental power distribution based on the free market and the human rights of habeas corpus.

Conclusions

In this volume I have brought together my papers on the political economy of Thatcherism, *alias* the supply side revolution in Britain. They set out my vision of what such a revolution should consist of and how it came to be supported or permitted by the British people (those who argue that only 40% or so actually supported the programme miss the point that another 20% or so refused to block it by voting Labour, the party that represented the status quo).

The programme was long term in its intended consequences, but it had to be sustained in the short term through three general elections. It, therefore, offers a fascinating source-book of material about how radical changes can occur in a modern democracy. This volume bears witness to my own long-standing fascination with it.

References

P. Minford, D. Davies, A. Sprague and M. Peel (1983), *Unemployment – Cause and Cure*, 1st edn, Martin Robertson (now Basil Blackwell), Oxford.

P. Minford, M. Peel and P. Ashton (1987), *The Housing Morass*, Institute of Economic Affairs, London.

1. A Return to Sound Money?*

I welcome this budget enthusiastically for the change of direction that it indicates. Not only are the changes to be implemented this year bold and appropriate, but explicit commitments have been made in the budget speech to these future actions:

1. Progressive reduction of the rate of growth of the money supply and of the public sector borrowing requirement (PSBR).
2. Further reductions of public spending to achieve this.
3. The progressive dismantling of exchange controls.
4. A review of the investment income surcharge ('justification . . . debatable'), of capital gains tax on paper gains, and of the capital transfer tax.

Some have commented that it is 'dangerous' to switch from direct to indirect taxes, because of the effect on the retail price index (3.5 per cent) and the supposed 'knock-on' effect on wages. No doubt there are some officials who hope that wages will react in this way and cause an early 'U-turn' towards incomes policy. The Treasury's forecast of accelerating prices seems to reflect some such reaction. These views illustrate a deep-seated unwillingness to apply straight-forward economic analysis. Clever officials suppose somehow that working people are incapable of recognising their own economic interests; that they and union leaders will not realise they are enjoying a rise in real post-tax wages, being misled by the drop in real pre-tax wages! Yet one only has to state this to expose its utter absurdity; needless to say, there is not a shred of evidence for it.

My only regret about this budget is that the forward commitments on the money supply and the PSBR are not made in explicit arithmetic form, year-by-year, for the next four years. It has been suggested that the Treasury opposed this, on the grounds that circumstances might change – and lead to a more inflationary ('expansionary') policy. Yet, this is precisely why we need this total

* First published in *The Banker*, **129**, 641, pp. 29–31, July 1979.

commitment and the implied total commitment to the elimination of inflation from our society by the next election. It is the absence of total commitment that allows inflation to run out of control, as the rest of this article explains.

My hope – and indeed my belief – is that ministers acquiesced in the omission of such detailed commitments only because of the speed with which the budget had to be put together. It follows that they should soon announce them. And the sooner that commitment is made, the sooner will the beneficial effects of these policies be felt on interest rates, wages and prices.

The Case for the Tories' Strategy

This is the first budget in this country drawn up explicitly according to monetarist principles. Previously, in the budgets of Denis Healey from late 1976 onwards, we have had half-hearted compromises designed to placate 'irrational financial markets'. Targets were enunciated for money supply growth and the PSBR, and were in practice broadly followed. However, they were not at the heart of the strategy, and were not paraded in the general exposition of policy that ministers adopted to the public at large. Mr Joel Barnett was occasionally allowed to make a few nasty arithmetic points but they were not allowed to obscure the main strategy. This was to increase public spending as soon as a social contract on wages could be 'delivered' by the unions. This contract would reduce inflation and so allow those ministers to 'expand the economy' without fear of upsetting the City.

Such policies have throughout the post-war period been dear to the hearts of senior civil servants. Indeed it is they that have been largely responsible for selling them to our political masters. They have succeeded to the extent that few politicians have been able to avoid paying lip service to 'responsible wage bargaining', private sector 'profiteering', 'joint consultation with unions and industry', 'invest-ment-led growth', 'increasing industrial efficiency', and so on.

With the advent of the new government, the predictable and cunning barrage by senior officials has begun, to 'educate' ministers and to bring them back to the complacent ways of previous macroeconomic failure. However, since these efforts were totally predictable, ministers should be quite able to use these officials constructively to carry out their strategies, largely because these strategies have been carefully worked out outside Whitehall; the academic opposition has a strong academic and research base and within the economics profession at large the tide has turned strongly in the direction of the policies this government is adopting. The evidence is now overwhelmingly seen to favour the view that markets work and that macroeconomic policies can have a major impact on inflation with at most a modestly stabilising effect on output.

It is by now familiar that the central assertion common to 'monetarists' (who are nevertheless a very diverse lot in their detailed support for this assertion) is that growth of the money supply must be controlled. Yet, the true reasons for the necessity of control are hard to grasp, being, in fact, rather technical. They involve us deeply in the area of expectations formation.

Textbook Monetarism . . .

The standard textbook view – vintage 1970 – of how the economy works went something like this. Imagine the economy starts off with full employment and an inflation rate of, say, 5 per cent. Now let there be some expansion in demand such as a stimulating budget. This raises output and employment. The resulting pressure of demand causes inflation to rise; initially not by much because people only gradually realise that prices are rising faster. However, as their expectations catch up with the faster rise, inflation rises more rapidly. If the growth in money supply is held constant (i.e., the budget deficit is financed by borrowing outside the banking system), then this higher inflation causes a tightening in financial markets; this, if allowed to continue, will contract ('crowd-out') demand and cause the inflation to fall back. The higher deficit will cause a higher price level and higher interest rates in the long run but not a higher inflation rate, because the money supply growth has been held under control.

By contrast, were the authorities to have allowed the money supply to expand so as to prevent any tightening in financial markets (a view associated with the 'real bills' doctrine that money should accommodate the needs of trade at constant interest rates), then no limit would intervene to prevent inflation rising. Strictly speaking, an economy with these policies would in time inevitably move into hyperinflation; in practice monetary policy would at some point have to tighten in the face of this worsening inflation. The basic point is that the absence of control over the money supply makes the economy exceedingly vulnerable to inflation.

. . . and its Refinements

This standard textbook model has been challenged from two main viewpoints in recent years. First, the link between budget deficit and money supply growth is closer than this model says because in the long run the extra bonds created by the deficit, if money supply growth is held constant, have to be absorbed by the private sector; to do this interest rates would have to keep on rising to induce investors to hold an ever-rising proportion of bonds in their portfolios. In the long run this would have to stop; therefore a higher budget deficit must in the long run be financed by equiproportionate expansion of money and bonds. The moral is: you cannot in the long run have an independent monetary and fiscal policy.

Second, the 'rational expectations' controversy has questioned the plausibility of the slow process by which agents in the standard model change their inflation expectations. Are they not as well able as the government to perceive the long-run implications of the change in policies? If so, why should they delay in changing their expectations? Whatever view one takes as to the realism of 'fully rational' expectations, this line of thought must lead to severe modification of the basic textbook process. In particular, it speeds it up sharply.

The overall effect of these two developments is to make monetary and fiscal control even more urgent – a short-run matter, in fact. In the textbook model there is room for the authorities to 'wait and see', 'keep options open', and so on – the familiar Whitehall lobby material and the essence of 'fine tuning'. Alas in the new view, lax policies today get translated into their corresponding long-run realities and, before the authorities realise what has happened, they have lost control of inflation – today.

This is in essence the rationale for control of the PSBR and growth in the monetary aggregates. It has little to do with the simple quantity theory of money but emerges rather from a fully articulated view of how the economy is likely to work.

It should be apparent why it is insufficient merely to cut the PSBR and money supply growth this year, in the pursuit of lower inflation.

These cuts must be part of a medium-term programme of sustained and cumulative reduction in the PSBR and monetary growth. The final year of the programme must, if the ultimate objective is a stable currency, envisage a PSBR compatible with the private sector's normal rate of acquisition of bonds and money (or 'net acquisition of financial assets' as this is sometimes called); the evidence for the UK suggests that this is very low in non-inflationary conditions, which suggests a PSBR target of zero as the desirable long-term aim. The equivalent rate of growth of the money supply compatible with zero inflation will be in the region of 3 per cent, the normal growth of real output; but it may vary somewhat between definitions of money, within a range, perhaps, of 2 to 5 per cent.

The issue that is repeatedly raised in opposition to this strategy is unemployment. It is suggested that it will raise unemployment considerably for some length of time; even if it is conceded that this would eventually reduce inflation, the unemployment cost, though temporary, is too large to tolerate, it is argued.

This argument is rooted in the textbook model I described earlier, for in that model the cut in money supply growth works to reduce inflation through the induced rise in unemployment. Yet, as I argued earlier, this fails to take into account the possibility that economic agents will change their inflation expectations 'rationally' in line with the change in policies. If any group of agents in the economy – be they financial agents, or firms, or trade unions – acts in this way, the whole process is sharply speeded up, and the output effects along the path become hard to predict but in any case are likely not to be the recession of the textbook model. They could in principle go either way, depending on the interaction of a variety of shock waves evoked by the change in policies.

Modest Output Effects

I have seen at different times simulations of versions of two 'big' models (the London Business School and the Treasury) under the assumption that agents in the foreign exchange market have rational expectations. These have tended to suggest that policies of permanently cutting the PSBR and money supply growth in parallel would have small output effects but would rapidly reduce inflation.

The reason for the reduction in inflation is clear; it is the anticipation of the long-run effects of the policies acting on immediate behaviour. The reason for the modest output effect is roughly speaking that the direct cut in demand arising from the PSBR cut (i.e., lower public spending or higher taxes) is off-set by higher private spending from (a) the cut in inflation, which directly raises consumption spending (largely an asset effect, but also due to the reduction in uncertainty that lower inflation brings) and (b) the cut in interest rates, which raises the capital value of financial assets and so leads to a diversification into goods.

The numbers in such simulations should not be taken seriously, but they make the point which is that the output effects will probably not be seriously negative for any period of time. In the same spirit, I have set out simulations from the UK model we have developed at Liverpool in which all agents are assumed to have rational expectations.

The simulations assume for illustration that the strategy over the coming five years is as follows:

	79/80	80/82	81/82	82/83	83/84 and after
PSBR as per cent of GDP at factor cost	5.3 (£8¼bn)	4.5	3.8	3.2	2.5
Money supply growth (sterling M3) per cent p.a.	13½	12	11	9½	8

The strategy with which they are compared assumes that the PSBR would have been held at about 6 per cent of GDP and money supply growth at about 15 per cent per annum. This would have implied inflation running at about 12 per cent per annum over the next five years.

Simulation Results

The broad simulation results are that in the long term inflation and interest rates would be some 7 per cent per annum lower with these policies than the 12 per cent per annum that would have otherwise occurred. There is some 'overshooting' of the path in 1981–83 and this should be ignored as unlikely. The level of output would be quite unaffected by 1984–85; meanwhile, there would be minor blips (of ± 1 per cent or so) to it reflecting interacting effects of asset changes and the net balance of public demand. These blips should also probably be largely discounted.

The bolder strategy – which it is to be hoped the Tories would choose – of cutting the PSBR to zero (and money supply growth correspondingly) would thus bring the prize of a stable currency within the grasp of this government before the end of its five-year term.

I stress again that no importance should be attached to the detail of such numbers. However, the policy point is: the gain in lower inflation from such a strategy is very likely to be large in the long run and to come through rapidly, while any temporary loss of output is likely at worst to be of modest significance. Looked at in this light, this budget heralds the start of a strategy which, if persisted in with determination and commitment, offers the promise of a return to a sound currency at a cost that we should be well willing to bear.

2. Is the Government's Economic Strategy on Course?*

The title of this chapter poses a simple question. This government's economic strategy is, at least in conception, a complete departure from the past; to understand it, and therefore to criticise it, we must examine in general terms the rational expectations view of the economy according to which, in our opinion, it is most clearly justified and which is the view we share. Our chapter therefore consists partly of general observations on this framework, interspersed with illustrations from recent events in the UK, and partly of more detailed analysis of current policies. We start with a general discussion of the rational expectations assumption. Then we draw out its implications for macroeconomic behaviour as an equilibrium process, and go on to describe the transmission mechanism for the UK as seen in the 'Liverpool model'. In the following section we consider the meaning of the 'lags' between money and prices, especially in the recent UK context, and review the case for 'immediacy' (rapid cuts in money supply growth) as against 'gradualism'. Next, we consider the role of stabilisation policy, while in the following section we review the political economy of policy choice. In the final two sections we make more detailed comments on the government's monetary and market strategies respectively.

The Rational Expectations Approach

The basis of our approach is the assumption that people use information efficiently in the pursuit of their interests. To make this operational, we suppose first that 'their interests' are 'normal' (i.e., they like more rather than less of commodities and leisure, they avoid pain, etc.) and, secondly, that given perfect knowledge they would know how best to pursue them. Let us call these respectively 'normality' and 'technical competence'. We suppose, thirdly, that

* Written with David Peel. First published in *Lloyds Bank Review*, 140, pp. 1–19, April 1981.

their efficiency in the use of information is absolute, that they know the *true* probabilities attached to possible outcomes, given all the publicly available information; this is 'rational expectations'. This concept is due to Muth (1961), arising out of his work with Modigliani in the 1950s; however, it was Lucas (1972) who first drew attention to its wide implications for macroeconomic and market behaviour.

The assumptions of normality and technical competence are standard in the economist's tool-kit. Yet they are the object of parody by non-economists and patently 'unrealistic'. Economists are parodied as 'believing in' *homo sapiens economicus*, an inhuman machine for self-gratification incorporating a mini-computer for the calculation of first and second order conditions of a maximum for multivariate functions.

Such parody misses the point; these assumptions constitute a powerful theory able to generate a multitude of predictions about economic behaviour. The economic literature of the past two decades is full of the successes (and occasional failures) of prediction by this theory – in fields ranging from consumption, through investment and employment decisions, to education and even marriage.

There is a vast methodological literature on the status of such 'unrealistic' assumptions: Can they be true or false? Does it matter that they violate known facts about certain people's behaviour? Our view is straightforward: *any* theory *must* be 'unrealistic'. A theory is a decision not to *describe* 'reality' in full (how would this add to knowledge?), but to find some general rule, relating *selected* events, which can reproduce reality reasonably closely in relevant respects ('fits the facts'). Therefore, all theory involves selection and unrealism. A good theory, we suggest, will provide a high degree of 'fact-fitting' performance for a low degree of 'complexity'; this is what we mean by 'successful approximation to the truth'.

The success of the normality and technical competence assumptions can be rationalised in various ways. Normality will by definition hold on average so, though there is an aggregation problem, we may expect aggregate behaviour to approximate to normality. Technical competence is another matter. It is possessed by few people, if one is to believe statistics on numeracy and literacy; yet people may consult experts or there may be patterns of behaviour passed on through generations or there may be instinctive cunning in matters of the pocket. What is clear is that there are strong incentives for households or firms to act with technical competence however arrived at. Research on the effects of incentives is steadily turning up examples of the various ways in which society embodies appropriate responses (e.g., Brunner, 1979). The unrealistic assumption of technical competence is therefore consistent with underlying pressures.

The rational expectations view has been widely criticised as 'unrealistic', 'not how people behave', etc.; this criticism has, oddly enough, been most vocally expressed by certain distinguished economists, who have themselves regularly assumed normality and technical competence (e.g., Solow, 1979). The answer is clear; *of course* it is unrealistic, it is meant to be. It is a very powerful assumption for generating predictions. This one assumption is a rich source of restrictions in economic models. The criticism is quite simply irrelevant.

The valid question is: how well do models incorporating this assumption perform relative to models incorporating some alternative? What these critics are claiming, in effect, is that they will do worse. Yet this claim is quite different, and to date it carries no conviction. The evidence on the contrary is accumulating that it is rather successful (e.g., Fama, 1975; Sargent, 1976a, Barro, 1977; Korteweg *et al.*, 1978; and Minford, 1980a); the gathering interest of the profession in this assumption, even on the part of 'Keynesians' (e.g. Tobin, 1980), bears witness to this.

It is not hard to see why it is likely to be successful. As with technical competence, there are strong incentives for households and firms to evaluate information correctly. Consultancy and forecasting firms exist with the sole object of selling such expertise; markets responding to those with such expertise transmit it indirectly in prices to individuals who do not have it. Research into this 'information industry' suggests that, while there must remain a normal profit to information-gathering which must prevent perfect informational efficiency (Grossman and Stiglitz, 1980), nevertheless competition in the industry will drive markets 'close' to this state.

The Nature of the Economy under Rational Expectations

These assumptions lead ineluctably to an equilibrium model of the economy (Lucas, 1975), that is one in which all markets clear continuously. For example, imagine a counter-case: the market for cars is in 'excess supply'. Dealers and buyers have a common information set, on which they will form expectations of future prices in the car market and elsewhere: given these expectations, the excess supply (i.e., cars remaining in dealers' hands) can occur only if it is not worth dealers' while dropping their prices to sell now. However, this is an *equilibrium* based on speculation about future prices.

If dealers had posted prices in advance ('contracts' to sell unlimited quantities at a fixed price), then they could be selling less than they expected. Under the terms of this contract they cannot reduce prices to raise their sales. Yet the point here is that they entered voluntarily into such a contract; customers chose to do business with them on those terms. Contracts do not imply disequilibrium; on the contrary, it is rare to find any transactions not to some extent covered by contracts of some form. Contracts do imply that the impact of particular shocks falls on parties in a specified way; the contract terms reflect expectations at the time of drawing them up. The questions raised by contracts are why agents choose to shift the impacts of shocks in the particular ways we observe. Nevertheless, we cannot ignore contracts in our equilibrium model.

Particular market structures – unions and monopolies – in no way interfere with the generality of equilibrium. On the contrary, a monopoly price (or union wage) is a particular form of market equilibrium in which the monopolist sets terms to maximise his discounted expected returns. The price will be varied according to changes in demand and supply conditions influencing these returns.

The general point is that, on our assumptions, the economy behaves in a way that reflects people's choices, given the framework imposed on them by laws and other government intervention. There is no 'slack' in this system, in other words, unless government itself has created it. Unemployment, for example, is voluntary. If a man loses his job owing to a surprise shift in demand against his firm, he then chooses whether to work elsewhere probably at lower net-of-tax wages (and with the costs of moving) or to take social security benefits. Wages fall to a level at which demand for labour equals the supply, given these benefits. Nevertheless, because government has created a system (i.e., of taxes and benefits) which generates slack, it can add further interventions which can reduce this slack. One popular candidate is monetary and fiscal 'stabilisation' (or counter-cyclical) policy, to which we turn later.

The Transmission Mechanism in the UK

The 'Liverpool model' incorporates the well-known features of the UK economy in a way that is fully documented elsewhere (Minford, 1980a). The key points are:

a.   Financial markets are 'efficient' – a term we use in the sense that prices equate expected returns across these markets nationally and internationally.
b.   Private expenditure is influenced strongly by the level of public sector debt held in portfolios ('portfolio balance'). This implies a tight link over the medium term between fiscal and monetary policy because a permanently-held fiscal deficit injects new debt continuously into private portfolios; if money supply does not rise in proportion, interest rates must rise continuously and this, of course, cannot be sustained indefinitely.
c.   Union wages are determined annually by contract, but non-union wages are determined in a continuous and informal manner (with 'wage-drift', etc.).
d.   There is no 'money-illusion'. All behaviour is concerned with real costs and returns.

Two simulations will suffice to illustrate the properties of the economy on this view.

A sustained 'deflation' in which the budget deficit is cut by 1 per cent of GDP and money supply growth by 2 per cent per annum (i.e. consistently with the fiscal contraction) shows the now familiar 'overshooting' of the exchange rate (a fall in competitiveness) because inflation drops unexpectedly, causing real wages to rise in an unplanned way. Inflation and interest rates drop at once. The resulting capital gain on government debt stimulates private spending so that output is not much affected over the first few years, rising a little at first then falling a little before settling down at its original level; this initial bumpiness reflects the bumpiness of the portfolio adjustment mechanism. There is only a very limited trade account reaction to the fall in competitiveness because this is expected to be temporary.

In the UK much is often made of wages as being 'inexplicable' and not influenced by broader economic pressures. Our work suggests strongly otherwise. Wages reflect two major forces: the changing equilibrium level of *real* wages, and the expected rate of inflation, mirroring monetary policies. Because wages are, presumably for good reasons, negotiated largely for a one-year contract period, sharp changes in monetary policies can cause unplanned changes in real wages as the exchange rate and inflation react. However, in the *next* contract period, wages are negotiated to restore equilibrium. Recent experience illustrates this: in the 1979/80 wage round real wages rose in an unplanned way as the exchange rate rose in response to the Medium-Term Financial Strategy, but the 1980/81 wage round has been correspondingly 'moderate', particularly in the manufacturing sector most exposed to foreign competition.

In the second simulation – a 10 per cent real cut in all social security benefits to the unemployed – real wages fall by 10 per cent and competitiveness rises by 18 per cent, permanently. Output rises by 6 per cent as the traded goods sector expands. Unemployment falls as more people choose to work rather than take benefits. These effects do not measure the contraction of the 'shadow economy' that would result; hence the increase in over-all 'true' output and employment is overstated to some (unknown) extent.

We see here the mechanism by which jobs can be 'priced back' into the market. For an equilibrium model, unemployment is voluntary. Given unemployment compensation, it may pay people, faced with an unpleasant change in the environment (a drop in the demand for their skills), to remain unemployed rather than move house or change occupation or make whatever changes are required in order to fill the jobs available. Their decision may be to remain unemployed for a longer period (e.g., given the chances that the economy may recover in such a way as to restore the old type of job, they may decide not to take an interim job) or to become *permanently* unemployed because available jobs are just not attractive enough. The UK social security system gives indefinite and generous support in a way that sharply undercuts up to half of the economy's available jobs. Our own calculations suggest that, allowing for benefits in kind and the cost of working, a man with a wife and two children would obtain *permanently* in benefits a living standard about three-quarters as good as he would on *average earnings*. Supposing he enjoys leisure – or more practically that he or his wife can find some part-time activity – then jobs paying average earnings or less will cease to be attractive. It is probably only habit, the desire to avoid upheaval, and the knowledge that the system must surely be changed in time, which prevent many more people from actually abandoning their existing jobs, rather than simply not making active efforts to find new ones.

The first simulation illustrates the monetary aspects of the model; monetary and fiscal policy permanently change inflation and interest rates ('money things') and have only transitory effects on real things. The second illustrates the real aspect of the model, or the 'supply side'; here a real measure to improve the workings of the labour market has minimal and transitory effects on inflation or other money things, but lasting real effects. In both simulations, the lags are relatively short, because once people realise that a change in the environment is permanent they adjust their behaviour promptly.

The Lags between Money, Output and Prices

It is often claimed that there is a long lag (around eighteen months to three years) between changes in money supply growth and the rate of inflation. This view is often justified by statistical analysis of the relationship between the two variables or simple inspection of graphs. Unfortunately, inferences from such analysis are likely to be erroneous, particularly from a policy viewpoint. This is because it has been shown (Sargent, 1976b; Minford and Peel, 1979) that there is an observational equivalence of reduced-form relationships (that is, those expressing the total effects, direct and indirect, of a change in policy or other circumstances) between prices and money or real output and money derived from either Keynesian or rational expectations models. In other words, the reduced form derived from a model in which expectations are adaptive and systematic monetary policy can drive real output above its normal level is indistinguishable from that generated from a model in which expectations are rational and systematic government feedback policy with respect to output is impotent.

Consequently, a researcher could come along, collect data on real output and money supply, examine the relationship between output, lagged output and money supply, and conclude that a

Keynesian policy of monetary expansion would raise output or that a feedback monetary rule from lagged output could ensure full employment. However, we know that such inferences are invalid in the rational expectations model which produced these 'relationships'.

The lessons to be drawn from this analysis are, first, that inferences from reduced-form relationships between inflation and money supply or output and money supply are potentially misleading from a policy viewpoint. The only reliable method of inferring the impact of monetary change on inflation or output is by investigation of structural models (that is, those setting out the full interrelationships at work in the economy). Secondly, temporary deviations of money supply from its target level will not be reflected in the anticipated or mean rate of inflation. This point is relevant to the current and lagged (temporary) distortion of the money supply figures. Only if agents form the opinion that the underlying rate of monetary expansion has changed will there be any significant implications for inflationary expectations and hence for interest rates, wages, prices and the exchange rate.

The Effects of the Government's Policies

These properties can be further illustrated by a simulation of the effects of a medium-term monetary plan of the sort announced by the government in the 1980 Budget. The assumptions made are as follows. At the time of announcement, the monetary plan is believed only partially; the rate of growth of sterling M3 is expected to fall by 0,2,3,4 per cent (fiscal years from 1980/81) thereafter to stay 4 per cent lower. However, from late 1981/82 full credibility is achieved, so that the figures expected for 1982/83 onwards are lower by 5, 7 and 8 per cent thereafter.

Our simulation shows that, from the announcement, the exchange rate moves very sharply in anticipation of the long-run effects of the policy on UK prices. This brings forward the drop in inflation virtually to the year of announcement. It also causes a sharp reduction in competitiveness, but this is eliminated rapidly from the end of 1981 and is therefore regarded as temporary, so has only a modest effect on the trade account in this model.

Notice that in this policy experiment the 'lags' from money supply to prices are *reversed*. Money supply growth declines gradually according to the monetary plan, but inflation declines sharply,

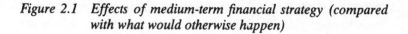

Figure 2.1   Effects of medium-term financial strategy (compared with what would otherwise happen)

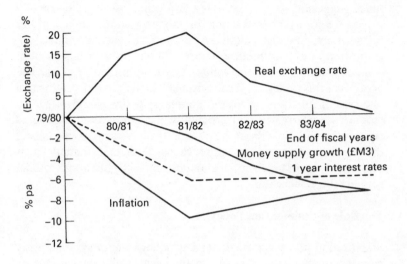

giving the impression that it is 'leading' the reduction in money supply growth. There is no significance in these 'lags'. They are the result of a particular policy regime change. The general point is that lags observed between money and prices will depend on the policy regime being pursued. In truth there is *no lag* between systematic expected money supply growth and inflation.

This raises an important question, posed by Kaldor and Trevithick (1981) among others, namely, if inflation can be controlled by monetary measures is it not preferable to bring the inflationary process to a halt suddenly ('immediacy') rather than slowly and gradually through moderate reductions in the planned growth of the money supply in successive years ('gradualism')? Assuming that as a practical political matter the authorities can engineer the cuts involved in the budget deficit to enable a policy of immediate reduction in the rate of monetary growth, there appears to be one major problem. The change in the rate of monetary expansion is likely to be largely unanticipated and consequently the potential emerges for large disturbances to output and relative prices. This dislocation may, however, be less severe than sometimes suggested as interest rates and other asset prices rapidly respond and as recontracting in labour markets takes place; furthermore, any dislocation would be short-lived since mistakes, being purely of a monetary nature, should be to a large extent compensatable after the new monetary commitment is clear. The benefits of this policy are those arising from the rapid transition to a low rate of inflation, while the gradualist policy can also lead to monetary uncertainty and credibility problems as it engenders constant speculation about the possibility of 'U-turns'. On balance, the rational expectations approach suggests that immediacy is preferable to gradualism; simulations of the Liverpool model support this conclusion.

The Role of Stabilisation Policy

Stabilisation policy can be defined as policy to alter systematically variables controlled by government, such as the growth of the monetary base and the size of the budget deficit, in response to movements in key economic variables such as inflation and output. Two types can be distinguished: 'feedback' policies where, as new information arrives, the authorities alter their targets for the *future* (e.g., raise the deficit or money supply target for 1981/2 because unemployment is higher in November 1980 than expected), and 'automatic' policies, where in response to current shocks (unexpected developments), the *current* outcomes for the target variables are allowed to diverge from targets to some extent (e.g., if an unexpectedly sharp recession lowers tax revenues and raises transfers, take no compensatory action to reduce current expenditure or raise current tax rates; or if private and public borrowing raises money supply growth, do not raise interest rates). The distinction is somewhat arbitrary in that it implicitly assumes there is some period which is the 'current' one after which the 'future' begins; yet it is a real one because of the institutional arrangements for taking government decisions (an annual budget with a November announcement of social security uprating, etc.).

Stabilisation policy must be carefully distinguished from policy changes. These are defined as unanticipated shifts in the *framework* of policy – either in the long-run targets for control variables or in the stabilisation policy responses – i.e., in the policy function itself.

However, on the assumption of rational expectations with shared information, not even the government could know when a policy change would occur, let alone plan to manipulate the economy via policy changes. Furthermore, *frequent* policy changes ('discretion') would make the 'policy rules' of no value for forecasting, for they would be too short-lived; *the* 'policy rule' would then become an expression describing the policy changes themselves in some useful way. For example, if 'U-turns' *always* occur two years from an election, then U-turns are *part* of this policy rule and cannot meaningfully be described as a policy change.

The pursuit of stabilisation policy therefore implies the selection of a policy rule for the foreseeable future. For a number of reasons, in particular the presence of anticipated real rates of return in supply functions, of asset effects in expenditure equations, and of multi-period contracts, the authorities through suitable choice of stabilising parameters can in *principle* reduce the variance of either output or inflation (Phelps and Taylor, 1979; Minford and Peel, 1981).

The question arises as to whether, in practice, this is wise. Karl Brunner (1981) has carefully considered the arguments against policy activism; from our perspective two points stand out.

The case for medium-(and long-) term monetary targets is that they reduce uncertainty. If there are no targets, agents in financial and other markets are forced to form predictions of money supply and so of prices from other sources, the behaviour of past governments, ministerial hints, etc., all of which must give an unclear guide to policy intentions. Clearly, announcement of monetary targets by the authorities will not lead to uncritical acceptance of them by agents. They will evaluate whether the targets are viable and act accordingly. However, on balance, the announcement of (viable) targets will lead to less monetary uncertainty and consequently less disturbance to the real economy than in the absence of targets.

Yet, if so, it is of paramount importance that the authorities actually carry out their announced policy. Then over time such enactment will lead to more credibility being given to government announcements with a corresponding fall in monetary uncertainty.

Stabilisation policy seems likely to conflict with this aim because it is inherently hard for agents to distinguish between temporary and permanent variations in government-controlled variables. These variables are subject to political pressures, which are notoriously hard to predict. A rise in the deficit in recession may turn out to be irreversible, as the recipients of the additional transfers or spending establish vested interests; or it may not if these recipients have not got the 'clout'. The information required to judge is not available largely because it is in the political and not the market domain. It follows that stabilising responses of monetary growth or the deficit will to some extent be interpreted as permanent changes and cause corresponding changes in inflation and interest rates which add to changes in both prices and output possibly more than offsetting the benefits expected.

A second problem, which is particularly important at times of rapid technological change, is that it may be hard for government itself to distinguish between temporary and permanent shocks to the economy. Then mistakes will cause it to misjudge the equilibrium level of output; 'stabilisation' responses may well thus raise the variance of output around its true equilibrium.

Weighing up the costs and benefits of stabilisation policy in practice is a complicated problem of second best to which we have no ready answer. However, our impression is that any such responses should be limited strictly to automatic fiscal stabilisers only, which are less vulnerable to our objections; and even these should be strictly controlled (that is to say, if the unanticipated loss of tax revenue and rise in transfers in the current fiscal year exceeds more than some percentage of GDP, it should be progressively 'clawed back' by reduced borrowing in other ways). In current circumstances, the overshooting of the PSBR is to some extent therefore condonable; it may also prove difficult to eliminate it entirely in 1981/82.

Finally, the best long-run objective for policy remains to reduce the original government intervention causing slack in the system. This would amount to putting social security on a funded true insurance basis, instead of as at present supplementing it out of general taxation. If this were done, the rationale for stabilisation disappears and the system would then be functioning appropriately with private agents' own reactions.

The Political Economy of Macroeconomic Policy

One frequently encountered reason given for the inevitability of a 'U-turn' system of government is 'the political business cycle'. According to this theory (Nordhaus, 1975) voters evaluate governments at election time on the current state of the economy – especially the rate of inflation and unemployment (and/or real disposable income). Secondly, economic agents in the economy have 'adaptive' expectations of inflation (i.e., based only on past inflation with no explicit allowance made for the impact of current and future policy). The optimal policy for the government on arriving in office is to deflate in order to bring inflation down, then around mid-term to stimulate the economy to bring unemployment down and raise real incomes in time for the election, leaving their successors (or themselves) to cope with the rise in inflation that is the lagged result of the policy. Such models then imply that we will observe a Boom–Election–Slump–Boom–Election cycle.

An average and rising tendency to inflation can be explained by reference to pressure groups operating to persuade governments to spend, and governments accommodating these expenditures by printing money, against which there is only a general interest (for any individual a weak one) (Brittan, 1977). As before, this policy will cause inflation with a lag, but by the electoral cycle the expansion of spending is concentrated in the latter part of the government's term so this is not a problem.

If, however, there were rational expectations, then, first, electoral cycle policies would not affect the economy in this way, but in any case there would be no point in them because voters would 'see through' them and evaluate the government's performance independently. As for rising inflation and deficits, pressure groups benefited would possibly vote for the government but the electorate as a whole would penalise the inflationary effect. We have accordingly developed an alternative approach to political behaviour (Minford and Peel, 1982).

We suppose that whilst governments are concerned to become re-elected they are also concerned to enact policies which are in accordance with the economic interests and subjective preferences of their political constituencies. Our view is that inflation, as a *tax*, has a differential impact on the parties' supporters (Hibbs, 1977) because Labour supporters tend to hold fewer assets in monetary form and more in the form of human capital (that is, the earning power of their labour and skills) than Conservative supporters. It is not for reasons discussed above that there is any exploitable trade-off between inflation and unemployment. However, the authorities can by suitable rules stabilise real or nominal shocks to the economy; we suppose Labour voters will prefer real shocks to be stabilised, Conservative voters nominal shocks.

This approach implies that Conservative governments are more likely to run lower budget deficits and hence have lower rates of monetary expansion than Labour governments. Also Conservative governments will tend to stabilise nominal shocks to the economy more than real shocks, with Labour governments doing the converse. Yet *neither* government should systematically generate an 'election cycle'. These implications are supported in data for the post-war period. Our model of the floating voter implies that the agent votes on (rational) expectations of inflation, disposable income and the variance of inflation and disposable income under the current government, relative to the magnitude of these variables anticipated under the opposition. Our explanation of opinion poll data produces statistically more satisfactory results than those obtained when actual inflation, unemployment and disposable incomes are used as explanatory variables (Frey and Schneider, 1978).

This suggests to us that a government policy of stimulating the economy a year or so before the election date would be misguided (and has *not* been followed, in general at least, by post-war governments). In other words, we consider that it would be folly, as well as unlikely, for the current Conservative government as the election approaches to endeavour to stimulate employment by expansionary monetary policy. Such policies would rapidly lead to increases in interest rates, wages and prices as agents in financial, labour and goods markets responded – with negligible impact on employment. Our work also suggests that the electorate would penalise such behaviour.

The Medium-Term Financial Strategy

It should be apparent from this analysis that it would be nonsensical for us to look at any one monetary statistic over any given period of time in assessing this government's monetary and fiscal policies. To borrow a phrase much loved by Sir Geoffrey Howe, we have to assess the 'broad thrust' of these policies – or, more precisely, what is the *permanent* change in policy and what merely temporary (stressed also by Karl Brunner, 1981).

The major innovation in economic policy made by this government has been the explicit announcement of a programme of monetary and fiscal targets over their period of office, the 'medium-term financial strategy' (monetary plan, for short). To our knowledge this is the first government anywhere, let alone in the UK, to do such a thing. Even after the most cynical discounting, such a programme carries some weight with markets because a government's prestige is intimately bound up with carrying out its promises (witness the seriousness with which party manifesto commitments are treated by both UK parties). In our view – reinforced by simulations with the Liverpool model (Figure 2.1) – this programme commitment alone, underpinned by the prospects of large Exchequer revenues from North Sea oil (making it that much easier to carry out the monetary plan), has accounted for the strength of the pound, hence the tough monetary environment of 1980, and the rapid fall in inflation.

There has of course been substantial overshooting of both the PSBR and the £M3 targets in 1980/81. As argued earlier, this has not detracted from the achievement of a substantial tightening of monetary conditions because of the effect on the exchange rate of the government's monetary programme backed up by North Sea oil revenues.

Nevertheless, as one of us has repeatedly warned (e.g., Minford, 1980b) such short-run failures of implementation are deeply damaging to credibility. The effects were clearly visible in the sagging prices of government bonds in December and January. Furthermore, the gains achieved on the inflation front by the markets' willingness to trust the government even partially to carry out their monetary plan can be wiped out very quickly if public borrowing and money supply do not soon show very clear signs of moving back to the levels in the plan.

A feasible profile for the PSBR for 1981/82 onwards depends critically on the shape of the recovery. The key requirement is that substantial progress is made in reducing the PSBR on a cyclically adjusted basis in 1981/82, so that the credibility of reaching the monetary plan objective in the medium term is fully maintained.

However, it is also essential to make short-run control of the money supply as independent as possible of short-run variation in the PSBR. Operating methods of monetary control have now been changed in principle but the practice is not yet known. The best hope of short-run control lies in limitation of the monetary base with interest rates being allowed to 'float' freely; this implies that neither Treasury Bills nor longer-term government bonds are issued on tap, i.e., at fixed prices whether at the Bank's discount window or by the government broker, but rather at market prices in quantities determined by the desired growth of the monetary base. Markets will adapt easily to such new procedures provided they are clearly followed from now on; anyone who believes otherwise is belittling abilities in the most profitable square mile of Britain.

The Market Approach

The programme to improve the operation of the market (the 'supply side') has made some short-term progress, but there is cause for long-term worry. This programme called for increasing incentives by cuts in marginal tax rates, the return of activities to the private sector ('Privatisation'), increasing the scope of competition both in the public and private sector, and sharp reduction in union monopoly power.

Progress to date includes large reductions in the penal higher rates of personal tax, the abolition of controls on foreign exchange, dividends, incomes and prices, some limited disposal of public sector assets of which the most economically significant is the council house sale programme, some toughening of merger restrictions, and the law limiting union picketing activities. There is also a more critical attitude to industrial aid, exemplified by the lower profile of the National Enterprise Board; though both the British Steel Corporation and British Leyland have succeeded in getting increased aid, this is being given under tougher performance conditions to managements committed to returning the operations to profits, much as if they had the role of a receiver, the appropriate one in present circumstances.

Yet to list these actions is to be conscious that there is little else in the pipeline, except vague suggestions; there 'may' be greater limits on union power, nationalised industries are to be put under 'pressure' to be more efficient, public sector activities are being 'reviewed' with a view to privatisation 'at the right time', and further tax cuts are 'hoped for eventually'. Furthermore, the agreement to maintain uneconomic coal pits and subsidise coal against imports represents a serious setback for market forces. It is hard to resist the conclusion that the government has, at least for the time being, lost its momentum on market issues.

The most serious problems, on which no action is in prospect, are in the labour market. Unemployment is unlikely to fall much below 2 millions even after the recovery. Though the shadow economy fortunately employs some unknown proportion of 'unemployed' time, this represents both a waste of resources and a social threat. Our analysis indicates that this permanent unemployment reflects incentive structures produced by union monopoly power, the tax/ social security structure and housing market distortions (restrictions on rents, on council house transfers, etc.) Union power probably raises real labour costs in union sectors by 12.25 per cent (Metcalf, 1977; Mulvey and Foster, 1976; Parsley, 1980). If we assume that this represents 50 per cent of the labour force, the Liverpool model suggests that this raises permanent unemployment by 0.4–0.8 millions. Real social security benefits to the unemployed (excluding earnings related supplement), grossed up for marginal tax rates paid by both employer and employee, have risen by about 65 per cent in the last 15 years. Real old age pensions, which to the extent that they are available to people able and willing to work act in a similar way to reduce labour supply, have risen by about 40 per cent in the last decade. The model suggests that every 10 per cent rise in real social security benefits relative to the marginal product of labour raises unemployment by about half a million. Estimates of the effect of the housing distortions are not available; but regional disparities in unemployment suggest it is significant.

The government must regain momentum in these areas. There must be further legislation to curtail and over a period eliminate the ability of unions to raise relative wages and enforce restrictive labour practices. But we would also suggest a series of cuts in real social security benefits available to the employable, accompanied in so far as limits on public sector borrowing permit by cuts in income tax rates and national insurance contributions. Every 10 per cent reduction in real benefits would save directly about £2 billions per year in 1981/82 prices; this would both contribute to restoring the monetary plan and make a significant cut in prospective permanent unemployment.

Though such a measure would directly hit the least well-off, the indirect effects would be to lower real wages generally and so increase job opportunities. Therefore, in its full impact, it reduces the real wages of those *in* employment as well as the unemployed and spreads employment to the unemployed. Furthermore, the additional tax revenue obtained from the additional resource utilisation would be available for redistribution in the form of tax cuts of the order of £3½ billions at 1981/82 prices for every 10 per cent cut in real benefits; it would clearly be sensible to concentrate these cuts on lower-income tax payers in order to reinforce the incentive effects of reducing benefits. Therefore, those unemployed who become employed will obtain higher real incomes than before.

Those who remain unemployed will be worse off, but their decision to remain unemployed will be a voluntary one; the question society must ask is whether the subsidisation of the unemployment decision is worth the cost in output and employment. In a free society it is impossible to force people on benefits to work, even on 'social priority' schemes; the unemployed regard such schemes with an enthusiasm reserved for labour camps. There is therefore a three-sided choice between low income subsidies, freedom and resource waste. We cannot say how society will resolve this difficult choice, which faces virtually all Western economies at this present time and is at its most acute in the Benelux and Scandinavian economies besides our own. We can only draw attention to the costs and benefits. Our present suggestions, however, seem to us a minimum response to the situation.

Our suggestions will no doubt strike many as being 'politically impossible', even 'naive'. We remind the reader that much the same was said of policies to control the money supply in the early 1970s, and it has taken nearly a decade of inflationary experience to convince our leaders that the politically impossible was necessary in the monetary area. As we face the prospect of *permanent* unemployment of the order of 2 millions, which cannot be eliminated by 'reflation', we would argue that measures such as these, 'tough' and unpalatable as they may sound, are the only way to create the necessary jobs to bring down unemployment.

While any forecast of the effects of such an alteration in policies must be inherently uncertain, estimates based on the Liverpool model suggest that a combination of a 15 per cent cut in real social security benefits to the employable and a 15 per cent reduction in the trade union wage mark-up over non-union wages (e.g. from 15 per cent to nil), each spread over three years from 1982 to 1984, would reduce permanent unemployment in the UK by around 1 and a quarter millions by the mid-1980s. Can we afford *not* to price jobs back into the market by such measures?

Conclusions

The rational expectations assumption is a powerful tool of analysis in macroeconomics which recognises the strong incentives people have to make efficient use of information and whose empirical successes to date suggest it is a useful approximation. On this basis, the government's role is to set a framework of law, taxation and public spending, such as avoids distortion between private and social costs and benefits; voluntary private choices would then equilibrate the economy optimally in response to shocks. Stabilisation policy can then be avoided, the budget balanced, and the monetary base kept at a constant growth rate.

This government set out from an unenviable initial position of major distortions in goods and labour markets, a high budget deficit, rapid monetary growth, high inflation and high unemployment. Its plans envisaged the reduction of distortions (the 'supply side') and an announced programme of fairly rapid reductions in deficit and money supply growth (the monetary plan). The supply side programme has already made considerable progress but now appears to be losing momentum; there are still severe labour market problems. The monetary plan, helped by the automatic tax revenue effects of rising North Sea oil prices, has had a dramatic success in reducing inflation via the exchange rate; but the overshooting of targets in 1980/81 has undermined credibility, and the plan must be restored in 1981/82 to avoid the risk of a serious setback to inflation and so to the prospects of output recovery. This reflects markets' forward-looking views and has nothing to do with any 'lags' between money and prices which at present are actually reversed.

Stabilisation policy in this second-best transitional path should be invoked only in the case of automatic fiscal stabilisers, and then only to a modest extent. This suggests that some limited overshooting of the deficit targets in the plan to date has had to be accepted because of the unexpectedly rapid rise in unemployment.

The government's strategy calls for cuts in taxation as soon as the monetary plan permits – these are necessary for the supply side programme. This is therefore not a fiscal stimulus prior to the election because that plan calls for declining deficits as a share of GDP. Nor would any such stimulus make sense electorally; voters see through such nonsense. The political basis of support for the government lies in a combination of its own natural support and an apparent shift in the interests of floating voters towards policies offering lower inflation and greater competition. There is no reason to believe that this basis has been eroded; but, if it had, altering course would not help this government at the next election, merely land it with the added handicap of inconsistency. The government's economic strategy is therefore on course *provided* that hints of weakness on the supply side and monetary overshooting are rapidly corrected. This proviso underlines our basic point: the economy is forward looking and the government must therefore stick to its plans in order to succeed.

Since we wrote this chapter the Chancellor has presented his Budget. This has put monetary strategy back on course in a manner that we fully support. On the market aspects, major problems remain and the Budget has worsened the tax benefit structure somewhat by lowering real tax thresholds but we welcome the renewed commitment to tax cuts to be financed by further public sector economies. ·

References

R.J. Barro (1977), 'Unanticipated Money Growth and Unemployment in the United States', *American Economic Review*, **67**, 2, March, 101–15.

S. Brittan, (1977), *The Economic Consequences of Democracy*, Temple Smith, London.

K. Brunner (ed.) (1979), *Economics and Social Institutions*, Martinus Nijhoff.

K. Brunner (1981), 'The Case Against Monetary Activism', *Lloyds Bank Review*, January, 20–39.

E.F. Fama (1975), 'Short-Term Interest Rates as Predictors of Inflation', *American Economic Review*, **65**, 2, March, 269–82.

B.S. Frey and E. Schneider (1978), 'A Politico-Economic Model for the UK', *The Economic Journal*, **88**, 2, June, 243–53.

S.H. Grossman and J.F. Stiglitz (1980), 'On the Impossibility of Informationally Efficient Markets', *American Economic Review*, **70**, 3, June, 392–408.

D.A. Hibbs (1977), 'Political Parties and Macroeconomic Policy', *American Political Science Review*, **72**, 4, December, 981–1007.

N. Kaldor and J. Trevithick (1981), 'A Keynesian Perspective of Money', *Lloyds Bank Review*, **139**, January, 1–19.

P. Korteweg *et al.* (1979), 'The Problem of Inflation', *Carnegie Rochester Conference on Public Policy*, **8**.

R.E. Lucas (1972), 'Econometric Testing of the Natural Rate Hypothesis' in O. Eckstein (ed.), *The Econometrics of Price Determination Conferences*, Board of Governors of the Federal Reserve System, Washington.

R.E. Lucas (1975), 'An Equilibrium Model of the Business Cycle', *Journal of Political Economy*, **83**, 2, December, 1113–44.

D. Metcalf (1977), 'Unions, Incomes Policy and Relative Wages in Britain', *British Journal of Industrial Relations*, **15**, 2, July, 157–75.

A.P.L. Minford (1980a), 'A Rational Expectations Model of the UK under Fixed and Floating Exchange Rates', *Carnegie Rochester Conference Series on Public Policy*, **12** (The State of Macroeconomics), 293–355.

A.P.L. Minford (1980b), 'Evidence to House of Commons Treasury and Civil Service Committee', *Memoranda on Monetary Policy*, HMSO.

A.P.L. Minford and D.A. Peel (1979), 'The Classical Supply Hypothesis and the Observational Equivalence of Classical and Keynesian Models', *Economics Letters*, **4**, 2, February, 229–33.

A.P.L. Minford and D.A. Peel (1981), 'The Role of Monetary Stabilisation Policy under Rational Expectations', *The Manchester School*, **49**, 39–50.

A.P.L. Minford and D.A. Peel (1982), 'The Political Theory of the Business Cycle', *The European Economic Review*, **17**, 253–70.

C. Mulvey and J.I. Foster (1976), 'Occupational Earnings in the UK and the Effects', *Economica*, **44**, 3, September, 258–75.

J.F. Muth (1961), 'Rational Expectations and the theory of price movements', *Econometrica*, **38**, 1, January, 315–35.

W.D. Nordhaus (1975), 'The Political Business Cycle', *The Review of Economic Studies*, **42**, 2, January, 169–90.

C.J. Parsley (1980), 'Labour, Unions and Wages: A Survey', *Journal of Economic Literature*, **18**, 1, March, 1–31.

E. Phelps and J.B. Taylor (1979), 'Stabilising Properties of Monetary Policy under Rational Expectations', *Journal of Political Economy*, **85**, 1, February, 163–90.

T. Sargent (1976a), 'A Classical Macroeconomic Model for the United States', *Journal of Political Economy*, **84**, 3, April, 207–37.

T. Sargent (1976b), 'The Observational Equivalence of Natural and Unnatural Theories of Macroeconomics', *Journal of Political Economy*, **84**, 3, April, 631–40.

R.M. Solow (1980), 'On Theories of Unemployment', *American Economic Review*, **70**, 1, March, 1–11.

J. Tobin (1980), 'Are New Classical Models Plausible Enough to Guide Policy?', *Journal of Money, Credit and Banking*, **12**, 4, November, Part 2, 788–99.

3. The New Classical Economics*

In the last five years economic policy in the Western World has shifted substantially 'to the right'; that is, it has given renewed emphasis to beating inflation and to freeing markets from government regulation and other interventions (such as high taxes, minimum wages and high unemployment benefits). This shift has not occurred only in the US under President Reagan and in the UK under Prime Minister Thatcher. It has also happened in Germany under Chancellor Kohl, in Japan under Premier Nakasone, and in Denmark, in Belgium, in the Netherlands, in Eire. There is only one major exception, France under President Mitterrand; but his attempt to socialise French economc policy came after a big shift to the right under Prime Minister Barre and is already in tatters, and in effect is being reversed as fast as possible.

The true reasons for this shift in policy may be many, and different in each country. The major reason is an intellectual one: our view of how the economy behaves has changed, and it is this change that has permitted and encouraged the shift in policy. Part of that change has been 'monetarism', the connection between the supply of money and the general state of the economy, with which most people are now broadly familiar. Yet there has been a further development at work, with which most people are *not* familiar: 'Rational Expectations' Economics, sometimes called the 'New Classical Economics'. This new view of the economy has taken over most of the insights of monetarism, of which it can be regarded as a development, but has transmuted them and added to them in ways that have led it to be called a true 'revolution' in our thinking, where monetarism was a 'counter-revolution'.

This chapter examines the constituents of the New Classical Economics, and considers the implications for policy.

What distinguishes the New Classical ideas from the previous classical thinking in economics, much of it so effectively revived by Professor Milton Friedman under the name of 'monetarism' (and

* First published in *Economic Affairs*, pp. 6–11, March 1985.

often dubbed the 'Old Time Religion'), which will be familiar to readers of *Economic Affairs*? They have a lot in common. First, they share policy prescriptions; that the government budget should be balanced on average over the business cycle; that the central bank should not print more money than is required for the normal growth of the economy; and that government expenditure should be limited to goods and services – such as defence and law and order – where private provision would be ineffective or dangerous.

Secondly, they share a view of how the economy works; that it is normally a self-righting vessel, in which people and firms freely pursuing their own interest will, by mutual trade, make the economy prosper on average and recover robustly from adverse shocks to trade.

Finally, they share an emphasis on the necessity of maintaining work incentives in dealing with inequality and poverty. Unemployment benefits, for example, should not be so generous as to encourage unwillingness to search for new work at realistic rates of pay (probably lower than the worker's last pay). Not least, tax rates must be kept down to rates at which they do not seriously discourage additional effort.

This outline of Classical Economics, the economics of Adam Smith's Invisible Hand, describes a shared corpus of thought with the New Classical Economics. What has changed is our understanding of how the economy works. And the change has brought to adherents of classical thought both more self-confidence and a deeper awareness of what economic analysis *cannot* deliver. I say 'change' in understanding, rather than 'improvement', because we now know not only more of what is likely to be happening in the economy's workings, but also how much *less* well than once was thought we are likely to be able to track those workings by econometric models.

The key to this change is in the theory of expectations. Virtually all economic behaviour and decisions depend on the decision-maker's expectations about the future. Yet the future is unknowable, the expectations subjective; what then can an economist say constructively about them? The answer seemed to be, until quite recently: not a lot. The Classical economists typically either assumed that expected future prices (etc.) were the same as current prices or that they bore some mechanical relation to them (e.g., changing by x% more or less). Ironically perhaps (in view of ultimate developments), it was Keynes who first put expectations in the centre of the economic stage with a sort of theory attached: expectations of future profit and of future interest rates are crucial to Keynes's theory of boom and slump, which still dominates modern business cycle thinking. Booms would occur when profit expectations were high and interest-rate expectations low; and vice-versa for slumps. But Keynes could do little better in theorising about these expectations than to attribute profit expectations to the 'animal spirits' of businessmen and interest-rate expectations to stock-market prejudice. This is, quite transparently, a cop-out: Hamlet, the Prince of the drama, is a *deus ex machina*, wheeled on and off inexplicably, even arbitrarily – decidedly not a 'general' theory.

There is however one famous passage in Keynes's book, *The General Theory of Employment, Interest and Money*, which went deeper, tantalisingly glimpsing a more persuasive theory. In it Keynes muses about the stock market and compares it to a beauty contest:

> Professional investment may be likened to those newspaper competitions in which the competitors have to pick out the six prettiest faces from a hundred photographs, the prize being awarded to the competitor whose choice most nearly corresponds to the average preferences of the competitors as a whole . . .
> It is not a case of choosing those which, to the best of one's judgement, are really the prettiest, nor even those which average opinion genuinely. thinks the prettiest. We have reached the third degree where we devote our intelligence to anticipating what average opinion expects average opinion to be. (p.156)

People Learn from Experience

So near to modern theory, and yet so far – as we shall shortly see. This passage, indeed, turns out to be Keynes's digression on the hopeless *irrationality* of expectations and how useless it is for economists to try to explain them. Some of Keynes's disciples adopted this view. Others in the 1950s modified it somewhat to allow for 'adaptiveness'. They argued that expectations, wherever they originated (in irrational prejudices, animal spirits, etc.) would gradually be modified in the light of forecast errors; the result was that expectations, for example, of inflation, would gradually tend towards eventual inflation if the situation remained unchanged for long enough, because people would *learn from their experience*.

This expectations theory was a distinct improvement on its predecessors, since it recognised that people learn systematically and that this applies to their expectations as much as to other aspects of their economic behaviour. However, it still embodied a basic behavioural irrationality: for example, even if it is as clear as daylight that a government is embarked on a spendthrift course of high deficits and hot central bank printing presses, the theory predicted that people would not raise their expectations of inflation to realistic rates until long after the inflation has hit those rates. It defied commonsense that people should be duped in this way.

This supposition of general and lasting delusion – or fooling all the people for a long time – also ironically implies that governments can engineer long-lasting booms and reverse incipient slumps simply by turning to such inflationary (euphemistically, 'reflation-ary') policies. The reason is that, because expectations of inflation take off slowly, so also does inflation itself; and so the extra money pumped into the economy has a correspondingly big effect on output in the early stages, rather than being absorbed in higher prices. By the same token, governments could stop booms from getting out of hand by a timely reversal of these policies once the upswing is well-assured but before inflation has taken serious hold. By such 'stabilisation' policy, governments could ameliorate, if not conquer, the business cycle, without sparking off inflation on any major scale.

Keynesian Nonsense

Claims to such powers on the part of governments have lain at the heart of the Keynesian approach to policy, and have underpinned most of British post-war economic policy until 1979 and most of US economic policy from the Kennedy era until Mr Volcker's in-auguration as Chairman of the Fed, also in 1979.

These claims would have appeared preposterous to the old Classical economists, and, who knows, perhaps also to Keynes himself in modern circumstances; they have, of course, always shocked followers of Conservative economic thought. Yet these followers had for a long time no theoretical tools with which to counter this nonsense. They were confronted with 'econometric evidence' that the adaptive expectations models fitted the data and that Keynesian policies worked to maintain full employment without provoking serious inflation. The non-Keynesians either had to put up with it or shut up; they grumbled through the 1960s but basically shut up. Professor Milton Friedman, the originator and leader of the monetarist counter-revolution against Keynesian thought, had by 1970 reached a sort of truce with the Keynesians, who in turn had incorporated many of Friedman's innovations into their models. In this truce, dubbed the Neo-Classical (or Neo-Keynesian) Synthesis, Monetarists and Keynesians agreed that stabilisation policies *could* work in this manner, because of the adaptiveness of expectations. Where they agreed to differ was, first, on how long it would take for the stimulatory phase of policy to produce inflation, and, second, how beneficial stabilisation policies would be in practice. The monetarists have typically argued, first, that big inflation effects would come through within two years or so of a stimulus – more quickly than Keynesians believe. Secondly, they said governments are incapable, even if they were willing, of *timing* their interventions correctly, so that they would be as likely to *worsen* as to improve the cycle. Finally, and most damagingly, they have charged that there would in practice be an inflationary bias in government policy; governments would be happier 'stimulating' than 'deflating' the economy, and this would cause a steady upward pressure on inflation.

Hence there have been substantive and obvious differences on *policy* between monetarists and Keynesians. Nevertheless, they both subscribed to an essentially similar view (or 'model') of how the economy worked, the crucial part of which was that when policies changed people would only change their expectations *gradually* and *after* the policies had taken effect.

Rational Expectations has Shattered the Keynesian–Friedmanite Truce

This intellectual truce has been shattered by the modern theory of 'Rational Expectations'. It says that people use all the evidence available to them in an intelligent manner to predict inflation, profits, etc., that is, both *before* the policies take effect and afterwards. Going back to Keynes's beauty contest, speculators in the stock-market are certainly worrying about what other speculators think and will think. Yet, what Keynes missed was that they each can work out the likely outcome for the profits which underlie stock performance and they know the others can too – much as the judges know what will wash as 'beauty' in the outside world of public opinion after the contest is over. This knowledge acts as a discipline on the market; 'silly' views could in principle take hold, but everyone knows that, if they did, they would sooner or later lead to a crash *and they will avoid them.*

The original idea was set out in 1961 by John Muth in a now famous article; but it took a decade before it really caught hold of economic thinking in a major way. Pioneering work on its implications for the behaviour of the economy really started around 1970, and by the middle 1970s a lot of work was under way.

When you think about it, the theory of Rational Expectations is – like all good theories – obvious commonsense.

New Thinking – New Policies

However, it has dramatic implications for policy. Because people intelligently evaluate the likely effects of government policies, it clearly implies that government does not have the power to stabilise the economy by the methods described earlier: policies to stimulate the economy will be 'seen through' and will generate inflation rapidly. If governments are seen to be committed to some unrealistically high volume of employment in the name of 'full' employment and to pursuing reflationary policies with that over-riding aim, the inflation generated will rise to a point of crisis in a short time and the policies will be unsustainable. While, if very carefully circumscribed, there may be some effective 'stabilisation policy', its evaluation is a highly complex matter and at the very least the chances of finding a successful formula remote, given our limited knowledge of the complex interactions between government and the behaviour of intelligently reacting people and firms. Robert Lucas (University of Chicago) and Thomas Sargent (University of Minnesota), two major pioneers in rational expectations work, have summarised it thus:

> Existing Keynesian macroeconomic models cannot provide reliable guidance in the formulation of monetary, fiscal or other types of policy. This conclusion is based in part on the spectacular recent failures of

these models and in part on their lack of a sound theoretical or econometric basis . . .
Models can be formulated which are free of these difficulties . . . The key elements of these models are that agents are rational . . .
[These models] will focus attention on the need to think of policy as the choice of stable rules of the game, well understood by economic agents . . . [They] will also suggest that policies which affect behaviour mainly because their consequences cannot be correctly diagnosed, such as monetary instability and deficit financing, have the capacity only to *disrupt* [my italics].

The implications go further and deeper. Suppose a government could work out such a formula for stabilisng the business cycle. Why should it benefit the economy? After all, if people were already reacting intelligently to the events – perhaps adverse shocks, such as a rise in oil prices – that had hit them, they can be regarded as having already done the best that could be done. Government, by smoothing out the reaction, would then be making matters *worse*. Again it is possible to find circumstances where the economy has problems which stabilisation policies could in principle improve, but the *practical* difficulties of design remain and these problems often have simpler cures.

The effect of generous unemployment benefits on unemployment is one such problem. In recession, these benefits will encourage more unemployment than otherwise and a lesser willingness to take wage cuts. People are acting rationally in exhibiting this unwillingness. Yet, of course, because the state is paying out the benefits, society as a whole is worse off if they do so. If stabilisation policy succeeded in reducing the recession, it would save society some resources. But a simpler cure for this problem would be to set benefits at lower amounts where the incentives to work are preserved reasonably intact. It would be a curious case of the tail wagging the dog if governments were to pursue vigorous stabilisation policies which risk triggering serious inflation, because they lack the courage to set benefits at realistic amounts.

Yet another implication of rational expectations is that the steady rise in unemployment we have observed over the last two decades in the western world cannot be attributed to 'governments not spending enough' – as by the same token it could not be eliminated by a sustained government 'reflation'. It must be attributed to the economy's inefficiencies which, in turn, must come from ill-advised government intervention in markets – since, left to themselves,

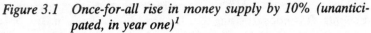

*Figure 3.1   Once-for-all rise in money supply by 10% (unantici-
pated, in year one)[1]*

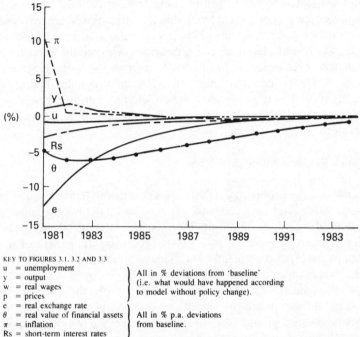

KEY TO FIGURES 3.1, 3.2 AND 3.3

u = unemployment	
y = output	All in % deviations from 'baseline'
w = real wages	(i.e. what would have happened according
p = prices	to model without policy change).
e = real exchange rate	
θ = real value of financial assets	All in % p.a. deviations
π = inflation	from baseline.
Rs = short-term interest rates	

private firms and people could make a good job of the economy.
This is the basis for 'supply side' policies, broadly defined as policies
to free markets from government restrictions. High tax rates
('marginal' ones – i.e., the extra tax on *extra* income earned) induce
people to work less; the interaction of taxes with unemployment
benefits can contrive to create very high 'marginal tax rates' on the
decision to work at all and induce unemployment, as well as a
burgeoning of the shadow economy.

Britain is a good illustration of a country where the problem has
been particularly acute. By the end of 1983 a family man with two
children would have had to earn about 85% of the average male
manual wage to be noticeably better off than out of work. These
out-of-work benefits continue indefinitely. So in effect, if such a
man decides to work, he will pay no less than 85% of his earnings
back to the state, a ridiculously high marginal tax rate! Furthermore, should his wife decide to work when he is unemployed, she

will lose no less than 90% of her extra earnings in taxes or reduced benefits. It is not surprising that the shadow economy in Britain is now estimated to have risen to some 16% of national income, a figure which makes it seem likely that the unemployed are involved on a major scale, since they have a particularly large incentive to take work undeclared to the authorities who would dock their benefits. This nexus of problems, known as the 'unemployment trap', has led to increased emphasis in Britain on containing the rise in benefits while urgently seeking new ways of cutting expenditure to make room for tax cuts, especially to bring the low-paid out of the tax net.

Quick Surgery Better than Slow

However, the problem of inflation has dominated policy discussion since 1979. And here, rational expectations has brought about a remarkable shift of emphasis. Monetarism emphasised the necessity – generally accepted by 1970 – of reducing the growth of the money supply to control inflation. Because of adaptive expectations this process was seen as slow and painful even by monetarists; if growth in the money supply were to be cut sharply, this would mean a very bad and prolonged slump and unemployment. They therefore advocated 'gradualism', i.e., reducing the rate of money supply growth by a few percentage points each year, the whole process stretched out over say a five- to ten-year period. In this way, the inevitable misery of squeezing inflation out of the system would, while admittedly stretched out over a protracted period, be prevented from becoming a traumatic crisis.

This prescription is now under challenge. A sharp once-for-all cut in money supply growth ('cold turkey'), if expectations are rational, would imply indeed a sharp shock to the economy: as the regime changes there will be big errors in expectations previously formed. However, new expectations would then be formed consistently with the new regime; inflation would fall rapidly, and the economy would rebound from the shock, admittedly not at once, but at a reasonable pace. By giving some warning of the regime change, it may even be possible for the government to mitigate the shock to expectations. In the electoral rhythm of democracies, 'cold turkey' started early after an election has a good chance of delivering results before the next one – the inflation results would clearly have arrived, and the recovery from the initial sharp shock would be well under way. Such, indeed, is a rough description of the policies practised both by Mrs Thatcher from the end of 1979, and by Mr Paul Volcker at the Fed from the end of 1980. Both involved sharp contractions in monetary policy, producing rises in interest rates to unprecedentedly painful heights.

By contrast, gradualism runs the serious risk of doing little to inflation but enough to unemployment to fail to impress the electorate and so dissipate early sources of political will to reduce inflation. Its *political* feasibility is therefore in doubt as a cure for inflation. Gradualism went wrong in the US under Nixon and Ford, in Canada between 1975 and 1981, in France under the Barre plan in the late 1970s, and in Italy under repeated attempts at moderate squeezes by the Banca d'Italia in the 1970s.

The Budget Must be Balanced

A final aspect of counter-inflation policy must be addressed – the role of the budget deficit, a big debate in the US today. The early Classical economists never questioned the necessity of balancing the budget on average over the cycle. Keynesians, of course, discarded this belief, but one of the by-products, even under monetarism, was the down-grading of this requirement. Monetarists believe that, provided money supply growth is controlled, failure to balance the budget will affect only interest rates. A sustained budget deficit, they said, would raise interest rates and thus reduce private spending but will not cause inflation.

Rational expectations has led to the reinstatement of the old Classical orthodoxy on budgetary policy. The monetarist belief, as far as it goes, is not questioned. The objection is that it does not go deep enough. Suppose a policy of high deficits and tight money is followed. The nation's debt will accumulate rapidly because deficits are high and, since not financed by printing money, must be financed by issuing IOU's in the only other form – government bonds or 'debt'. This goes on year in year out, as long as the deficits stay high (and money is not printed any faster). Yet clearly it cannot go on indefinitely like this. Sooner or later, either the nation's savers will refuse to hold any more government debt; or they will demand higher and higher interest rates as the price of holding more and more of it. And, in this case, the process will eventually be stopped by the pressures of rising interest rates. When this point comes, high deficits will only continue to be possible if money is printed faster to hold interest rates down. At this point, there will be, contrary to the dicta of the monetarists, higher inflation for sure.

If people expect inflation, inflation expectations will be high today! This will both give an added upward twist to interest rates and will cause the inflation to start much earlier, because people will start a 'flight from money' which itself will trigger rising prices.

Figure 3.2   Permanent unanticipated rise in PSBR by 1% of GDP (balanced finance)[1]

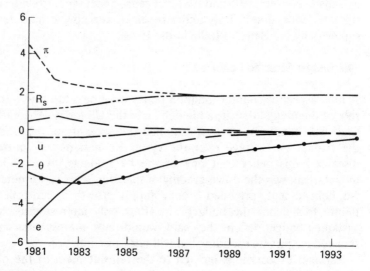

SEE FIGURE 3.1 FOR KEY

So the budget deficit does matter because of the political feasibility of permanently refraining from printing money to finance it. Prudent anti-inflation policy includes containment of the deficit to an amount that can be comfortably financed at steady interest rates without printing money.

This has been a primary maxim of Mrs Thatcher's policies. Indeed, more attention has been paid to reducing the budget deficit than to the short-term movements of growth in the supply of money, because it has been felt that, provided the basic source of monetary temptation so to speak was bolted down, then control of money supply itself would be easier over the long term and, most importantly, market confidence in that control would be assured.

President Reagan's policies contrast with Mrs Thatcher's. The budget deficit has been allowed to rise far beyond the wildest early projections, and the consequences for money supply control have been shrugged off by the White House; Paul Volcker, Chairman of the Fed, has been left to do the best he can with it. The White House would like him both to control the money supply, financing the deficit by massive $50-billion per quarter bond issues, and keep interest rates down. From a rational expectations perspective this is possible only if there is confidence that at some future date (now that the election is over) the budget deficit will be brought down without printing extra money. Yet by 1985 the public sector's debt could have nearly doubled in real value since the end of 1980, assuming inflation is held down by continued tight money; debt interest alone will be running at over $100 billion per year. It is a tall order for the markets to believe a future American President will order a rise in taxes or cuts in spending of up to $100 billion a year to balance the books without resort to the money printing presses. The risks are obvious: a collapse of confidence in the Fed's future capacity to control the money supply (because of a political incapacity to control the deficit) would precipitate a renewed inflationary crisis in the United States – with all that implies for the rest of us.

Realism and Evidence

Some would argue that Rational Expectations is an unrealistic concept; that people are unlikely to use information as efficiently as the theory postulates, and that instead they use rules of thumb which are rather like 'adaptive expectations'. Others in similar vein say that, while people may indeed use information efficiently, they do not know how the economy works, and this uncertainty causes them to make systematic errors in their expectations; in practice, the best they can then do is again something that is rather like adaptive expectations.

Clearly, for individuals, this criticism has some force. We all

Figure 3.3   Effect of unanticipated rise in real benefits by 7%[1]

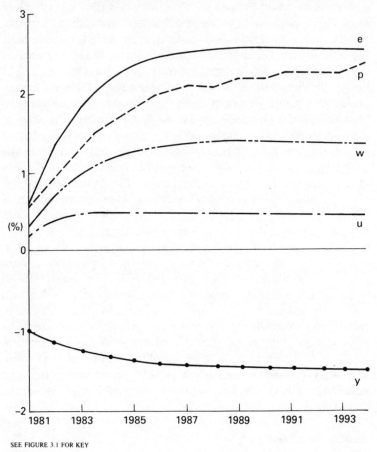

SEE FIGURE 3.1 FOR KEY

know an Aunt Agatha or Uncle Fred who would be prime candidates for non-rational expectations or worse. However, this objection misses the force of the argument that there are strong incentives – because people's livelihoods and firm's profits ride on them – for forecasts to be accurate; hence, when it matters, people and firms will pay professionals to produce a good forecast. These professionals will invest resources in the forecasting business because of its returns; extra business will be channelled towards the advisers who make the better forecasts. And the *best* forecasts possible are rational expectations forecasts! Thus the competitive process itself will at the least produce a strong tendency for forecasts to move towards 'full rationality'. Even if Rational Expectations is, strictly speaking, inaccurate as a description of expectations, it is likely to be a useful approximation, certainly more so than the assumption that people use forecasts which could easily be bettered by the application of sophisticated techniques and more inform-ation. In this respect, assuming firms have rational expectations is like assuming firms maximise profits; they may not exactly do that all the time but it is a useful approximation to complex behaviour.

Economists have rough-and-ready tools at their disposal and they have to make do with such powerful approximations. The majority in the economics profession today are adopting Rational Expect-ations into their tool-kit; and they are reporting good results on the whole. Financial and commodity markets seem to behave more or less as the theory would predict; they appear to respond to new information rapidly and with well-informed assessments. Since interest rates and the exchange rate are set in such markets and play a major role in general economic behaviour, in the business cycle and inflation, at the very least rational expectations has clearly contributed this important dimension to our understanding of how the economy behaves.

Yet it does not stop there; wages have also been found widely to be determined crucially by rational expectations of prices, so that the inflation process itself is now seen as driven powerfully by rational expectations of future policy. Economic research all over the world is going on at a hectic pace in these and other markets to re-examine experience in the light of the new approach; and it is steadily gaining ground. We, in Liverpool University, have found it to be a highly effective way of modelling and forecasting the British economy. (Figures 3.1, 3.2 and 3.3 illustrate the view of the 'Liverpool Model' of certain key policy changes.) We have had our share of mistakes but we have succeeded in predicting both the sharp slowdown in inflation that has occurred under Mrs Thatcher and the vigorous recovery now in progress. Both predictions were greeted with general incredulity by mainstream 'neo-Keynesian' forecasters when we started to make them regularly in early 1980; it was the rational expectations methods that convinced us our predictions had to be right.[2]

The time cannot be far off when these methods will become part of the tool-kit of the 'mainstream forecasters'. There is always a time lag – a 'diffusion process' – before new methods are generally adopted in practical work. They would certainly yield dividends in forecasting the US economy and the world economy generally. As it is, by a curious irony policymakers such as Mrs Thatcher and President Reagan have made considerable implicit use of these ideas in reinforcing and justifying their 'conservative' hunches and instincts, whereas practical economic forecasters in industry and the City of London have been rather slow to adopt them into their procedures.

Let me leave you with a thought about *politics*, an implication of the rational expectations approach where it might be thought to be fairly irrelevant. One of the pieces of the 'conventional wisdom' among economists has always been that to win elections politicians should depress the economy soon after a general election to squeeze inflation down in time for the next general election and then should boost the economy as this new election approaches. Inflation will still be low because it takes time to react to the boom, but incomes will be booming because of the pre-election stimulus.

According to the rational expectations approach, this is bad advice to give politicians because rational voters will see through this behaviour. They will see that inflation will revive after the election and penalise the offending politicians at the election. It is better, or best, on the new view, for politicians to present a coherent programme, to try no clever tricks on the electorate, and to be honest about problems and tough solutions. Mrs Thatcher's re-election in 1983, when, according to the conventional political/economic wisdom, she should have been massively defeated, is a good example of this principle at work. And it had obvious relevance for President Reagan in November 1984. Pursue this thought about the rationality of voters a bit more and you will start to get optimistic about the frontiers of the 'politically possible' in economic policies in a democracy. Rational economic policies, after several decades of increasing government intervention and resulting market malfunctions, may be once again within our grasp.

Notes

1. Glossary of terms in Figures 3.1–3.3: π = inflation, y = output, u = unemployment, Rs = short term interest rates, θ = private sector financial wealth, e = real exchange rate, w = real wage, p = price level.
2. We have documented some of this experience in a new book for economists – *Rational Expectations and the New Macroeconomics* by Patrick Minford and David Peel, published by Martin Robertson, Oxford, 1983.

References

John Muth (1961), 'Rational Expectations and the Theory of Price Movements', *Econometrica* **29**, pp. 315–35.

Robert Lucas and Thomas Sargent (1978), 'After Keynesian Macro-economics' in *After the Phillips Curve: Persistence of High Inflation and High Unemployment*, Federal Reserve Bank of Boston.

Kent Matthews (1983), 'National Income and the Black Economy', *The Journal of Economic Affairs*, 3, 4, July, pp. 261–7.

4. Monetary Policy in the UK under Mrs Thatcher*

In 1979 Mrs Thatcher inherited a monetary mess. Inflation was rising rapidly from an initial rate of over 10%. The policy of wage controls that had been used to hold it down in 1978 had crumbled in the 'winter of discontent' of that year when graves went undug and rubbish piled up in the streets. Large public sector pay increases had been promised by the Clegg commission under the previous government. The budget was in crisis; already the deficit was up to 5% of GDP and it would clearly rise sharply more with these pay awards on top of the usual spending pressures.

The advice from Professor Milton Friedman (1980) was to reduce the money supply growth rate gradually and to cut taxes in order to stimulate output. The first part was accepted but the second was not because the deficit was seen to be important in conditioning financial confidence. Until the deficit could be reduced by other means taxes would have to stay up and perhaps even go up. This was the view not merely of the Treasury but also of the financial markets; in Liverpool we saw it as a rational expectations effect, given the growing pressures for monetary financing of a long-lasting deficit.

This was the background to the policies pursued. As we shall see little importance was attached to the operating method used by the central bank, whether monetary base control or interest rate setting in pursuit of monetary targets. So that with this, and the emphasis on fiscal policy support, the debate on monetary policy in Britain took a very different form from that in the US for example, though it perhaps had a rather European character. I propose first to describe the intended policies and their rationale in more detail. Secondly, how they turned out in practice. Third, whether any alternatives might have had better results. Finally, I shall consider future policy and, in particular, the UK attitude to the EMS.

---

* First published in *Finanzmarket und Portfolio Management*, 4, pp. 43–6, 1988, with additional part from IEA *Inquiry* 5 ('A Monetarist's Agenda'), October 1988.

The Thatcher Government's Monetary Plan

The key problem was seen to be the lack of long-term credibility in counter-inflation policy. The previous government had instituted monetary targets, starting in 1976 in conjunction with the IMF support arrangement. It had also managed a substantial reduction in the budget deficit; the Public Sector Borrowing Requirement (PSBR), the usual measure of deficit in the UK including government net lending to the private sector, was reduced from 10% of GDP in 1975 to below 4% in 1977. Nevertheless, the policies lacked long-term durability. Incomes policy which had been emphasised as the key bulwark against inflation crumbled as widely predicted it must in a free economy. The money supply target for £M3, a wide aggregate, was generally 'achieved' by using a tax on high-interest deposits, the 'corset'; excess money showed elsewhere, notably in rising M0 growth. Also, budgetary discipline was based on cuts without any long-term strategy for reducing the size of the public sector; so they were seen as temporary pain to be reversed once the pressure (e.g., of the IMF) was off.

Thus, the problem of a credibly durable monetary restraint on prices was one of fundamental political economy, not merely a technical matter of the central bank fixing appropriate targets. If the central bank had been constitutionally independent or even fiercely committed to price stability in practice, with a high profile Governor respect for monetary probity, matters could have been different; analysis of Switzerland or the US or the Federal Republic of Germany would, for example, focus mainly on the central bank for this reason. However, the Bank of England commanded no such position; formally an executive arm of the Treasury, it was staffed by Keynesians and had as Governor a lawyer whose main personal interest was regulation and who had no intuitive grasp of monetary theory.

To achieve durability – and it was hoped to convince people rapidly of that prospective durability – policy was cast in the form of a Medium-Term Financial Strategy or MTFS. This consisted of a commitment to a 5-year rolling target for gradually decelerating £M3 (the corset having been removed together with exchange controls and incomes policy) backed up by parallel reduction of the PSBR/GDP ratio – the original plans are shown in Figures 4.1 and 4.2, together with eventual outcomes. Announced in the 1980

Figure 4.1   Annual percentage growth in Sterling M3

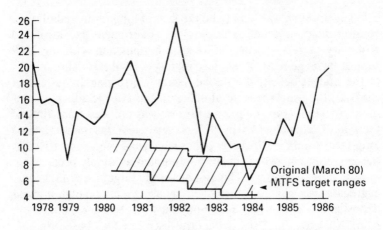

Figure 4.2   Four-quarter moving average of PSBR/GDP (%)

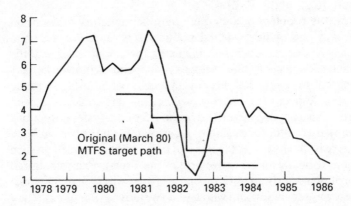

budget, it carried the full authority of the Prime Minister and notionally of the Cabinet, so that future deviations should be seen as a seriously embarrassing breach of promise to the electorate. On the optimistic view that it would be totally credible, market expectations of both short- and long-term inflation should drop, interest rates should fall rapidly, and any recession should be short-lived, possibly non-existent, as the falling money growth was offset by falling inflation so keeping up real money balances and consumer purchasing power.

The basic analysis could not be faulted. It rested on the logic of (1) the government's 'intertemporal budget constraint', whereby deficits today must be paid for by taxes, money expansion or economies tomorrow; (2) the political pressure for money creation to relieve a rising debt/GDP ratio with its consequence in rising interest rates and future tax burdens. This analysis was later spread widely by Thomas Sargent and Neil Wallace in their well-known paper 'Some unpleasant monetarist arithmetic' (1985) which was applied even in the US context, assuming a constitutionally independent central bank and no rise in interest rates because of 'Ricardian equivalence' (whereby future taxes are perfectly anticipated and offset by higher current savings). The point is that if one assumes any reasonable termination of the rising debt/GDP ratio, whether because of a limit on distortionary taxes or on available savings (the Sargent and Wallace case), then money financing is eventually required in the absence of quite implausibly severe cuts in public expenditure.

Monetary Policy in Practice

Logic was not enough; the MTFS not only failed to command credibility, fully or even to a significant extent, it also failed to be carried out in its own literal terms. Yet policy turned out to be more fiercely contractionary than the gradualism intended; it was closer to shock tactics than gradualism. A paradox indeed! Tougher, yet less credible, apparently the worst of both worlds.

Trouble came from two directions: technical design and politics. Technically, the choice of £M3 was an error because, after deregulating the banks (including their offshore links, with no exchange controls), high-interest deposits became the major weapon in the banks' battle for market share; as the banks' fortunes ebbed and flowed, so did £M3. In 1980–81 it overshot its targets massively (Figure 4.1). Yet M0 – the most narrow monetary aggregate, consisting of currency in circulation and bank reserves – was unaffected by deregulation and told a quite different story, of sharply tightening monetary conditions (Figure 4.3); its growth rate halved in the 12 months to mid-1980 and halved again in the next 12. It is obvious from data on the economy (see below Figure 4.5) which story is the true one; the recession, the rapid fall in inflation, and the strong exchange rate all confirm M0 as the accurate indicator.

Politically, the pain of recession, especially in the manufacturing sector, undermined the already insecure position of the 'monetarists' in the Conservative party, and Mrs Thatcher faced substantial internal opposition. The days of the MTFS and perhaps even of Mrs Thatcher herself seemed numbered.

So the MTFS was widely written off at this time as a failure because its targets had not been achieved and a temporary interlude before traditional politics returned. Meanwhile, the Chancellor, Sir Geoffrey Howe, doggedly persevered with the attempt to keep the MTFS 'on course'. Interest rates were kept up to reduce the money overshoot, and the PSBR was brought down on its track even though swollen by recession. Policies close to shock tactics were implemented by these means, perhaps mainly by accident but to some degree surely by intuitive survival instinct: that is, given that recession was connected in popular debate with the monetarist policies, it was vital to get results on inflation in short order as justification – to be hung for a sheep as a lamb, and better still to be applauded for the sheep of much lower inflation.

Whatever the reasons, the rapid fall in inflation – down to 5% by end-82 – restored the fortunes of Mrs Thatcher and her supporters. In early 1981, too, the technical problems were appreciated; with the arrival of Sir Alan Walters and his circulation of an influential paper by Professor Jurg Niehans of Berne University (Niehans, 1981), the decision was taken to loosen monetary policy in order to weaken the exchange rate, to stabilise M0 at a growth rate around 5%, and permit output to recover. To enhance credibility, the budget of 1981 increased taxes by 2% of GDP to cut the PSBR even though the recession still had not ended. This cut was crucial in finally creating market confidence in the policies' durability; long-term interest rates which had fluctuated around 14% for two years began to fall at last during 1981 (Figure 4.4). Output also started to recover in spring 1981.

This episode was the furnace in which the current monetary policy of the UK was forged. Those now running that policy have fashioned it with that experience in mind. The key elements are:

1. The PSBR must be kept down to sustain market confidence.
2. M0 is a reliable indicator of monetary conditions.

Figure 4.3   Annual percentage growth in M0

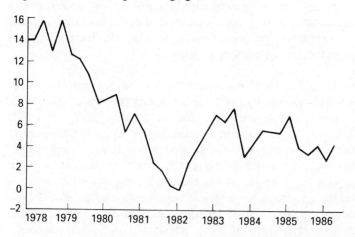

Figure 4.4   Long-run rate of interest, based on gross yield of 2.5% consols

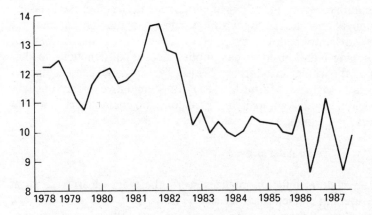

3. Rapid movements in the exchange rate may contain monetary signals and will in general not be permitted, unless M0 confirms systematically after the event that they should.
4. In controlling monetary conditions what matters is that interest rates be moved *symmetrically* as dictated by targets (without political intervention for example to hold interest rates down) and that market participants can understand the system's

signals in forming their expectations. Monetary Base control –
a method according to which M0 should be kept rigorously to a
fixed path – was rejected in favour of a system using M0 as the
key monetary indicator to guide interest rate changes; this was
an extension of familiar methods.

Though much ink has been spilt on such monetary control methods
per se, from the modern perspective of rational expectations these
key features of symmetry and efficient signalling attach to a wide
variety of short-term control methods, and there is no reason to
prefer Base Control over the method currently used, in principle.
Difficulties arise under the current method only when ambiguities
creep into the practice, as has occurred recently with uncertainty
about the European Monetary System (EMS) and the exact status
of exchange rate targets; but these problems also arise in base
control systems, as the Swiss experience shows.

Since 1982 these principles have been pursued with the objective
of keeping inflation below 5%; no strong efforts have been made to
drive it to zero, because of fears that these might destabilise a
smooth recovery and falling unemployment. The emphasis in policy
innovation switched to the supply side – deregulation, union laws,
privatisation and tax cuts. Nevertheless, even the process of
keeping inflation down has implied occasional deflation, so that
over the whole period from 1979 to 1986 Matthews and I estimated
(Matthews and Minford, 1987) the cumulative effect of tight
monetary and accompanying fiscal policy on unemployment was no
less than 1 million, just over 4% of the labour force.

Was There an Alternative?

The counter-inflation policies were therefore clearly far from
costless in conventional terms. With hindsight it is natural to ask
whether an alternative strategy could have conquered inflation at
less cost. Some argued for incomes policy; however, past experience of this in the UK is hardly encouraging. As argued earlier,
in a free economy (and as shown by Bean *et al*, 1987, Britain is low
in corporatist features), such policy can only be a temporary
expedient; apart from the costs it imposes in distorting markets
while in force, it cannot therefore provide a durable mechanism
either for controlling inflation or for reducing its unemployment

cost. Hence policy credibility would not have been enhanced, and so long-term interest rates would not have come down. As for inflation, though it might have been held down in the short term, so limiting the contractionary effect of monetary tightening, as controls crumbled inflation could well be higher than otherwise. So the contractionary effect would merely be displaced in time.

A more interesting possibility is that advocated by Hayek and new Classical economists (Sargent, 1985) of proper openly proclaimed shock tactics. In a recent paper, a colleague and I (Minford and Rastogi, 1988) took the calculations of Matthews and Minford (1987) for the effects of the policies actually pursued and re-computed them assuming shock tactics.

As we have seen, credibility was only established as the PSBR/GDP ratio actually fell; the rules the markets believed on the basis of available information to be governing the authorities' actions were that this ratio would be kept constant at its current level and that M0 growth would be set to keep the debt/GDP ratio constant at its current level. Our model gave a good fit to this period assuming these rules, which is some evidence that the markets did indeed believe these rules to be in operation.

If so, then to change expectations once-for-all policies should cut the PSBR/GDP ratio immediately to its zero-inflation value and cut M0 growth in line. While this would represent a big shock to expectations, it would be the last and the economy could recover uninterrupted from that point on.

The simulations that follow assume that from the beginning of 1980 public expenditure was cut and taxes raised sharply in order to bring the PSBR down at once to approximately 0.5% of GDP on a cyclically adjusted basis. (Since inflation is planned to fall to zero, also in short order, inflation adjustment is irrelevant.) Money growth (M0) is cut in parallel – implying a steady growth of around 1% pa for stable prices – with temporary exceptions designed to prevent excessively violent changes in monetary conditions in any one year.

From 1981 onwards fiscal and monetary policy is sustained in this mode; whereas in 1980, of course, the policy is a shock on a major scale, from 1981 it is fully anticipated for reasons discussed above.

The story of this alternative strategy is clearly told in the charts of Figure 4.5, comparing the model's prediction of what would have happened under shock tactics with what actually happened.

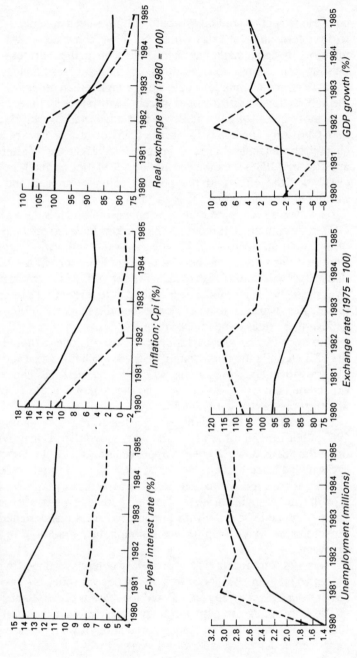

Figure 4.5 Simulation of shock tactics

64

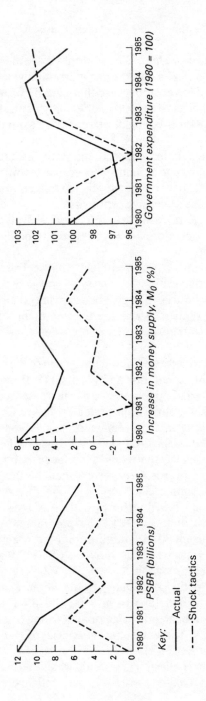

Figure 4.5 Simulation of shock tactics continued

Key:
———— Actual
— — ·Shock tactics

PSBR (billions)

Increase in money supply, M_0 (%)

Government expenditure (1980 = 100)

65

The basic picture is clear. There would have been a deeper recession in 1980–81 and a quicker rise in unemployment, reaching 3 million by 1981. However, because there are no further negative fiscal/monetary shocks after 1980, unemployment starts to fall sooner, and by 1984 it is falling decisively away from the 3 million mark.

The inflation rate falls more rapidly and settles at zero from 1982. It does not drop at once to zero in 1980 because the world recession and other negative shocks on the supply side reduce money demand in 1980–81 and cause 'defensive' price rises.

The real exchange rate similarly rises more sharply in 1980 but, thereafter, drops back more quickly as there are no more negative fiscal/monetary shocks.

We have found, rather in line with new Classical advice, that the short sharp shock that cannot be reversed – and so bypassses issues of credibility – can be argued to give better results than gradualism. The question that remains is whether the treatment was too brutal to be a practical possibility even in the honeymoon period of the first 6–12 months.

The scale of the cuts needed would have been of the order of 10% of total government expenditure and 4% of GDP. By contrast, even with the 'Clegg awards' – public sector pay increases recommended by the Government Commission under Professor Clegg – actual government spending in 1980 remained roughly constant in real terms (i.e., deflated by the GDP deflator). It is not that difficult to imagine a crisis package that could have been politically viable: withdrawal of Clegg awards, freezing of all benefits in money terms, general 10% programme cuts, raising of the discount factor on capital projects, and bringing forward the tax rises of the 1981 budget (worth 4% of the GDP). The programme here in fact assumed that government expenditure followed roughly its actual path and that tax rates were raised by 4% of GDP from 1980 and remain at this level throughout.

Judgement of political viability would require an extended discussion which would take us too far afield. Yet, when the opposition has itself been practising or advocating cuts, experience shows it can be done; witness the recent policies of Haughey in Eire and Lange in New Zealand in just such circumstances.

In summary, the policies here would have caused substantial dislocation during 1980–81, with the real exchange rate appreciating about twice as much as it actually did and GDP falling 7%, also about twice as much. However, the recovery would have been faster with inflation eliminated; by 1985, GDP would have been nearly 5% higher. Would such a cure have been so much more painful than what actually happened, that its speed and long-term gain would still not have seemed attractive?

Future Directions

We have argued that British monetary policy, in its efforts to bring inflation under control, has taken a form adapted to the institutions and political economy of Britain. It has emphasised the fiscal support needed, has put M0 in the role of key indicator with the exchange rate in a supplementary role, and has used a traditional indicator intervention system. The policy evolved out of the experience of the 1979–82 inflation battle.

We also argued that immediacy or cold turkey would have given better results especially for unemployment than the combination of announced gradualism and near-immediacy in practice.

The discussion so far has been mainly historical. In the last eighteen months, monetary controversy has flared again and, though the view set out here has ultimately won out as the basis of UK monetary policy, it has been challenged from two directions.

First, there has been pressure both from our EEC partners and from within the UK to join the EMS. The reasons given are political – we must join it or risk being left out of the full EEC councils – and economic – the UK will enjoy the benefits of exchange rate stability and the anti-inflation discipline of the Sterling/Deutschemark link.

The second challenge comes from those, especially City economists, who are concerned about the rapid growth of credit and the broad money supply measures. This has been reinforced by the sharp increase in the current account deficit on the balance of payments, and by other signs of over-heating – tighter capacity, skilled labour shortages and fast-rising house prices. The once reviled £M3 measure has therefore made a comeback in these circles.

The EMS Option

The argument against Britain joining the EMS is that the EMS is not a true fixed-rate system or monetary union; as a semi-fixed-rate system it is similar to the later stages of Bretton Woods and liable to repeated currency crises. These, to be controllable, require monetary policy to veer sharply as crisis occurs and probably also need exchange controls in devaluing countries; furthermore, the intervals between devaluation produce over-valuation for their currencies. All this may be worth enduring if domestic monetary policy is unable unaided to control inflation; but otherwise its cost is too high. A system of monetary union is attractive since it would reduce monetary transaction costs in the common market. Yet the time for the UK to join in EMS would be when it could make it a genuine monetary union with the DM at least; that, of course, requires convergence of monetary policy and inflation. It is in that sense that the time is not ripe. However, it may equally not be far off since it is no longer fanciful to speak of such convergence occurring.

The case for joining the EMS has been further weakened by recent events. Its advocates claim that it would hold down UK inflation, although this could be costly in terms of exchange controls and the difficulties with maintaining the exchange rate at its EMS limits. What they did not anticipate was that UK inflation would exceed 4 per cent even though the pound was strong against the Deutschemark. It has required a tightening of UK monetary policy to restore monetary stability, undermined by the exchange rate target. It now seems that not only is the EMS awkward to manage in a free market context, but it does not even keep inflation down.

The EMS has also become entangled with EEC proposals for 1992 integration and harmonisation. Unfortunately, it has become quite apparent in recent months that the Brussels view of integration is not one of comprehensive deregulation and competition, but rather of comprehensive regulation on common standards (harmonisation), with Brussels wielding greatly enhanced political and regulative powers. The plan seems to be to have uniform worker, and positive trade union, rights, to prevent the more competitive parts of the EEC undercutting their more unionised brothers; to force common tax systems, so that there can be no tax havens undermining the revenue base of the high-spending corporatist countries of the EEC, and to move towards a fortress Europe in trade matters, heralded by recent aggressive 'anti-dumping' tariffs against some Japanese and South Korean video makers.

In the light of this EMS could become a Trojan Horse, out of whose belly would issue Brussels' demands that the UK pursue other policies to support the EMS efforts to hold the pound within particular bands. For example, were we now in the EMS, we would be told by our European partners that our tax cuts should be reversed; that it would be 'helpful' to raise VAT or to place exchange controls on non-EEC currencies. The EMS would be the excuse that our more socialist and corporatist partners have been longing for, to put a spoke in the wheels of the UK's supply side reforms.

In short, EMS has been undermined by becoming entangled in a hidden agenda of essentially anti-competitive corporatist policies, in addition to its deficiencies as a monetary regime. In the light of these considerations, there is no compelling reason to abandon the MTFS.

The Credit Boom

Has the credit surge destroyed the MTFS's credibility? It could be argued that the EMS and exchange rate targets have not merely failed to control UK prices, they have positively destroyed the MTFS by fomenting a monetary explosion, shortly to become a price explosion.

This view completely fails to understand the role of banks and other financial intermediaries in a freely competitive banking and financial system. Competing banks will drive the interest rate, not just on their savings deposits, but on their current account deposits, up to the rate at which they can lend minus the cost of intermediation (which is relatively small in the UK where there are virtually no formal reserve requirements). As the High Street bank and building society war hots up, non-interest bearing current accounts will probably give way to explicit interest payments. The recent changes whereby banks forego charges on accounts in credit is the first step in this direction.

Once interest is paid on deposits, they cease to be 'money'. Consider currency. It pays no interest, so it will only be held to facilitate transactions (such as small-scale purchases) that cannot be paid for by clearing arrangements like credit cards or cheques. The advantage of the latter is that you can buy without surrendering interest until the moment of settlement. However, currency must be used for certain purchases. It is held ('demanded') for this purpose – demand for currency will fall when interest rates rise because it is worthwhile to economise on currency (by going more often to the bank, for example), and demand will increase as the number of transactions rise. This demand is quite clear and determinate.

As long as no interest rate is payable on current account deposits, they are like currency – held only for transactions that require payment by cheque, and with a determinate demand affected by interest rates and the volume of transactions.

Compare people's attitude to deposits with full interest payable. They will be indifferent between holding these and some other deposit, say in a unit trust, or indeed holding equity in a company. All these assets are priced so that they yield an equivalent return to the holder, after allowing for their riskiness. They are a part of the great market for savings.

Now comes the difficult bit of the analysis. The demand for any one of these interest-bearing assets is not given or easy to determine. There is literally an infinite number of asset-liability combinations in which the private sector can hold its savings; and each is as good as the other from its viewpoint. For example, suppose a new unit trust springs up offering a particular mix of shares and bonds in its portfolio; it is priced so that people buy its units, and the trust buys these shares and bonds from existing holders in the private sector (we hold the government's operations constant, to study this manoeuvre within the private sector). Now there are more private sector assets and more liabilities; but savings are the same, and so are interest rates. As a result nothing has changed to make people want to spend more or do anything differently. All that has happened is a reshuffling of balance sheets.

Obviously, something must determine the structure of balance sheets. Such things would be the costs of different sorts of intermediation and the ability of different intermediaries to improve the mix of risk and return faced by savers, e.g., because they can deal in economic quantities of stock. The structure goes on changing until no new intermediary opportunity is available. Yet the point is that all this reshuffling makes no difference to the overall return available in the market.

It does not affect the analysis that some types of deposit are used in settlement systems and so provide a service in transactions.

Settlements will be priced at the marginal cost of supplying this service in a competitive system. Some of the deposit holders will use their deposits for transactions. However, this is not reflected in the return they get, because this return is fixed by the rate of interest less the cost of intermediation. These holders in effect get a bonus, or 'surplus', although their demand for these deposits could be predicted. The overall amount of these deposits cannot because, as we have seen, the structure of balance sheets can take myriad forms and be affected by, say, a small change in the technology of intermediation.

In summary, though many deposits continue to be used in transactions through clearing systems, they cease to be money with a determinate demand, and become savings vehicles with an indeterminate demand. The banks become just like unit trusts, distinguishable only by the bundle of 'deposits' that they invest in (loans rather than shares). Just like the unit trust in our earlier example, should banks expand credit and deposits, nothing other than the balance sheet structure will have been affected. Credit and wide 'money' measures will be driven by the supply-side technology of the financial system and be of no significance for consumers' savings and firms' investment plans.[1]

In particular, if, as is surely the case, the high street banks are being compelled by competition to make themselves more efficient, it is hardly surprising that they seek to expand their operations sharply, raising their interest rates to consumers, improving their loan services to firms. This shift in bank technology is just the sort of thing to shift private sector balance sheets to expansion on both sides.

It is therefore an implication of financial competition that money changes its form and, in particular, the only money left is currency. Hence the government's decision to target M0 in the MTFS, and the abandonment of the wider measures, described briefly in an earlier section. As for the credit explosion school of thought, it is clearly wide of the mark, using concepts appropriate to a financial environment that has now passed away into the history books.

Mechanisms of Control, Rules and Relationships

Is there some new framework that could be set in place to institutionalise the experience and analysis set out here? In Britain, an oral tradition has generally been preferred, partly because of Parliamentary sovereignty which enables the legislature to nullify any rule. However the next Chancellor will inherit the framework of the MTFS, balanced budget in normal times and an M0 target range to be kept inside through interest rate movements. This is a simple and ancient recipe, revived and adapted for our times. Also, it is a departure from the pure oral tradition. While it can at any time be overthrown by ministers and Parliament, this would bring a serious loss of prestige to Mrs Thatcher's Government. It seems doubtful that anything much more binding could be achieved by more formal commitments than now exist (such as the Gramm-Rudman-Hollings amendment on the budget in the US).

The Chancellor could reconsider a totally fixed target path for M0, a monetary base control system to strengthen the commitment to monetary stability. This might help to avoid a repeat of recent ambiguities. An evolutionary approach still seems the best way now, as it did when considered six years ago. First, let him succeed in keeping inside the target range, and then gradually narrow the range, until eventually the path is quite rigorously controlled, as in base control. As argued above, the key thing is to act regularly on interest rates to achieve a medium-term money supply growth rate –short-run fluctuations with a narrow range are of little significance.

The heart of controlling the monetary base is that it is demanded for transactions purposes by individuals, firms, and not least banks. There is no need to increase demand artificially by placing compulsory ratios on banks or anyone else. Banks will have cash ratios of their own for transactions reasons, and they may observe a variety of other 'prudential' balance sheet ratios to reduce their exposure to risk. These are part of the normal commercial demand for cash and other assets; they require and would be assisted by no official intervention. Indeed, artificial ratios act as a tax on the banking system, reducing its efficiency in intermediation. At present, there are no official cash or other ratios on British banks (other than a nominal 0.5 per cent 'non-operational reserve' requirement, an unnecessary relic from the past). Long may this continue!

One institutional route that could well lead to greater monetary certainty in the long term would be through a stronger Bank of England. The Bank was nationalised by a Labour Government. It did not much distinguish itself in the early days of Mrs Thatcher's

Government, however, becoming identified with irredentist Keynesianism. This has now changed and it may be possible to create again in the Bank the bastion of monetary independence and stability, guardian of the MTFS on its monetary side, just as it once was pre-war and as is the Bundesbank in Germany. For now, control of monetary policy must rest with Mrs Thatcher and her Chancellor; these are the safest hands. However, the Bank's role should evolve until, perhaps, even formal privatisation and the issue of competing private currencies can be considered.

Notes

1. Those who would like a fuller, more technical but still readable account of all this, should read two articles by Professor Eugene Fama (1980 and 1983), who teaches finance at the University of Chicago.

References

C.R. Bean, Layard, and Nickell (1987), 'The Rise in Unemployment: a Multi-Country Study', in *The Rise in Unemployment*, Blackwell, pp. 1–22.

E. Fama (1980), 'Banking in the Theory of Finance', *Journal of Monetary Economics*, **6**, 39–57.

E. Fama (1983), 'Financial Intermediation and Price Level Control', *Journal of Monetary Economics*, **12**, 7–28.

Milton Friedman (1980), 'Memorandum on Monetary Policy', House of Commons Treasury and Civil Service Committee, *Memoranda on Monetary Policy*, HMSO, 17 July, 55–68.

K. Matthews and P. Minford (1987), 'Mrs Thatcher's Economic Policies, 1979–87', *Economic Policy*, **5**, Oct., 57–101.

P. Minford and A. Rastogi (1987), 'A New Classical Policy Programme', mimeo, University of Liverpool, published in A.J.C. Britton (ed.) (1989), *Policymaking with Macroeconomic Models*, Gower, pp. 83–97.

J. Niehans (1981), 'The Appreciation of Sterling – Causes, Effects and Policies', ESRC Money Study Group Discussion Paper, ESRC, London.

T. Sargent (1986), 'Stopping Moderate Inflations: the Methods of Poincare and Thatcher', ch.4 of *Rational Expectations and Inflation*, Harper & Row, New York; an earlier version appeared as 'The Ends of Four Big Inflations', in R.E. Hall (ed.) (1982), *Inflation*, Chicago University Press, Chicago.

T. Sargent and N. Wallace (1981), 'Some Unpleasant Monetarist Arithmetic', *Quarterly Review*, Fall, Federal Reserve Bank of Minneapolis, 1–17.

5.   Trade Unions Destroy a Million Jobs*

I.   The Central Analysis and Argument

It is not original to suggest that unions create unemployment. It has been a widespread claim by economists – including many associated with the Institute of Economic Affairs – who have urged more freedom for market forces. What they have generally had in mind was that unions raise wages for *unionised* workers, some of whom as a consequence will lose their jobs (or equivalently other *non-unionised* workers will fail to get jobs in unionised industries). The workers displaced will find it hard to gain employment in the non-union sectors because of the limited opportunities there and will, for the most part, be unemployed.

What has been lacking in this argument is two-fold. First, there has been some vagueness about why workers would not find jobs in the non-union sector, since they would drive non-union wages down there until there was full employment. Second, the order of magnitude of the unemployment which could result from union power has not been indicated; this is obviously very important because, if the magnitudes are trivial, the ordeal by fire required to reduce union power would not be politically attractive.

In the course of our researches at Liverpool[1] we have devoted considerable effort to examining these two matters. This chapter describes our examination. Our first conclusion has been that the operation of the tax and benefit system prevents wages in the non-union sector from dropping much, because benefits are 'flat rate' (i.e., regardless of previous earnings) after six months, and that for low-income jobs they may be so close to net earnings that the jobs would become unviable and unattractive for workers if wages fell very far. Hence the non-union sector has only a small ability to absorb workers displaced by the union sector.

Upon estimating relationships which incorporate the role of the

* First published in *Economic Affairs*, pp. 73–8, January 1982.

74

tax and benefits system, our second conclusion has been that *the substantial rise in union power since the early 1960s has raised unemployment by about one million.* This is a round number probably at the upper end of what politicians and practical men may have suspected, but, if correct, it must weigh heavily in the political scales against the fuss involved in reducing union power.

Challenge to Wishful Thinking

Our work is bound to be controversial at this stage because it challenges much wishful thinking. Yet it will be a long time before all the additional evidence has been sifted – particularly the immense amount of potential information in the Family Expenditure Survey – which may settle all the interlocking issues involved. However by the time such research has been done, it may be too late to take the necessary action. Already the tide of union power has swept in irresistibly. Some recent events have suggested it may temporarily be receding, but who can tell what access of strength it may gain in the next economic upturn and beyond? Now may be the last major opportunity available to politicians to push the tide out once and for all. To lose such an opportunity on the chance that our estimate of the effect of union power may be much too high would be a dangerous gamble. Compared with it, the risk that the highly unpopular union movement will be able to resist successfully and damagingly the necessary legislation to cut their powers seems a risk substantially less to be feared.

Union Monopoly and Unemployment

The basic ideas in our work are simple enough. A union exists to raise the wages of its members to an 'optimal' amount, given, first, that higher union wages means fewer union jobs, and, second, the wages their members could get in the non-union sector. The union typically determines an optimal union wage which is some way above the non-union wage. A monopolist raises his price to the point at which his profits are maximised; this point will be above that which would have been set by free competition and will reduce the size of the market. So with a union monopoly.

Workers who lose their jobs as a result of their monopoly power will then seek jobs in the non-union sector. These additional supplies of labour force wages down there, until supply is equal to demand. However at this point, we note that the social security system guarantees a minimum income regardless of work and that taxes apply to workers with very low incomes. As wages in the non-union sector fall, they become progressively less attractive (after tax) to workers forced out of the union sector; some, perhaps many, will not be prepared to take the jobs on offer for such rewards. They will go on the dole. The major way in which supply is equated to demand in the non-union sector by falling wages is through the contraction of supply. Demand rises as wages fall, but the tax and social security system imparts a 'floor' to wages, which causes major withdrawals from the labour market as wages get too close to this critical level. Consequently, *wages cannot fall enough to create much additional demand*.

This analysis is sometimes criticised on the grounds that the resulting unemployment is labelled as 'voluntary'. Many people feel, rightly, that unemployment is a tragic misfortune and cannot be regarded in any meaningful sense as voluntary. Consequently, they feel inclined to dismiss the analysis.

However, such a feeling is inspired by a complete misconception. There is nothing in the analysis to suggest otherwise than that unemployment is unpleasant and degrading. The point of the analysis is that *the alternatives to unemployment, non-union jobs at non-union wages, are even less attractive*. What is more, workers who take the jobs in the non-union sector would, of course, prefer to work in the better-paid union sector. It is a technical convention in economics to call the decisions of these people 'voluntary', because they are doing their best even in poor circumstances, but they could just as well be described as involuntarily forced out of the union sector.

No amount of relabelling however will avoid the basic problem society faces: how to create permanent jobs for pay that people will accept. The analysis clearly indicates that one major way to do this is to *reduce the power of unions to raise union wages*. As union wages fall, the demand for union labour rises, people are withdrawn from the non-union sector, non-union wages rise and more people are prepared to work in it.

The Estimated Effects of Union Power

In Part II, we detail our analysis. It is basically that during the 1960s the world environment was kind to Britain, world trade grew fast and our terms of trade were favourable. British governments raised both social security benefits and taxation on labour substantially. Furthermore, union power increased sharply towards 1970. During the 1970s we have had a substantial worsening of the world environment, a slow-down in world trade, and a deterioration of our terms of trade (if to a modest extent offset by North Sea oil). Yet union power has continued to increase, though more slowly and, though real benefits have stabilised, labour tax rates have continued to rise. The opposite – a reversal of the trends in the 1960s – was required to prevent unemployment from rising as it has done in the 1970s.

We can inspect the effect of union power in various dimensions. The unionisation rate in 1963 was 43%; by 1979 it had risen to 56%. Our estimates indicate this would have raised total real wages, once fully worked through, by 13% compared with what they would otherwise have been. The effect on output would be to reduce it by 8½%. The effect on the PSBR is correspondingly severe: an increase of £6½ bn at 1981 prices. The effect on unemployment, coming both through the increased substitution of mechanisation for labour (about 650,000) and through the contraction of output (about 350,000), would be about 1 million.

To produce such a rise in unemployment our equations suggest that non-union real wages would have been depressed by about 13%. Hence the increased union power would have had its effect by reducing the living standards both of non-unionised workers and of those becoming unemployed and deciding to sign on rather than take non-union employment.

Conclusions

Even if our estimates are remotely near the truth, it would seem clear that *union power, even if only a modest nuisance in the 1960s, has become a major obstruction by the early 1980s.*

Monopoly power in the labour market from the union side now rates as a major allocational issue. Monopoly power in goods markets was the major allocational issue in the post-war period, resulting in important legislation such as the Restrictive Trade Practices Act of 1956, new institutions such as the Monopolies

Commission and tax changes like the successive tariff-cutting 'rounds'.

In British history the trade unions have been the instigators of major social reforms. Once they were a 'countervailing force' in an economy where major employers held the whip hand in negotiations, but their historical role as social reformer is no longer relevant. The need for countervailing force has disappeared in an economy where employers' monopoly power has been heavily curtailed by the stronger competition in goods markets and the emergence of industrial relations institutions such as the industrial courts. It is hard to escape the conclusion that the public interest requires measures to deal with labour market monopoly power in an analogous way to goods market monopoly power. A corollary is that, since the power is vested in the unions by exceptionally favourable laws, *it is no use hoping that non-legal measures – such as incomes policies, 'confrontations' or exhortations – will have any effect on the problem.* Only changes in laws and institutions which take away union power will remove its effects on unemployment, output and the interests of non-unionised workers.

To my untutored mind, it seems a simple and attractive course to abolish the 1906 (Immunities) Act, except for the peaceful picketing clause (a suggestion I owe to a prominent economic journalist, Andreas Whittam Smith), to abolish the closed shop, and to institute a Labour Monopolies Commission. Good legal minds can probably do better; but the essential is that *only the law can take away a force that the law has strengthened* to the point of inflicting severe damage on the British economy and our working people, *especially the poorer*.

II. The Assumptions, Calculations and Equations

The issues we are examining are not short-term matters; in the UK both the rise in unemployment and the rise in union power have taken place over two decades, in the course of five economic cycles. While it may be defensible to suppose that, in the short term of a year or two, there can be excess supply or excess demand in the markets for goods and labour, it is extraordinarily hard to defend such a supposition for longer periods.

Our analysis is concerned with the long-run determination of employment, unemployment and real wages, and we assume that in the long run there is no excess supply or demand for labour or goods. Our long-run assumptions are captured in Figure 5.1. It shows, first, a supply curve of labour to the UK economy associated with the average real non-union wage, Wc/P on the vertical axis; the quantity of labour is on the horizontal axis. The supply curve is drawn flat at low wages because the ratio of real benefits (shown as B/P) to real wages becomes critically high for a large section of the population, but at high wages the benefit/wage ratios drop to irrelevance for the vast majority so that the only effect of benefits is to raise somewhat the length of time spent between jobs in 'search'. At these high wages the supply of labour approximates to what we may call the 'labour force', shown as $\bar{L}$; those capable of working would wish to do so under appropriate terms, and would mostly register as desiring work at unemployment benefit offices.

Figure 5.1   The effects of an increase in union power (dashed lines represent situation after rise in union mark-up)

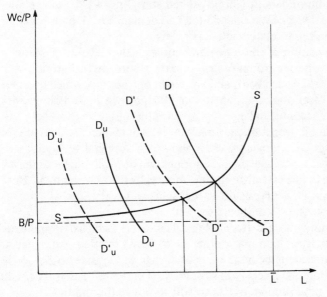

This supply curve of labour shifts to the left if real benefits rise or if income tax rates (T_L) rise (reducing disposable wages corresponding to the gross wage shown on the vertical axis), or if the labour force is reduced. We must also allow for the rigidity of the housing market and the dispersion of employment opportunities; a mismatch between population centres and opportunities will shift the SS curve to the left if mobility is obstructed by housing.

The demand side of the diagram is drawn up on the simplifying assumption that there is a constant 'union mark-up' (the percentage by which unions raise unionised workers' wages above non-union wages) at all levels of non-union wages and other relevant variables. The expositional advantage of this (clear over-) simplification is that it allows union and non-union firms' demand curves for labour to be put on a single diagram. With union real wages uniquely related to non-union real wages, the demand for union labour, though truly related to union real wages, will also be uniquely related to the non-union real wage, as shown by the D_uD_u curve. The demand for non-union labour will be related straightforwardly to the non-union real wage. We can add the two demands for labour together to obtain the total demand curve, DD.

The position of these demand curves – the 'level of demand' – depends on four groups of factors. First, there are the international ones; world trade (WT), and our terms of trade (π), which together dictate what domestic demand and output will be consistent with current account balance at given non-union real wages. An expansion in world trade, for example, would increase demand for British goods from abroad; if these are supplied at higher real wages, the additional export earnings will be available for domestic demand to increase also, raising imports by the same amount. Both D_uD_u and DD curves shift to the right, and real wages will rise, as will labour supply and employment.

Secondly, there are technological factors (k) which determine the productivity of labour and other costs. A rise in other costs, such as raw material or capital, both of which we assume to be set in international markets, will shift the DD curve to the left. A rise in the marginal product of labour will shift it to the right.

Thirdly, taxes on labour paid by firms and other implicit labour costs levied on employers (such as sickness benefits and redundancy costs), which we denote by T_F, will shift the DD curve to the left.

Finally, we come to the union mark-up. A rise will shift the D_uD_u

curve to the left, since a given non-union real wage will now correspond to a higher union real wage. The DD curve will be shifted to the left by the same amount (there will be no change in non-union labour demand at given real non-union wages).

What determines the union mark-up? Our analysis is straight-forward enough; each union is a maximising monopoly which faces the problem of working out an optimal time-path of real wages for its members, given that actions it takes today will have effects far into the future. In principle, therefore, all the factors determining the demand for labour in both sectors and the total supply of labour will come indirectly into each union's analysis. Complicated as this problem is, the essentials of the solution are clear enough; in particular, the mark-up will rise the less easy the employer finds it to substitute other factors of production including non-union labour for union labour. 'Union power' is measured in principle by the difficulty of this substitution, but this is not helpful in practice since this difficulty is unobservable. In practice, we resort to the only available index of union power, the proportion of the labour force which is unionised, and suppose that it is likely to bear some rough relationship to the true measure.

We can put this whole framework together easily enough. Employment and real non-union wages are determined in the long run at the intersection of the supply curve, SS, and the demand curve, DD. Unemployment is the difference between workers who register, $\bar{L}$, and those who are employed. This again is an over-simplification, because not all in the labour force register for a variety of reasons, especially lack of eligibility and dislike of the unemployment status, but registered unemployment will be highly correlated with the difference between $\bar{L}$ and employment.

The Mechanics of Estimation

In the short run, the economy will not jump quickly to any new long-run equilibrium, for the traditional reason that there are costs of adjusting labour demands (and possibly also labour supplies, though we do not find them important). These costs of adjustment cause both employment and union real wages (so also average real wages) to move relatively sluggishly; our estimates suggest that adjustment takes between 2 years (quarterly data) and 4 years (annual) for 90% to come through.

It is convenient for us to assume that in the non-union sector day-to-day (as opposed to *long*-run) supply is always equal to day-to-day demand; hence our model assumes 'continuous labour market equilibrium' in the sense that this residual market always clears and there is no excess supply. However, this is less important than it seems. Our analysis still has the conventional economic characteristic: that it takes time to get to the long run. Other analyses which would share our long-run framework but assumed 'short-run disequilibrium' (excess supply or demand) could well produce similar results. So our analysis does not appear to rest crucially on the assumption of continuous market equilibrium.

What our analysis gives us is two basic equations and one group of equations:

1. An equation for total average wages (union and non-union) which, using real wages as the supply price of labour, says it depends on the volume of unemployment, real benefits grossed up for direct taxes, the size of the labour force, and the unionisation rate. To allow for one-year nominal wage contracts over a proportion of employees, the size of inflation forecasting errors also enters the calculations; unexpected inflation causes workers who contracted in advance to suffer an unexpected drop in real wages. Finally, the last period's real wages enter because of the adjustment costs noted earlier. This is the 'supply equation' in the analysis.[2]
2. An equation for unemployment, regarded as depending on the demand for labour; this is the demand equation in the analysis. Unemployment is related inversely to real wages grossed up for labour taxes on the employer, technological progress, the volume of output, and lagged unemployment.
3. A group of equations determining the level of output.

These are the equations of the Liverpool macroeconomic model. They have the property that in the long-run output must be such that there is current account balance; hence long-run output (and so employment) will depend, as in the diagram, on world trade, and the terms of trade, as well as all the other factors entering the SS and DD curves. Output in the short run depends on the fiscal, monetary and international shocks hitting the economy which cause fluctuations around the long-run equilibrium (discussed in our other reports and not important here).

These equations follow in summary form. They have been successfully tested for stability, autocorrelation and sensitivity to differently weighed benefit and tax series; the inclusion of a time trend in the wage equation and of the labour force in the unemployment equation also makes no difference to the other coefficients of these equations, both variables being quite insignificant.

Statistical Appendix[3]

Full details of the wage and unemployment equations are in A.P. L. Minford (1981), *Labour Market Equilibrium in an Open Economy*, SSRC Project Working Paper 8103, University of Liverpool (published in Oxford Economic Papers, **35**, 4, November supplement, pp. 207–44, 1983).

The wage and unemployment equations were estimated for quarterly data from 1964:2 to 1979:2, and also for annual data from 1955 to 1979.

Quarterly equations (t-values in brackets, constant and seasonal dummies not shown; Two Stage Least Squares):

$$w = -.28P^{ue} \quad -.027u \quad +.125(b+T_L) \quad +.46UNR$$
$$\quad\ (0.09) \qquad (2.1) \qquad\quad (3.1) \qquad\qquad (2.4)$$

$$-.03N \quad +.77w_{-1}$$
$$\ (0.1) \qquad (11.8)$$

$\bar{R}^2 = .98 \qquad DW = 1.77$

Box-Pierce statistics (BP) (16 degrees of freedom) = 15

$$u = -2.3Q \quad +1.1(w+T_F) \quad +.01T \quad +.7u_{-1}$$
$$\quad\ (4.1) \qquad\ (2.8) \qquad\qquad (2.8) \qquad (9.5)$$

$\bar{R}^2 = .96 \qquad DW = 1.95 \qquad BP(16) = 13$

Annual equations (t-values in brackets; Three Stage Least Squares):

$$w = 3.95 \quad -.034u \quad +.12(b+T_L) \quad +.95UNR$$
$$\ (0.8) \qquad (0.9) \qquad\ (3.0) \qquad\qquad (2.8)$$

$$-.6N \quad +.72w_{-1}$$
$$\ (1.3) \qquad (4.5)$$

$\bar{R}^2 = .97 \qquad DW = 2.47 \qquad BP(6) = 2.3$

$$u = 49.1 \qquad -3.4Q \qquad +1.8(w+T_F) \qquad +.08T$$
$$\quad (2.4) \qquad\quad (1.7) \qquad\quad (1.1) \qquad\qquad (1.2)$$

$$+.53u_{-1}$$
$$\quad (2.9)$$

$$\bar{R}^2 = .87 \qquad DW = 1.5 \qquad\qquad\qquad BP(6) = 11.2$$

The output equations for the Liverpool model are set out in
A.P.L. Minford (1980), 'A Rational Expectations Model of the UK
under Fixed and Floating Exchange Rates', Carnegie-Rochester
Conference Series on Public Policy, **12** ('On the State of Macroeconomics'), Spring, pp. 293–355.

Notes

1. Financial support for this work from the Social Science Research
   Council is gratefully acknowledged.
2. The unionisation rate (and so the union mark-up) enters the supply
   equation though it entered the demand curves in the diagram, because
   the diagram is in terms of the non-union wage, whereas the estimation
   is in terms of the (observable) total wage over all sectors.
3. Variable definitions: w = log of real wages, u = log of unemployment,
   P^{ue} = unexpected inflation, $b + T_L$ = log of real benefits grossed up for
   employee taxes, UNR = fraction of employees unionised, N =
   working population, Q = log of output/trend, $W + T_F$ = log of real
   wages grossed up for employer taxes, T = time.

6. High Unemployment is not Permanent*

It has become fashionable in polite circles to say that unemployment is now going to be always with us and that society must 'adjust' to it by compulsory part-time work, early retirement, 'creative leisure planning', and so forth. This talk is ill-informed or, to put it impolitely, rubbish. This essay is an attempt to explain why. It will be dismissed by the fashionable as 'optimistic', 'on another planet' and with similar phrases; but the more reflective will, I hope, take note of the lessons of economic history and commonsense economic analysis to which I shall try to draw attention.

I. Frictional Unemployment

Unemployment can usefully be divided into three categories. First, there is 'frictional' unemployment, by which is meant the inevitable unemployment arising from the ceaseless change in the structure of industry and employment, as people leave jobs in one firm or industry and are relocated in another. Job-change must take a minimum of time, and during that time people will be temporarily unemployed, unless they are in the fortunate position, as many are, to have found another job before they leave their previous one; during this period of unemployment, the job-changer will be searching for a new job and will settle for one when the prospects of finding a better one by searching longer are just outweighed by the extra searching costs he would incur. In Britain just over a third of all jobs on average change hands each year. Some jobs change hands more than once a year, making up for the more than two-thirds that change hands less frequently than once. This figure has been fairly steady for 20 years. The volume of 'frictional' unemployment will then depend on the minimum period the average person would require to find a new job (allowing for those who have done so). In practice, the period people take will usually be

* First published in *Economic Affairs*, pp. 17–23, July-September 1984.

substantially more than the minimum (the reasons are discussed below). Yet let us conceive of a minimum period as the condition where there is no significant incentive to delay finding a new job. As a rough guide in Britain we could use the 1950s when it took people about 3 weeks on average to find a new job. If a third of the labour force change jobs each year and take on average three weeks, unemployment will average about 2% of the labour force ($33\frac{1}{3}\%$ × $\frac{3}{52}$ = 1.9%, which will be the percentage of the labour force out of action on average over the year). This was roughly the British rate in the 1950s.

Clearly, this frictional unemployment is not a constant. In periods of more rapid change in the structure of employment or when there are sharper regional disparities, necessitating more distant or complicated job shifts, the rate will rise. However the evidence suggests that the major variations in unemployment do not come from this source; indeed, if they did, we would not worry about them much, because we would know that the system was coping effectively with the problem.

II. Cyclical Unemployment

The major variations arise from the two other categories of unemployment, which can be termed 'cyclical' and 'induced'. The cyclical is familiarly the unemployment which arises in recessions or depressions, international business cycle fluctuations in activity. We are now just emerging from the 1980–82 world recession, the most severe since the war, which pushed US unemployment up about 4 percentage points from the 1979 cycle peak when it was 6.2% to the 1982 trough when it was 10.5%. It is a plausible judgement that, by the end of the world recovery, US employment will be back down to around 6% again. This is widely regarded as the frictional rate in the USA, higher than in Britain because of its large size and the consequent complications of job-swaps, often inter-state.

What happens in a recession and why does unemployment usually rise so sharply? The world market system is a network of a myriad separate price signals, to which producers, consumers and investors are continuously reacting. They make their plans based on current prices derived from them and from other information. In a period when plans are (on average) being fulfilled, the world economy will be in a relatively tranquil state, growing at a steady rate (or recovering steadily from the last recession). A recession is triggered when plans are frustrated by a widespread adverse shift in prices; for example, crucial raw material prices may rise faster than expected or retail prices may suddenly slow down. One reason for recession is that, in such a highly decentralised system as the world market economy, the *interpretation* of such price shifts is immensely difficult. *If* people think they merely reflect less or more *inflation*, they will pay little attention, merely marking their own prices up slower or faster. Yet if they think they reflect 'genuine' changes (reducing the profitability of their operations), firms will react by making real changes in their plans, such as cutting down on their plant and labour force, and consumers by reducing their consumption. A recession occurs when enough people and firms think the adverse price shifts are genuine and react adversely to them (even though in the event it will transpire that on average these price shifts could *not* have been adverse: a wind that blows against some *must* blow fair for others). The business cycle, on this view, is the result of mistakes made in interpreting surprise shifts in the price environment; mistakes which are inevitable in a decentralised system which, nevertheless, is desired for its economic flexibility and political freedom.

Two other explanations could perfectly well co-exist with this one in an overall view of recessions. They assume that *interpretation* is not the problem when shocks occur. Rather, according to one of them, the problem is that people and firms are tied into previous contracts which prevent them from doing the best in the new situation. They would, for example, like to cut their prices (or wages) in response to a worsening environment. However, these prices (or costs) have been fixed, so instead they have to cut back on *supply* (output and employment). In the other rival explanation, the problem is rather that different groups will react to the shocks at a different pace. The gainers from an oil price rise, such as oil sheikhs, for example, may be slower to spend their extra resources than losers are to cut back their spending. Demand thus drops today relative to tomorrow, requiring a fall in the rate of interest and other pressures of recession designed to cause producers to shift output from the present into the future.

These explanations have very different implications for the role of fiscal and monetary policy.[1] What they have in common is that activity contracts in response to unexpected changes in the environment (and vice versa) which frustrate previous economic plans.

When activity contracts, unemployment rises as people take longer to find jobs. They do so because, while they could persuade firms that are cutting back to take them on or to keep them on at sharply lower wage rates (perhaps in a different job paying much less), they would rather spend longer and wait for something better as the economy picks up than to settle for such terms. To take an extreme example, a person trained as an accountant may be able to pick up a job washing-up in a restaurant, but he may decide that such work would lower his chances of getting another accountant's job in six months or so. The extent to which people will wait in this way during recession depends largely on the nature of the social benefit system; if it is generous relative to their previous income, waiting will be lengthened and cyclical swings in unemployment will be the wider.

Cyclical unemployment, however, like frictional unemployment, is not serious, because 'what goes up comes down'. Clearly we would like to moderate the extent by which it goes up, and there is a highly charged technical debate about how far this is possible, but it is the third category of unemployment which is really at the back of people's minds when they speak of 'high' unemployment lasting into the indefinite future. Will it?

III. Induced Unemployment

This category is the unemployment induced by intervention, invariably government or government-sanctioned, in the labour market. It is usually well-intended. The government is pressured to 'help the poor', for example, by fixing minimum wages, by instituting incomes policies which raise wages of the low-paid, by raising unemployment benefit or by giving legal protection to union action for 'decent living standards'. Yet such intervention is disastrous. Most of it damages the very group, the poor, it is designed to help. All of it increases unemployment among the poor. And, even though higher unemployment benefits would raise their living standards if unemployed, the diminution of their chances of a job increases their general dependency on hand-outs and diminishes their dignity as members of society.

How does this intervention create unemployment? If unemployment benefits are high relative to in-work incomes, there is an incentive to spend longer 'searching' for a new job. The intention of politicians in introducing most current unemployment benefit systems was indeed that, in *recessions* (when finding a job similar to the one you have just lost is *hard*), workers should be protected from having to change their working habits sharply. It could be argued that this is no bad thing – we might not want our temporarily out-of-work doctors or draughtsmen scratching around for washing-up jobs for six months or a year at a time.

However, suppose that in 'normal' times people generally take longer to find new jobs because of generous benefits; longer searching would permanently raise the unemployment rate. Instead, say, of taking 3 weeks on average, they might take 5 weeks. In Britain this would raise the unemployment rate from 1.9% to 3.2%.

This is perhaps not a serious effect. There is quite a lot of evidence that the sort of benefit systems in operation in the states of the USA has a small effect of this sort. Typically, the benefit systems give support for only a few months (usually 6 months and at maximum a year) before running out; the incentive to prolong unemployment in normal times is thus modest.

However, in some European countries unemployment support works essentially like a minimum out-of-work income available indefinitely even to people not seriously looking for a new job. Britain is one of these countries. Belgium is another. Also, there are incipient signs of imitation in France and Germany, which still in the main have US-style social benefit systems. In these countries a low-paid worker can find himself little or no better off in work than out of work. This cripples the incentive for low-paid workers who have lost their jobs to look for new jobs at the lower wages necessary for them to be profitably re-employed. They will 'search' for very long periods, possibly indefinitely, unless they get so fed up with being unemployed (and working spasmodically, perhaps part-time or in the shadow economy) that they finally take a job they cannot truly 'afford' to take.

The effect on unemployment can be dramatic. If 15% of the labour force are low-paid enough to come into this category, in a recession when many of them may lose their jobs, the bulk may end up effectively *long-term* unemployed because it will not really pay them to lower their wage expectations sufficiently to get a new job.

Unemployment among this group will only fall either if real benefits fall or if net wages (after tax) rise over time. One of these results will probably happen eventually, either because of growth or because of the drain on public finances, but it could take a long time.

Once a country has a benefit system of this minimum-income type, other factors can aggravate unemployment. Higher labour taxes will be one; these will now, instead of lowering workers' take-home pay (which would otherwise fall to preserve jobs), raise labour costs to firms (since workers will not take a cut), and destroy jobs. Union power will be another factor. Without this benefit system, people who lost their jobs in the unionised industry (because wages there are pushed up) find jobs in the non-union industries where wages are consequently depressed. Yet *with* this benefit system, wages will not *fall* significantly in the non-union sector because workers can get almost as much out of work; hence jobs will not be created there to offset the loss of union jobs and unemployment will rise when union power rises. A final example: if the country's products command lower prices abroad because of stronger competition, this too under this benefit system will create unemployment – because wages cannot fall enough to allow firms to reduce their prices to match the competition and they will therefore contract their operations and their labour forces.

The Historical Experience of Unemployment

So much for economic analysis. What of the relevant historical experience?

Figure 6.1 shows UK unemployment for the 120 years from 1851 to 1971. There are three phases. Up to World War I unemployment fluctuated fairly regularly ('cyclically') in the range of 2–10% around an average of about 5%. In the interim period, the rate rose dramatically to a peak in the Great Depression of 1931–33 before falling steadily to World War II, it then fluctuated narrowly until 1971 around an average of about 2%.

A number of features should be emphasised. First, the massive technological revolutions of the 19th century did *not* cause unemployment. Unemployment showed no upward tendency throughout the 60-year period to 1911. New jobs were created as fast, on average, as technology displaced old ones. This relationship between technology and jobs is obviously relevant to the current

Figure 6.1   UK unemployment rate, 1851–1971

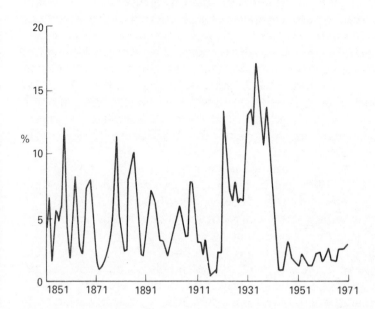

scare about the micro-processor revolution causing unemployment.

Second, the Great Depression stands out as an exceptionally bad economic cycle. It is increasingly agreed today that the reason for its severity was the failure of US monetary policy to avert a massive collapse in the US banking system. This diagnosis indeed, even more than 'monetarism', is the major claim to fame of Professor Milton Friedman, whose painstaking research with Anna Schwartz on US monetary history uncovered the full extent of this failure. Yet even in the Great Depression, a massive economic shock if ever there was one, it is startling how vigorously recovery took place in the 1930s. And, moreover, recovery quickly followed depression *without* Keynesian public expenditure policies. Instead it came with the ordinary 'automatic' or self-correcting processes of declining credit costs and reviving credit demands, notably for housing. The Great Depression illustrates that a severe shock will generate a severe cycle, *but not a permanent decline.*

Third, there is strong evidence that during the Great Depression British unemployment was substantially higher than it need have been because of the operation of the social security benefit system.[2] Benefits were fixed in money terms as flat amounts. As prices and wages fell in the early 1920s, the value of benefits relative to prices and wages rose dramatically. This weakening of the inclination to seek work seems to have been a major cause of the 'rigidity', or failure to fall much further, of wages in the late 1920s, of which Keynes made so much in his 1936 *General Theory*. It did, of course, mean that real wage costs were inflated by workers' unwillingness to lower nominal wages.

Finally, the low average unemployment after World War II up to the early 1960s and its low variability seem to indicate both a reduced frictional rate of unemployment and a more benign post-war cycle in a world with monetary policies disciplined by fixed exchange rates tied to a dollar set by fairly strict US monetary policies. This post-war low unemployment has been adduced as evidence of the success of Keynesian policies, but policies in the dominant US economy were not at all Keynesian until the Kennedy/Johnson era from 1959 onwards. And it was precisely from this time that the benign cycle began to break up, leading first to world inflation and finally, after a time-lag, to the worsening cycles of the 1970s.

We come to more recent experience below. What of the theories of 'long cycles'? Could we be poised on the edge of a long wave of depression, echoing previous long waves? The evidence on long waves as well as the supporting theory has been carefully assessed by many people (most recently by Professor Michael Beenstock in his *The World Economy in Transition*, Allen & Unwin, 1983); it does not stand up. The theory is impressionistic and unconvincing. The major version, that of Schumpeter, suggested that technological advances come in waves which cause a slump as they displace the old technologies, but there is no strong reason to suppose that technological advance, even if wave-like, would cause slump rather than boom. The evidence of these waves is statistically non-existent. (There are too few observations, even though the eye if sympathetically inclined can 'see something' in some commodity price movements.) Also, the unemployment chart gives no hint of a long wave.

This long historical evidence of almost a century disposes of three fashionable ideas:

1. that technological advance causes unemployment;
2. that there are long waves in activity and unemployment;
3. that Keynesian policies are necessary and sufficient for keeping unemployment down (they are neither).

1955 to 1981

We may now examine the most recent experience of unemployment in OECD countries for more insights.

Figure 6.2   Unemployment in five Western economies from 1955

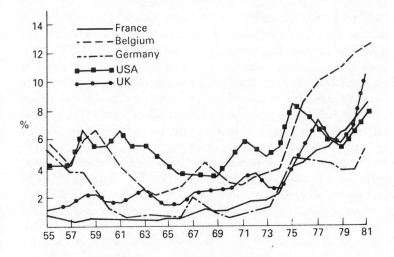

Figure 6.2 shows the unemployment since the War in a number of western economies. On the basis of our earlier analysis, we would expect to find that countries with benefit systems that are related to

earnings rather than flat-rate in nature and relatively modest in amount will cause *less* unemployment following both shocks hitting the world economy and long-term deterioration in their national trade advantages.

This result is indeed what we find. The USA – with a fairly limited earnings-related system – has experienced, in common with other countries, severe cyclical recessions in 1975 and 1980–81, and these have raised unemployment sharply during these two recessions.

The experience of France and Germany – with similar, though somewhat more generous, systems – is only a bit worse.

In the UK and Belgium, however, unemployment has risen much more, to over 13%. Both have benefit systems that provide more or less indefinite support at flat rates which substantially undermine incentives for low-income workers, and their capacity to adjust costs in industry to remain competitive by lowering real wages is correspondingly very limited.

Furthermore, the UK and Belgium have shared a steadily worsening long-term *trend* in unemployment since the mid-1960s. This trend has reflected not merely a deterioration in trading advantages vis-à-vis the New Industrialising Countries (as well set out by Professor Beenstock), one common to all the Western economies. More particularly, the trend reflects a steady rise in taxes, union power and real benefits in the context of this damaging benefit system. Figures 6.3–6.6 show some relevant statistics for the UK and Belgium: first, union membership as a proportion of the labour force (an index of union power) and the level of benefits grossed up for the taxes and rates on employment paid by employee and employer (e.g., if benefits are £100 per week, income tax and employees' national insurance contributions take 30%, and employers' national insurance (etc.) contributions are 10%, this figure would be £100 ÷ 0.9 ÷ 0.7 = £159 per week). This latter can be regarded as the minimum cost to a firm of employing a worker, since the firm will have to pay the worker at least as much as his benefits plus his taxes and pay employer's taxes on top of that.[3]

Briefly, what more recent Western experience shows is that the old Western economies face a common problem of 'transition' from old-style manufacturing to service and high technology areas. This transition entails a fall in the real wages of unskilled workers and a rise in the wages of workers with the new skills. Some countries, especially the USA, have managed this adjustment more smoothly

Figure 6.3 Union membership as percentage of labour force, UK

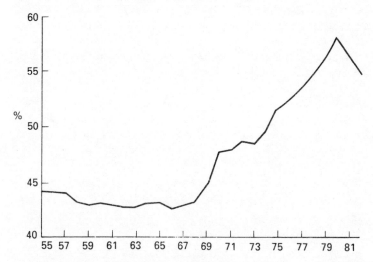

*Figure 6.4 Real benefits grossed up for all labour taxes, UK.
(Minimum real cost of labour)*

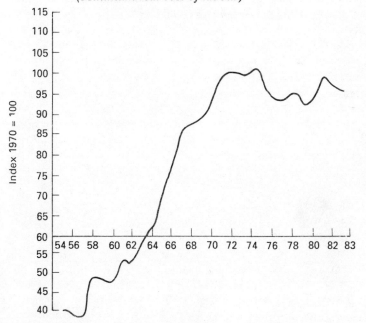

*Figure 6.5   Union membership as percentage of labour force,
Belgium*

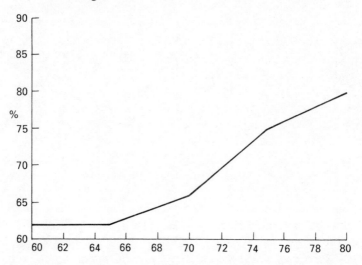

*Figure 6.6   Real benefits grossed up for all labour taxes, Belgium.
(The minimum cost of labour)*

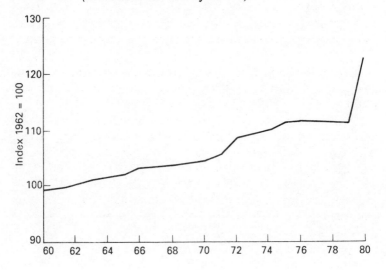

than others, including the UK, mainly because of more realistic social benefit systems.

The tenor of the analysis so far is that the prospects for unemployment in each country will depend crucially on how far it hinders the adjustment of the structure of employment. It is therefore impossible to make unqualified statements about any individual country, except when policy trends are very clear. Certainly, at the least there is nothing inevitable about high unemployment in 1990 in *any* country. But equally it is possible for the governments of any of these countries to *create* the conditions for continued high unemployment.

The US, perhaps most clearly of all, looks like a country where adjustment will continue to proceed smoothly. The cyclical recovery there will probably, over the next three years or so, bring unemployment down to the frictional rate there of some 6%. Already, it is down to about 8% and falling quickly.

At the opposite end of the spectrum, unemployment should still fall in Belgium and the UK as their cyclical recovery proceeds, but it would be very surprising if by 1986 it fell below 8% in either. Also, 8% is well above the minimum frictional rate in both. To bring it down faster will require more determined policies of cutting taxes on lower-paid workers, setting benefits at a lower percentage of take-home pay for these workers, and curbing union power. While none of these policies are easy to implement politically, a package of all three can be designed which is acceptable in its effects on the distribution of income so that it benefits society and the majority without making any group intolerably worse off.

This formula may sound cryptic; in concrete terms it means that the price of cutting unemployment benefits – and lowering the living standards of the poor if they remain unemployed – is cutting taxes on the low-paid, so that an unemployed man who *takes* a job will be better off working than he would have been before. With such a package, society can reasonably say it has improved the relevant *opportunities* for work and pay of poor people while raising the penalties for turning down those opportunities.

This is a highly defensible position politically and morally. *With* such policies, unemployment could be down to 4% by the late 1980s. *Without* them, this improvement would take a lot longer, perhaps another 10 years of slow adjustment, as productivity gradually rises relative to benefit levels. And, if any government *reversed* them, it would prevent unemployment falling at all.

In the middle of the spectrum are countries like France and West Germany, whose policies appear to be in some flux, not obstructive to change yet but flirting with these damaging welfarist notions, having been hitherto fairly tough in these matters. Work-sharing is now widely sought by unions in these countries (even in West Germany). If this and similar policies are pursued, they will obstruct the creation of the necessary new jobs by raising costs, and will at best *conceal* some unemployment without reducing it. These tendencies appear to be gathering strength. If so, the prospects for unemployment there, too, are little better than in Belgium and the UK. They, too, will show a slow fall as the cyclical recovery now evident gathers strength.

I should end by confronting one last persistent question. Is a world 'recovery' truly possible without a large co-ordinated programme of Keynesian stimulus applied internationally?

The evidence is there already. US recovery is in train, as UK recovery has been since early 1981. In the UK it has occurred with tight money and continuously falling public sector deficits. In the US the budget deficit has been rising while there has been confusion about the money supply because of institutional changes in banking practice. Some economists would say that the US government has stimulated the economy in a Keynesian manner by loose money and a rising budget deficit. This is clearly not true. If it were, world (and US) real interest rates would not be at the unprecedentedly high rates they still are. Nor would we have the still present threat of a world debt and banking crisis.

The truth must, on the contrary, be that money *has* been tight and that the high US budget deficit has, within that tight money market, forced developing countries out of the world capital market by penal interest rates. The net contribution to world demand of this process of large deficits has been virtually nil.

To return to the question I posed, the world recovery *is* occurring despite generally tight policies. The non-Keynesian process of recovery is one in which, as producers and workers price their products back into the market, inflation falls, interest rates fall, financial confidence is rebuilt, and spending revives as a result. This non-Keynesian recovery has happened in the UK and the US, and it is significant that it has *not* happened in countries such as France and

Eire, which tried deliberately to engineer recovery via Keynesian inflationary policies.

In short then, governments must not be tempted from the medicine of tight money by the illusion that loose money will help unemployment. Rather, they must design their taxes, benefits and union laws (in other words, good micro market policies) to further rather than hinder adjustment in the labour market needed to bring down unemployment. If they do, the long-term outlook for unemployment is bright. Even if they do not, the labour market will not break down – but it will take a lot longer to do its job.

Notes

1. Discussed in my 'Macroeconomic Controls on Government' in *The Taming of Government*, I.E.A. Readings 21, 1979 and, in rather more detail, in Patrick Minford and David Peel, *Rational Expectations and the New Macroeconomics*, Martin Robertson, 1983.
2. See Daniel Benjamin and Leuis Kochin, 'Searching for an explanation of unemployment in interwar Britain', *Journal of Political Economy*, 1979, and the same authors, their critics, and their effective response in the *JPE* in 1982.
3. These facts and the analysis here are set out more elaborately in a recent book, *Unemployment – Cause and Cure*, which I wrote with David Davies, Michael Peel and Alison Sprague, Martin Robertson, 1983.

7. State Expenditure: A Study in Waste*

I. The Nature of the Problem

In the debate currently raging over expenditure, a number of protagonists are losing sight of the essential economic arguments. Separate issues are being muddled together and emotion and frictional heat generated in the process. The purpose of this paper is to clarify the debate by analysing the mechanisms with which we are trying to achieve our social objectives by state expenditure and by enquiring whether we could design mechanisms that achieve the same objectives better. My purpose is not to attempt to persuade anyone, least of all politicians or the British public, to change their objectives. Some may wish to do that, and all of us have varying ideas about social objectives at different times, but they lie outside the scope of my discussion.

Briefly, I shall simply assume that the British people care about the poor, the disabled, the sick and the old, that they wish to achieve civilised and widely shared standards of education, that they wish the realm to be adequately defended, law and order to be preserved, economic infrastructure to be maintained, and other equally obvious purposes. I shall also take it as axiomatic that they would like more rather than less of all these desirables but that, with the finite resources of the economy, *given* the mechanisms of production and consumption, they recognise the necessity to allocate priorities as these resources expand and contract and that they are fully capable, through the political process widely defined, of this exercise in allocation. Give the people the information about what they can have, and they will choose wisely and in the general social interest.

My focus is thus on the mechanisms of production and consumption which condition people's choice. They are the proper

* First published in *Economic Affairs*, Supplement, pp.i–xix, April–June, 1984. Part III omitted, except conclusion.

focus for the economist, since it is likely that others will neglect them – out of technical ignorance – while the economist may see something useful that could 'add to the cake' from which they are choosing.

II. Principles for Action

Let us consider first what an 'ideal' system would look like. Transitional arrangements can be considered at a later stage in the light of this analysis. Too much discussion considers incremental changes in expenditure of a few percentage points from the system we have; these bring little improvement but create practical difficulties, so providing an easy excuse for their rejection.

Let us enumerate our objectives:

1. *Efficiency in production* wherever at present the state sector is a producer.
2. Optimum provision of *public goods*, which can only be provided by the state.
3. For private goods, *efficiency in consumption* wherever government is at present a consumer.
4. To ensure that the poor have 'good' education, 'good' health care, and are at all stages of the life cycle supported above 'subsistence' income, while preserving incentives to obtain work and, once in work, to work for higher wages. Call this objective, in short, *the efficient relief of poverty*.

Now let us see what can be done to achieve each objective.

1. Productive Efficiency

The rule should be: *no* state production. All present productive facilities operated by government, national or local, should be privatised in a competitive framework. If a productive facility is a 'natural monopoly', it should be operated privately after a periodic tender. It should be owned by the state and treated as 'infra-structure'.

The only exceptions would be on 'security' grounds, as with police, armed forces, judges and part of the civil service. Even though there would no doubt be gains in efficiency from having private companies offering policing to the state as consumer, and tendering for the 'police contract' for an area such as Merseyside for, say, five years, it is obvious enough that the public prefer to trade any such gains in efficiency for the sake of political security and control. Suppose, for example, that the private security company's employees broke the law or took bribes; who would police them? The public prefer instead that carefully selected representatives be given the task of building up to a force with standards of public morality and service especially inculcated. What I am saying here is that public production of these goods is itself a 'public good' i.e., the public security cannot by itself be provided privately.

Let us now go through a representative list of state production activities and set out illustrative guide-lines for their treatment (Professors Michael Beesley and Stephen Littlechild, 1983, provide an illuminating and detailed discussion of the relevant principles).

British Airways is an interesting case: it has been argued that it should first be made profitable and *then*, when the market is 'ripe', privatised. BA itself has taken this view and used it to oppose giving routes to its private competitors, such as British Caledonian and British Midland. Their argument is wrong, and for two reasons. First, the market is in as good a position as the state to judge the potential profitability of BA; if it is not, the state could easily release the information. A 'fair' price would then be set *today* for BA, which takes account of probable near-term losses (to be met by the taxpayer anyway if BA's sale is delayed) and long-term profits. The price would be as 'fair' to the taxpayer as to the private buyers, and would therefore be as good a saving in net tax as the taxpayer would get by hanging on to BA. So there is no justification for a delay in privatisation here.

Secondly, the *method* BA proposes for increasing profits (monopoly) is directly opposite to the objectives of privatisation – namely, the achievement of efficiency via competition. The price for BA will, of course, be less if competition is allowed; *but the taxpayer will gain* compared with the no-competition high-price situation. Competition must therefore go ahead as *part* of the privatisation process.

British Leyland is a similar case. BL has asked for more time before privatisation and wishes the car cartel to be prolonged indefinitely so as to make it a more 'viable' proposition. Both arguments are again wrong. BL should be privatised now, the cartel abolished and free trade in cars established, including Japanese cars. The British car industry has had years to 'adjust' itself to Japanese competition.

The British Gas monopoly of North Sea gas purchase should go (this is planned but still being opposed), its area boards put out to tender, and its retailing activities (showrooms and maintenance) sold. The area companies that get the tender will then buy the gas at world prices and retail it competitively to homes and businesses in their area. The national gas pipeline 'grid' to each area could be treated as national infrastructure, and its operation and maintenance put out to tender with the private sector.

To the Central Electricity Generating Board similar principles apply. The area boards should be put out to tender and its retail activities sold. The national grid could remain state-owned, and its operation put out to tender by a private company, which would act as a middleman between areas with excess electricity to sell and areas with a shortage.

The National Coal Board has no 'natural monopoly' features. Coal extraction and retailing is a normal private sector activity. The NCB would be best privatised in geographic blocs which would compete with one another. Import quotas should go, so that the world price of coal prevails domestically.

Of the last three industries in particular, it is worth pointing out that by protecting them the state has given *negative* protection, or heavy penalties, to other (mainly manufacturing) industries, so that the form which the waste here has taken has been that of *contraction in manufacturing* – a particularly obvious and unpopular manifestation of waste.

British Rail is a combination of a natural monopoly or infrastructural element (the railway track) and a perfectly ordinary industry (railway services). Track provision should be treated as an infrastructure decision, like roads, and co-ordinated with road planning; this can be regarded as a 'public good'. Its operation and maintenance (including signalling and stations) could be put out to tender to the private sector by geographical areas. The provision of railway services could be competitive and unregulated, just like coaches on the roads or airlines at airports and on the airlanes. Any company would be free to set up a railway service, buy rolling stock, hire sheds, and run its trains at chosen times and prices. BR's rolling stock and sheds would be put up for sale; no doubt they would be bought by these newly entering companies which would probably include management groups currently in BR.

The provision of education services is, as far as production is concerned, an ordinary service industry. There is no reason for it not to be competitive; that is, suppliers should be free to set up schools or universities in any area and with any mix of subjects they wish to offer. As with other service products, the public will carefully monitor the type and quality of products on offer – and private market services evaluating and advising on them would spring up, such as there now are for 2500 private schools. Schools, universities or technical colleges which failed to be profitable would contract in size, while profitable ones would expand or take over the unprofitable, or else other companies would enter to take advantage of profitable opportunities so highlighted.

All this could in principle take place with the state buying public education as now, just as it buys defence products from the private sector according to price and quality. However, I will argue later that, from the consumer's point of view, this is not an efficient way for education purchase to proceed. I recommend the equivalent of means-tested vouchers, freely transferable *anywhere* in the education system. The purchase of education would then be just like buying a holiday package only with the worse-off having a subsidy directly tied to it. Schools and universities would have to predict their market, set their prices, and adjust supply, just like a holiday operator – or existing private schools.

Health, too, is an ordinary service industry. Entry into it – by doctors' partnerships, hospitals, ambulance services, nursing firms, etc. – should be free. Again this would be perfectly possible even if the state continues to buy health services *en bloc* as with the current NHS. Yet, again, we will argue later for the equivalent of means-tested national health insurance, the analogue of education vouchers; poor people would be able to buy essential health services with virtual 100% insurance. Better-off people would take out private health insurance. All would buy health services just like any other private service.

Enough should have been said to illustrate our principles. The reader may find it instructive to apply them to other types of public production listed in a recent Public Expenditure White Paper (not directly dealt with here). He will find their application clear and **straightforward**.

2. Public Goods

Apart from defence and law and order the main group of public goods is 'infrastructure' – by definition capital equipment. Some people have jumped from this observation to the argument that state *capital* expenditure is *always* a good thing while state *current* expenditure involves waste. As our arguments should have made plain, this conclusion does not follow and is wrong. Some current expenditure is on public goods: defence and law and order are prime examples involving mainly current expenditure. Much public capital expenditure – e.g., by the nationalised industries – is *not* on public goods; if these industries were privatised, expenditure might well be cut back because of unprofitability in a competitive environment.

'Infrastructure' then is capital equipment that the state ought to provide. How should it decide what and how much? The answer follows from a discussion of clubs: the state is acting like a club and while it has no difficulty in raising club fees (taxes), it must simulate the club decision – evaluate whether people's benefits from the investment exceed their costs, so that in principle they would be willing to subscribe the club fee for installing the equipment. Such 'social cost/benefit analysis' is now standard in infrastructure decisions; but political judgement also comes in, and rightly so, as it would in club management deciding what it could 'sell' to its 'members'. The members are the taxpayers and their attitude to the facility and their resulting tax bill will affect their view of the politicians who decided.

This decision process is clearly vague and in national services prone to error. As far as possible, therefore, clubs to decide infrastructure should be set as narrowly as possible. Local roads, for example, require *local*, not national, decision for the main beneficiaries are local. Where a road or a bridge serves a clearly defined group and is likely to be highly utilised, a *toll* is possible; such projects can be 'privatised' efficiently.

This will still leave important infrastructure for national decisions. However, if the rest of our suggestions were adopted, state officials would have fewer distractions and pressures from other industries or services wrongly in the government sector and the decisions on infrastructure might be improved. One problem in particular would disappear: that of a chronic government finance crisis as cash-hungry open-ended programmes starved departments of cash for necessary infrastructure. This crisis problem appears to have become endemic in the government sector and to result in running down infrastructure programmes for purely cash reasons. This procedure is irrational, for the cuts should really fall in the ways we have been describing.

3. State Consumption

The main services bought by the state for the people and passed on at free or subsidised prices but still not public goods are health and education services.

The statement that these are not public goods requires some qualification. There are elements of 'public good' in both: if your neighbour catches bubonic plague, you and many others suffer. If someone is unable to read or understand the spoken language, he may cause others a nuisance (e.g., by disregarding public safety orders). A lack of general education impoverishes society and not only the individuals involved. Yet these aspects are easily handled *without* public purchase of health and education services for all; minimum standards of hygiene and preventative medicine (such as inoculation), and of education can be set and subsidised directly. Inoculations for bubonic plague would naturally be 100% subsidised; and education vouchers subsidise education directly. Thus the specific 'public good' elements are best handled by specific measures and subsidies, and we so assume in what follows.

The inefficiency involved in the state passing on these services free or with a general subsidy is discussed above. If everyone had equal income, the answer would be clear: let each spend his own chosen resources on health services (via health insurance and education). The inefficiency would disappear, the specific 'public good' elements being taken care of as assumed.

This brings us to the core of the 'welfare state' debate. Income is unequal; under this system, therefore, the poor would have *less* access to health and education than the better-off. Some go on to argue that to maintain *adequate* (others would say *equal*) access for the poor, the state must buy health and education and then redistribute them, but as we have seen, state provision involves inefficiency, which imposes a cost on society.

Assuming – as we do – that one objective is to give the poor access to 'necessary' health and education, can we resolve the apparent conflict between this and efficiency in consumption? The answer is: *yes* it is *not* necessary to have state purchase to achieve *any* given objective of access to the poor. The efficient way to proceed is to give the poor the means to buy these services, and (since these means are intended not to be diverted to *other* expenditure, whether food, opera or bingo) to *tie* these means to these services (by education vouchers or subsidising health insurance). Society can decide the degree of support it wishes to provide for the poor and then allow them and everyone else to spend this support and their own resources on buying health and education services produced privately – with the advantages of choice.

This support – given society's preferences – should be means-tested. Society wishes to help the poor, and not the better-off; indeed, it is precisely the open-ended subsidy given to all that causes the chronic financial crisis in health and education.

We now examine how this would work in health and education.

Health The assumption will be that health services are paid for by the individual and that he buys full health insurance, structured in a normal way with near 100% insurance for very serious bills. The concern of society is then that poor people will skimp on private health insurance. This danger could be allayed by providing a means-tested subsidy to health insurance – which could be payable on production of the health insurance certificate and evidence of income.

A serious problem with this method of payment is that yet another means-tested benefit is piled on top of an already complex tax/benefit system, worsening the poverty trap. There is a better way to achieve the same effect. The concern of society is two-fold: to help the poor to achieve an above-subsistence living standard but without damaging incentives *and* to ensure that within their income the poor spend adequately on health. The former help is best given by a Negative Income Tax (NIT) which makes net income slip back very slowly as gross income falls towards the subsistence level; this principle is illustrated in Figure 7.1.

This NIT maintains the incentive to work harder and earn more, albeit with a high marginal tax rate (say, of 70%). It also protects the poor in a general sort of way, i.e., via income. It is assumed to

*Figure 7.1   The Negative Income Tax maintains incentives and can
ensure access to welfare*

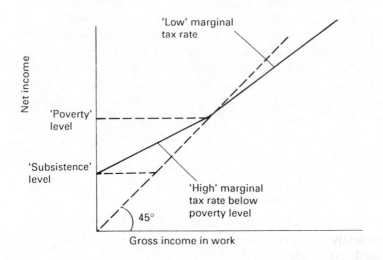

replace *all* means-tested benefits including rent and rate rebates,
and Family Income Supplement.

Given the NIT, the assurance that the poor receiving NIT are
spending adequately on health can be provided simply by making
payment of NIT contingent on the production of a certificate of
medical insurance to a specified minimum scale. Such a scale could
also be made compulsory by law, as in the wearing of seat-belts.

Primary and secondary education   The same principles apply here.
Assuming that the NIT is in operation, society is concerned that the
poor would skimp on education for their children – which is indeed
illegal, but clearly possible. Again, the simple remedy is to make the
payment of NIT also conditional on the production of receipts for
school fees for children below the minimum school-leaving age.

Higher education   This is quite different in that it yields a direct return to the graduate. There is no case for a *general* subsidy to higher education, since in general the skills and knowledge acquired carry a market price reflecting their social value. If society feels that particular subjects of social value (e.g., the study of ancient cultures and languages) are being insufficiently studied, a specific subsidy to these subjects is justified; but that is all. Students may borrow to finance their education and grants should therefore be replaced by loans. Students will also no doubt work in vacations (as many do now) to help finance their studies. Universities will be forced to compete on price for students' registration, which will lower costs, increase efficiency in teaching, and produce a better allocation of resources between subjects. Students will work harder in the knowledge that their own resources are at stake.

4.   The Efficient Relief of Poverty Over the Life Cycle

We have seen that NIT can relieve the poverty of people in work efficiently, while carrying with it conditionality on education and health standards. I have also considered the major areas of government consumption, but not three important areas of state expenditure; the transfer payments made by DHSS to the unemployed, to state pensioners and to the disabled. We now consider these in turn.

Unemployment benefit (including supplementary benefits paid to the unemployed)   As in the relief of poverty for people in work we set NIT with a marginal tax rate of no higher than 70%, already a high figure, to avoid crippling incentives, so with unemployment benefit a ceiling is required on the marginal tax rate levied on going to work at all. This aim could be achieved by a 70% ceiling on benefits as a fraction of previous net earnings. If introduced at a time when taxes on the low-paid were being *cut*, as the ideas set out in this article will make possible, then, while the introduction of this ceiling would indeed lower benefits of people remaining unemployed, the tax cuts would raise the net wages available to them if they opt to take a job. The improved job opportunities would be welcome, while the drop in benefits would increase the incentive to take advantage of them. Such a change would be highly defensible for society, both practically and morally. In the longer term unemployment insurance could be left to the individual to take out himself in the private market, for society will already be providing NIT (the safety net) for those who take jobs. It is then a private decision whether to take one of these jobs or to spend more time unemployed; there is no case in principle for a public subsidy to that decision.

Pensions   These forms of income are in the same category as health, a matter for personal investment but one that society is concerned that everyone should undertake and also that the poor may skimp. As with health, belonging to an adequate pension scheme could be compulsory by law, and evidence of belonging should also be made a precondition of receipt of NIT.

Sickness and disability insurance   Similar principles apply. This could be made compulsory and receipt of NIT again conditional on evidence of minimum insurance.

III.

. . .

Conclusion

The object of this paper has been to review the functions of the state sector and to identify the scope for reorganising its activities to eliminate economic waste in achieving society's objectives. My quest has been solely for improved economic efficiency.

I have been able to identify a mass of economies which would make possible substantial tax cuts and also permit government to carry on, without a constant 'cash crisis', its proper function of providing public goods such as law and order and infrastructure. 'Cuts' to date in the government sector appear to have been carried out without careful planning in a continuous atmosphere of crisis and have fallen largely on 'easy targets' such as infrastructural programmes.

The programme represents a carefully thought-out strategy for effective and deep cuts which would achieve our social objectives *better*. This strategy ought therefore to be one with which no-one – except numerous pressure groups with a specific interest to declare – can take issue, except on grounds of economic analysis, on which however I believe it to be valid at least in basic principles. My claim is that it would benefit the people – probably massively – rich, poor and in between. The changes proposed are large and fundamental and they would require time to carry out. But, if the British economy is to regain real dynamism, we have to embark on them soon with a view to completing them early in the coming decade. That is the challenge.

References

M. Beesley and S. Littlechild (1983), 'Privatisation: Principles, Problems and Priorities', *Lloyds Bank Review*, July, pp. 1–20.

8. The Poverty Trap after the Fowler Reforms*

What is the aim of income-support systems? I shall take it that, in the eyes of the voter who pays for them and whose judgement is therefore paramount, the aim is to help the poor without damaging incentives more than necessary. That there is a trade-off between poverty-relief and incentives seems unavoidable; the relevant question is how to improve it and where to be located along that best trade-off. The method used in this paper for assessing this trade-off is to compute efficiency losses of various proposals, assuming that they are all constrained to provide a minimum living standard to those in need. No account otherwise is taken of distributional aspects: it is assumed that there is no desire to reduce inequality for its own sake, over and above the provision of such minimum help. Efficiency losses are computed in the usual manner of public finance by assessing the loss of 'consumer surplus', that is the income-compensated effects on supply and the consequent 'welfare triangles'. Given that they are all subject to the constraint of providing the same minimum support (the 'safety net'), the proposals are judged purely by their efficiency or welfare loss.[1]

Many people feel strongly about distributional aspects, treated in this particular way here. No claim is made here that this treatment is necessarily right, morally for example. The reason the assumption is chosen is that it appears relevant to policymakers because it is close to values espoused by voters at the present time. Obviously, such a claim is hard to test except by politically revealed preferences at elections: but there is no evidence that the current level of social support through benefits, essentially unchanged now for a decade in real terms, is far enough away from what voters want to constitute an electoral liability for the government.

All proposals are subject to the same revenue constraint also; in the present context this is given by the probable availability of a

* First published in A. Bowen and K. Mayhew (eds) (1990), *Improving Incentives for the Low Paid*, Macmillan for NEDO, pp. 121–37.

budget surplus to distribute in various ways, but this, of course, in no way alters the ranking of the proposals, which is what interests us.

The Present System of Tax and Benefit

The present system is, after the Fowler reforms, close to a negative income tax. The main difference is administrative; people in work have to claim from the DHSS instead of collecting automatically from the Inland Revenue. Supplementary benefit (SB; now Income Support, IS) sets effectively a minimum income level which could be seen as a further difference; hence the marginal tax rate becomes 100% at this level.

The current situation is pictured for a family man with two children and a non-working wife in Figure 8.1. Sir Norman Fowler improved incentives for families, both to take work (the unemployment trap) and to take better-paid work (the poverty trap);

Figure 8.1 Couple with two children – the tax benefit system

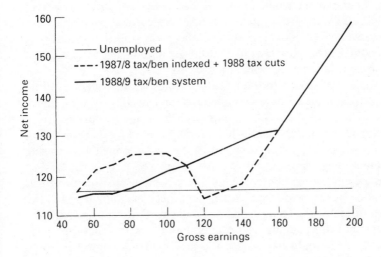

and it is for families that these incentives are, at least on paper, the poorest. Nevertheless, existing marginal rates for these remain uncomfortably high over various ranges, as the figure clearly shows.

I begin by considering reform of the unemployment trap. This seems to be a relatively easy problem in principle, if not necessarily in political practice. Then I turn to possible reforms of the poverty trap. I begin with a critical review of the Basic Income Guarantee proposal. Then I set out my own gradualist proposal.

My assumption in considering poverty trap reform is that the Chancellor has a choice of various routes through which to cut taxes over the next five years; the basic issue is what priority to give to raising thresholds, cutting the standard rate, or cutting the withdrawal rate for benefit in the poverty trap. Hence the background to the discussion of tax structure is one of an improving government revenue constraint.

Reform of the Unemployment Trap

Workfare – that ugly, but convenient, American neologism meaning working for benefits – is a way of preserving the support level for the unemployed while ensuring that they take any 'approved' opportunity for work; if they refuse it they lose benefit, so the effective marginal tax rate on work becomes zero (because if they do not take the work they technically get nothing from the state, so nothing is taken away when they work).

Workfare is close to the Beveridge rules in our system, so little applied in practice; it also is similar to the Swedish system, and is widely used in the USA. apparently with some success (Burton, 1986). Given that there is little scope at present for other changes in the tax/benefit system, it seems to me to be a highly promising avenue for getting the long-term unemployed into work. Restart has begun along this route and has been useful in its effect. Politically, the response to Restart has been encouraging; and the step of making YTS an 'approved' scheme (such that refusal of a place on it disqualifies for benefits) has met with general popular approval. I would like to see the new unified scheme become a similarly approved one or, if not, to ensure that benefit officers make refusal of a place on it a cause for action on benefit entitlement.

The ingenious idea of the Action credit (Ashby, 1988) has

recently been put forward, whereby the unemployed may work part time without losing benefit and put the proceeds into a saving account, to be released when they get a full-time job. For the unemployed, this quite clearly creates an increased incentive to work legitimately part-time and thence to take a full-time job.

There are two problems. First, this incentive may not be sufficient to dominate the alternative of benefits plus work on the side, especially since the income is not received until the full-time job is obtained.

Second, and more important – since this first problem does not stop Action credit from being at least a marginal improvement – the position of the short-term unemployed must be considered. They now would have an enhanced incentive to stay longer on the dole, since the benefit package is augmented by the part-time work return; it could become highly attractive to qualify for this programme by becoming long-term unemployed. Thus could a subsidy to the long-term unemployed condition produce more long-term unemployed.

This second problem seems too potentially worrying for this idea to be adopted; even as a temporary, 'unrepeatable' scheme for today's long-term unemployed only, it is dangerous. For the temporary scheme of yesterday has a way of acquiring long life; look at the 'temporary employment subsidy'!

Meanwhile, workfare will push the long-term unemployed back into the labour market, while maintaining their living standards at the SB/IS rate. Some, one hopes many, will opt instead to take non-workfare jobs and claim Family Income Supplement (now Family Credit). Either way the reintegration of the long-term unemployed into the labour market will at last occur, as intended by law and endorsed by popular morality. As a footnote to this discussion, the treatment of those who take up unemployment and supplementary benefit, even though they intend to and have been working for most of the year, could be reconsidered. Clearly, benefit is not intended to be drawn by people who are deliberately engaging in regular spells of unemployment; yet under the present rules and practices, such behaviour is not necessarily prevented. The questionnaires filled out as a condition of benefit should test for this behaviour, and it should be penalised. Otherwise, we have here another form of the (part-year) unemployment trap.

Reform of the Poverty Trap

1. The Basic Income Guarantee (BIG)

BIG comes in varying sizes (Parker, 1989, discusses a large selection of schemes). The smallest award a modest fixed income to all including the unemployed; all further income is to be acquired by work. Such schemes amount to a cut in unemployment benefits and a consolidation of existing child benefits into the BIG. I, in effect, put forward such a proposal in my '70% benefit cap' notion (Minford, 1983, 1985); but it did not get a rapturous welcome, because of the widespread desire to underpin the living standard of the unemployed, who are seen – often, no doubt rightly – as victims of misfortune, even if they could adjust more rapidly by finding new work. So small BIGs will not get far for the present at least.

Large BIGs take on board the constraint that BIG must be no less than the SB rate. These constitute a massive negative poll tax to the whole population. This requires a substantial marginal tax rate on that whole population to finance it, even assuming no adverse supply effects. However, adverse supply effects there will surely be for two reasons.

First, a jump in the standard rate by 10 percentage points or more (costings are uncertain and differ) would have a substitution effect for sure – that is an effect due to the change in the relative price of leisure, ignoring the effect of lower net income (Brown et al, 1986, for example set the substitution elasticity at around 0.15 and their number is fairly typical: Minford and Ashton, 1989, have 0.13 for the average employed male). Though small for each household it would, when spread across all, be a significant slice of GDP. True, among low income groups the marginal tax rates would fall to the standard rate, which would produce some compensating substitution or relative price effects among them; but though welcome, this would be unlikely to produce as much in value as the effect on the average- and higher-paid, simply because the latter are much more productive.

Second, there would be a negative income effect on work for those on low incomes – see Figure 8.2. This is the effect on leisure due to the change in net income; here net income would be raised for this group by the payment of BIG – the 'negative poll tax' effect – and so this group's demand for leisure would rise and their work

Figure 8.2   Basic Income Guarantee illustrated

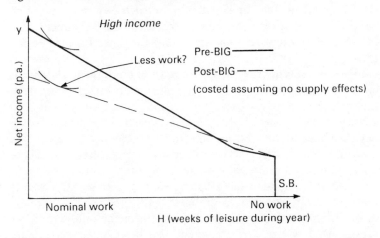

High income

Pre-BIG ——————
Post-BIG —— —— ——
(costed assuming no supply effects)

Less work?

Net income (p.a.)

S.B.

Nominal work   No work

H (weeks of leisure during year)

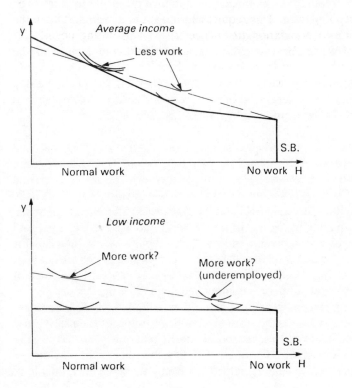

Average income

Less work

S.B.

Normal work   No work   H

Low income

More work?

More work?
(underemployed)

S.B.

Normal work   No work   H

effort fall. For the majority on middle incomes the income effect should be small; but for part-timers on such pay rates it will be seriously negative. For the higher earners the income effect would be positive, but this has to be set against the powerful substitution effect.

Figure 8.2 sets out the qualitative possibilities if the tax needed is costed assuming no supply effects. While the net effect on supply of the higher and lower-paid is ambiguous because income and substitution effects go in opposite directions, that on the majority is negative because of substitution with negligible income effects. So there are clear dangers of serious negative effects on output. These are examined more formally in the Appendix.

These would not only be damaging to the economy in themselves (besides output loss, remember that the pure efficiency losses relate to substitution effects, all negative except for the minority of less productive low paid). They would also drive up the necessary standard rate of tax. Politically, the implied rate looks too high to be accepted by the floating voter, who would be unwilling to pay the price for such redistribution.

BIG is, in short, a radical gamble that the reduction of the marginal tax rates at the bottom of the pay scale would beneficially compensate for the damage done higher up by the increased marginal rates needed to pay the cost. Politically unacceptable, it would also be economically dangerous.

Can monitoring produce a 'partial BIG'?   BIG lowers the marginal tax rate for those in the poverty trap, while raising it for those beyond it. However, Hermione Parker now proposes a 'partial BIG' (Parker, 1989), under which a certain payment would be made unconditionally as in BIG, but it would be less than current benefits. Extra payments would be made conditionally (called 'cash and care') by local benefit officers, who would assess 'need'. This proposal is intended to square the circle: basic benefits are cut as in small BIGs, to keep down costs, and yet benefits are provided at current levels to the poor employed in genuine need.

If this screening process worked as intended, those who could genuinely work harder for more money to support themselves and their family would not get conditional benefits and so would face the general marginal tax rate, so avoiding the poverty trap. Those in genuine need would be helped but being, *ex hypothesei*, unable to work harder for more money, they would not be constrained by the poverty trap; as soon as they could help themselves, conditional benefit would be withdrawn and they would avoid the poverty trap thereby.

There is a parallel with screening the unemployed under Restart and the Beveridge intentions embodied in existing law. There, the unemployment trap is avoided in just the same way, but screening of the unemployed and their ability to get a job is clearly much easier than screening the ability to earn more in an existing or alternative job. The former requires evidence of unsuccessful job applications and interviews, as widely practised in Switzerland, Sweden and, now increasingly, here. The latter requires little short of a complete 'appraisal' of the employee by one or more employers. Its practicality is doubtful and its cost would certainly be considerable.

A scheme, such as Parker's partial BIG, which relies on this for its effectiveness, is therefore flawed, but screening may nevertheless be a useful adjunct to a practicable scheme, by reducing the impact of the poverty trap.

2. A Gradualist Proposal

The problem with BIG can be summarised by looking at Figure 8.3, which is a reworking of Figure 8.1. For a typical family man there are two critical points, assuming that he works. There is the minimum support rate, which he gets however low his income sinks; this is the intercept of the net income line with the left-hand axis – amount b. Then there is the point at which he loses all benefits in work (benefit withdrawal is complete), and his marginal tax rate becomes the standard rate, plus national insurance. This is the kinked point on his net income line, c along the horizontal axis. BIG proposes to replace the existing line with a straight line going through point b. Yet, necessarily as the illustration makes clear, this can only be achieved by lowering the slope of the line for those currently on standard rate. This is necessary to pay for the increased support for those in the poverty trap and those currently outside it who will benefit from the lower withdrawal rate. One way to lower the marginal tax rate in the poverty trap without raising it elsewhere is to reduce the minimum support level, b. This is illustrated by the line running through point b'. (Its marginal tax rate would in fact be

Figure 8.3 Structure of tax reform proposals

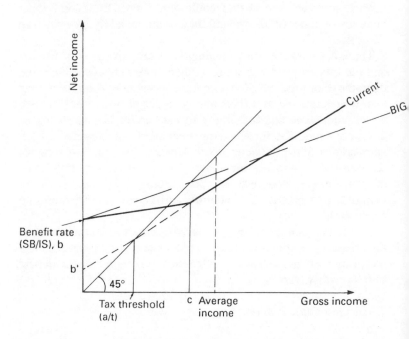

slightly less than the current standard rate plus NI because the taxpayer pays less in poverty support; but this is not drawn in, for simplicity.)

This proposal would be unacceptable because the safety net principle would be violated, given that current benefit rates are generally believed to be approximately right to sustain families in normal health.

However, the safety net principle is designed to relieve 'absolute poverty'. That is, while living necessities may change over time as society changes and becomes richer, the amount set to maintain health will not vary proportionately with average income; it will probably rise little, and over a five year period, it could be regarded as fixed in real terms.

Now suppose b is fixed in real terms (i.e., indexed to prices) while the economy grows and average real income rises. Suppose too that tax thresholds are indexed to prices. Then over time the number of households in the poverty trap will fall, but more significantly the number just above it will fall fast too. This means that not only will the poverty trap be a less serious problem because it affects less people, also it will become worthwhile to repeat the Fowler-style reduction in the withdrawal rate, because less people will be drawn into the trap compared with the beneficial effect of higher incentives on those within it. The possible arithmetic of when it pays to lower the withdrawal rate is worked out in the Appendix, but a possible rule of thumb would be to accept the Fowler judgement that it was right to lower the withdrawal rate at the expense of roughly doubling the number of families in the poverty trap to its current 450,000. The Appendix suggests that this could well have been about right.

The reasoning is that any further reduction in withdrawal rate beyond the Fowler point would increase numbers in the trap too much relative to the benefit in better incentives for those already in it. However, if the calculation is done for an increase in the withdrawal rate to pre-Fowler levels, welfare falls slightly, implying that the current number is close to an 'optimum' one (given the constraints on policy choice from fixing the benefit at b) – the best of a bad job. This is a rough judgement, given the imprecision of our estimates; but underlying it is the steep increase in population density just above the group currently in the trap (illustrated in Figure 8.4 (b)), and it will therefore generally pay to prevent the trap pulling these extra large numbers in.

If this notion is accepted, then it would follow that as the numbers in the trap fall with rising incomes, the withdrawal rate should be continuously lowered to maintain those numbers.

My gradualist proposal is then to lower the withdrawal rate annually for those in the poverty trap as average real income rises. In effect, this means that point b would be indexed to prices while point c would be indexed to wages. Thus the marginal tax rate in the poverty trap would fall each year by approximately the rate of real wage growth, times b/c (about 0.7 currently on average). At current productivity growth of 4% a year, this would cut the rate by around 11 percentage points over the next five years, but there is a further source of cuts in the withdrawal rate. This is income tax cuts. It is shown in the Appendix that standard rate cuts dominate threshold rises, because the former give a stronger incentive boost. Suppose then that the standard rate is cut by 5 more points over the next five

Figure 8.4   Changing the withdrawal rate as net incomes rise

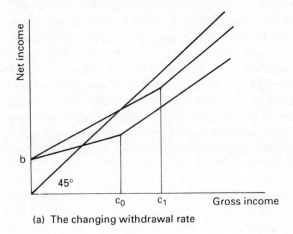

(a) The changing withdrawal rate

(b) The shifting population density function over gross income

years. We must calculate the consequential rise in net income of someone at point c, receiving no benefit.

Typically, this is now about 2% for a 5% cut in standard rate. The withdrawal rate can now be cut by 2% because benefit income can be higher up to point c.

The mechanism of these adjustments to the withdrawal rate is illustrated in Figure 8.4. The formula for the withdrawal rate is $[c(1-t)-b]/c$ or $1-t-(b/c)$ where t is the average tax rate paid by someone at point c (the point at which benefits have been totally withdrawn), and b is the minimum support level of benefit. Hence the change in the withdrawal rate is $-$(change in t) $+b/c$ (the proportional change in c).

Tax cuts could well reach 10p – making a standard rate of 15p – given the present fiscal outlook. If so, then the total cut in the withdrawal rate would reach a worthwhile 15 percentage points over the next five years.

This may seem slow progress, but the problem with faster progress is that it would draw too many new people into the trap, at a cost in efficiency greater than the gain from better incentives for those in the trap already.

Incrementalism appears to be inevitable from an efficiency viewpoint.

Would such slow progress provoke social unrest? This is a fear of some, who feel that those in the poverty trap could strengthen the tendencies towards production of an 'underclass'.

Yet as far as this aspect goes, monitoring must have a role to play. In the giving of unemployment benefit, the policing of moral hazard is important not only for efficiency reasons, but also for reasons of social behaviour (idleness and the black economy must breed underclass attitudes). So in the giving of in-work benefits, there is a case for monitoring that the receivers are making reasonable efforts to maximise their own sources of income.

This could act as a check on underclass tendencies, as well as improving the incentives within the poverty trap. As with un-employment benefit, the fact that the taxpayer gives must entitle him to monitor that it is given to those in true need, and not to those who could help themselves. Monitoring or 'screening' of this type would in terms of Figure 8.3 have the effect of cutting the numbers subject to the poverty trap, since anyone found to be capable of supporting themselves would lose in-work benefit eligibility. If screening was perfect, as noted above in the discussion of Parker's partial BIG, then the poverty trap would disappear, since those capable of self-support would pay the standard rate of tax, not receiving benefit, while for those not capable and so receiving benefit, incentives would not arise. Of course, screening of this sort can never be more than modestly effective, as argued earlier, but it could produce a useful alleviation.

Conclusion

Incremental progress appears to be by now both politically possible and capable of improving incentives at the bottom while not sacrificing those higher up. Under this approach high marginal tax rates will remain for the employed in the poverty trap for some time to come, but not for the unemployed if workfare is introduced. The cost to the economy of these high rates for low-paid workers is probably quite small, as the numbers involved are small and their productivity is low; even though their substitution effect may outweigh their income effect, the value lost is modest. To attempt to retrieve it by BIG risks losing far more resources from substitution higher up the scale; and the redistribution involved would be unlikely to please the voters.

The proposal made here is to maintain the minimum support levels constant in real terms and to lower the withdrawal rate in the poverty trap so as to keep the numbers in the trap constant. (To lower the numbers in the trap would mean an undesirably higher withdrawal rate, and to lower the withdrawal rate faster would raise numbers undesirably.) This implies that the withdrawal rate can be reduced by the rate of growth of real wages plus the percent effect of tax cuts on the net income of the marginal man outside the trap. To strengthen incentives in the trap and to help counter the development of an underclass culture, monitoring of efforts made to maximise private income would be advisable.

Appendix   The Arithmetic of Poverty Trap Reform

The proposal made here is incrementally to cut the safety net level of support relative to average income, by indexing it to prices not wages for an indefinite period. I assume that cutting the support level in real terms is not popularly desired. In terms of Figure 8.1, our illustrative starting point, it would steepen the net income curve in the lower ranges without flattening it higher up – unlike BIG. I also propose a tough work-testing/workfare scheme that de facto eliminates the 'incentive' to be unemployed; BIG schemes aim to tackle incentives of the unemployed without this.

Let us examine the argument arithmetically, using some recent estimates of labour supply responses. Clearly, strong value-judgements are involved in redistribution. However, let us, in normal public finance manner, leave distribution effects on one side, at least for a start, and measure incentive effects only – i.e. substitution effects and consequent welfare loss. (To this measure we may perhaps add a cruder one, that of total work effort produced or lost; this measures effects on the measured GNP rather than welfare in money metric form.) These measures give us something to put in the balance for those who wish to redistribute, as opposed to those who are content to provide an absolute safety net.

Table A8.1 shows the price elasticities (substitution and income) for various groups culled from my General Household Survey (GHS) study with Paul Ashton (Minford and Ashton, 1989). The weights are the share in value-added of each group. One way to proceed would be to take different schemes of tax reform and compute welfare losses.

Table A8.1 Elasticities and weights in GDP

| | Elasticity | | Weight |
	Substitution	Income	
Employed			
top rate	0.50	−0.45	0.12
standard rate	0.13	−0.16	0.86
poverty trap	0.40	−0.39	0.01
Unemployed	0.80	−0.65	0.01
Weighted Average	0.13	−0.20	1.00

Source: Minford and Ashton, 1989

A more transparent method is to proceed from the optimal tax end. If we assume no cross-elasticities of supply, which seems quite reasonable here since relativities between occupations at the same general pay level will not be disturbed, then we can make use of the Ramsey reasoning (Ramsey, 1927). Welfare costs from a marginal tax rate, t_i, on the ith person equal $e_i V_i t_i^2$ where e_i is the elasticity of supply and V_i is the value-added by the person.

Minimising welfare costs subject to the revenue constraint yields the well-known Ramsey formula that the ratio of the tax rates of two groups should equal the inverse ratio of their elasticities: $t_i/t_j = e_j/e_i$. The GHS evidence suggests that for those with normal marginal tax rates elasticities are both fairly low and similar; elasticities rise with the marginal tax rate. If so, then the optimal marginal tax rate will be equal, since at equality elasticities will be roughly equal too. But the Ramsey rule also sets benefits and tax thresholds to zero since this minimises the marginal tax rate.

This clearly gives us an (impractical) ideal. Note that equal tax rates can be achieved either by BIG or by my proposals. However, under mine, the proposed marginal rate is the result of levelling down to the standard rate. Under BIG, the rate is much higher, representing a lowering for those in the poverty trap but a substantial rise for the millions more outside it. Obviously the welfare costs of BIG are higher. How much higher depends on the exact proposals, not pursued further here.

A last interesting question is how total welfare costs of these proposals compare with the present situation, which though not ultimately optimal may yet be the best feasible option for now. Obviously my proposals offer lower welfare cost, but since cutting benefits in real absolute terms is not suggested to be feasible, or desirable on safety net grounds, no progress in that direction is immediately possible. As for BIG, very rough calculations on a thorough-going and generous scheme – Table A8.2 – suggest a rise in welfare costs, since though elasticities are higher among the unemployed and low-paid their numbers and value-added are very low relative to those of the standard rate taxpayers whose incentives are worsened. Notice that Table A8.2 also suggests there would be a fall in work effort under BIG, compared with now.

The question remains of whether there is any other incremental-ism that could help matters temporarily, while retaining the levelling-down aim. Here, we note the fact that those in work in the poverty trap face much higher marginal rates than those just outside it on standard rate; they also seem to have higher elasticities. This

Table A8.2 Possible welfare costs of BIG (assuming 50% equal marginal tax rate, current benefit rates) compared with present situation.

Working People	Unemployed	In Poverty Trap	High Income (top 5%)	Others Employed	Weighted Total
Weighted in Current GDP (*Source: Table A8.1*)	0.01	0.01	0.12	0.86	1.00
% Change in Net Marginal Wage	+230.00[1]	+230.00[2]	−17.00[3]	−33.00[4]	−25.80
Substitution Elasticity (*Source: Table A8.1*)	0.80	0.40	0.50	0.13	0.11
Substitution Effect on Hours (%)	+184.00	+92.00	−8.50	+4.29	−1.96 (−3.80)[5]
Weighted Substitution Effect on GDP (%)	+1.84	+0.92	−1.02	−3.70	
Welfare Change (% of GDP)	+0.92	+0.46	−0.51	−1.85	−0.98 (−1.90)[5]

[1] Assumes replacement ratio of 85% currently
[2] Assumes withdrawal rate of 85% currently
[3] 50% v. current 40%
[4] 50% v. current 25%
[5] Figures in parentheses show effects excluding the unemployed (i.e. assuming that worktest/workfare became operative under the current system).

might suggest that, as taxes are cut, priority (over standard rate cuts) can be given to raising thresholds especially for those in the poverty trap, since this will take households out of the trap and put them on the standard rate portion of their budget line. It was for this reason that I was anxious to see Nigel Lawson when Chancellor retain his 1987 Green Paper proposals on transferable allowances, which would have taken many families out of the trap. In fact, what follows shows that while the Green Paper proposals would have reduced welfare costs, this would not be true of a general rise in thresholds, because these would transfer too few out of the poverty trap relative to the worsening of incentives for those on standard rate. Over such a general rise in thresholds, standard rate cuts should have precedence.

The possibility of increasing the taper, as Fowler effectively did in his reforms, can also be considered. This has the difficulty that it puts more people into the trap, while reducing the marginal rate for those already in it. The balance of costs depends on how many are in each category. At present the balance looks unfavourable, as there are large numbers just outside the trap, and only some 450,000 in it, but this could change back with fast-growing incomes.

This arithmetic is set out with a little algebra in what follows.

Let there be two groups of households: i employed at standard rate (t_i), j employed in the poverty trap (tax, i.e. withdrawal, rate t_j). Elasticity of hours = e. Number of households = n. Value-added per household at zero tax rates = V. Benefit rate = b. Tax threshold = a/t_i. Total revenue to be raised = R.

Optimal Tax

Revenue constraint is $R = (-b + t_jV_j - t_j^2V_je_j)n_j + (t_iV_i - t_i^2V_ie_i - a)n_i$, where the terms with squared tax rates allow for the effect of rising tax rates on the tax bases, V_j and V_i respectively.

Loss function is $C = 0.5 (t_i^2V_in_ie_i + t_j^2V_jn_je_j)$.

Minimising the Lagrangean, $L = C + pR$, with respect to t_i, t_j yields:

$$0 = dL/dt_i = V_in_i (t_ie_i + p[1 - 2t_ie_i])$$
$$+ dn_i/dt_i \{ 0.5 [t_i^2V_ie_i - t_j^2V_je_j]$$
$$+ p [b - t_jV_j + t_j^2V_je_j + t_iV_i - t_i^2V_ie_i - a]\}$$
$$0 = dL/dt_j = V_jn_j (t_je_j + p [1 - 2t_je_j])$$

$$+ dn_i/dt_j \{ 0.5 [t_i^2 V_i e_i - t_j^2 V_j e_j]$$
$$+ p [b - t_j V_j + t_j^2 V_j e_j + t_i V_i - t_i^2 V_i e_i - a]\}$$

Note that $dn_i/dt_s = - dn_j/dt_s (s=i, j)$.

In the region between the optimum and zero tax rates, the arc elasticities are likely to be similar and close to those estimated for our average employed person. The terms dn_i/dt_s are the effects on the numbers of households in the poverty trap – see Figure 8.3. $a=b=0$ minimises C with respect to a, b. $dn_i = 0$, since people cannot claim benefits and n_i, n_j are fixed groups.

Hence for $e_s = e$
$$t_i e/(1 - 2t_i e) = p = t_j e/(1 - 2t_j e)$$
so that $t_i = t_j$.

Incremental Change from the Current Situation

Let e_s be as estimated for current tax rates. Suppose b and R are constrained. Then varying a or t_j implies a corresponding variation in the standard rate t_i.

Inspection of Figure 8.3 shows that raising tax thresholds and so a, must reduce numbers in the poverty trap until the threshold, a/t_i, reaches the point where the poverty trap segment crosses the 45% line.

Lowering t_j will raise numbers in the poverty trap while lowering the marginal rate on those within it.

Changing t_i will have a negligible impact on numbers in the poverty trap ($dn_i/dt_i = 0$) but will change incentives for others of course.

I. Varying t_j

From the revenue constraint we have

$$dt_j \{n_j V_j (1 - 2t_j e_j)$$
$$+ dn_i/dt_j [b - t_j V_j + t_j^2 V_j e_j + t_i V_i - t_i^2 V_i e_i - a]\}$$
$$= -dt_i \{n_i V_i (1 - 2t_i e_i)\}$$

And $dC/dt_j = t_j V_j n_j e_j + 0.5 (t_i^2 V_i e_i - t_j^2 V_j e_j) dn_i/dt_j + dC/dt_i . dt_i/dt_j$

Our estimates are: $e_j = 0.2$, $e_i = 0.07$ (based on Minford and Ashton, 1989); and (based on official statistics and Liverpool calculations)

$V_i = 200$, $V_j = 100$, b=110, a=15 (all in £ per week, 1987 prices); $n_j = 0.45$, $n_i = 22$, dn_i/dt_j (for a cut in t_j) = 2.5 (all in millions); $t_i = 0.25$ and $t_j = 0.85$.

a.   A cut in t_j – increasing numbers in the poverty trap but lowering the withdrawal rate further as in the Fowler reforms:

In this case we estimate $dC/dt_j = -26.0$ (£ million per week), implying that further cuts in the withdrawal rate would reduce welfare; for example, a reduction of .05 would cause an increase in welfare costs of $.05 \times 26.0 \times 52 = $ £68 million per year.

b.   Returning to pre-Fowler levels:

For a rise in t_j (back to pre-Fowler levels) dn_i/dt_j is much smaller (about 0.7) so that $dC/dt_j = +3.5$, implying that a return to pre-Fowler levels would raise welfare costs. The optimum therefore must lie somewhere between current and pre-Fowler levels. Since dn_i/dt_j falls steeply as we move away from the current level back towards pre-Fowler, this optimum is likely to lie close to the current level.

II.   Varying a

Revenue constraint:

$$da\{dn_i/da\ [b - t_jV_j + t_j^2V_je_j + t_iV_i - t_i^2V_ie_i - a] - n_i\}$$
$$= -dt_i\ \{n_iV_i\ (1 - 2t_ie_i)\}$$

And

$$dC/da = 0.5\ (t_i^2V_ie_i - t_j^2V_je_j)\ dn_i/d_a + dC/dt_i.\ dt_i/da$$

Hence, given also $dn_i/da = 0.02$, we obtain $dC/da = 0.4$ (£ million per week), indicating that raising tax thresholds would slightly raise welfare costs because of the corresponding rise in the standard rate. In other words, priority should be given in tax cuts to lowering the standard rate rather than raising general thresholds. This particular result is however rather sensitive to the assumptions. Also, if the rise in tax thresholds were concentrated on married couples as in the Green Paper proposals, then dn_i/da would be much higher (about 0.3) and dC/da would turn negative. In any case, the sums are finely balanced.

Notes

1. I am grateful to Paul Ashton for assistance and comments on the calculations in this chapter; I remain responsible for errors.

References

Peter Ashby (1988), 'Proposal for the Action Credit', St George's House, Windsor.

Charles V. Brown, E.J. Levin, P.J.Rosa, R.J. Raffell, and D.T. Ulph (1987), 'Taxation and Family Labour Supply' - Final Report of HM Treasury Project.

John Burton (1986), 'Workfare', Institute for Employment Research, Buckingham University.

Patrick Minford and Paul Ashton (1989), 'The Poverty Trap and the Laffer Curve – What Can the GHS Tell Us?' CEPR discussion paper no. 275, revised December 1989.

Patrick Minford, David Davies, Michael Peel and Alison Sprague (1983), *Unemployment – Cause and Cure*, Martin Robertson, now Basil Blackwell (second edition, with Paul Ashton as added co-author, 1985).

Hermione Parker (1989), *Instead of the Dole: an Enquiry into Integration of the Tax and Benefit Systems*, Routledge.

F.P. Ramsey (1927), 'A Contribution to the Theory of Taxation', *Economic Journal*, **37**, pp.47–61.

9. Housing Reform to 'Create' Jobs*

The housing market in Britain is the object of massive government intervention. This involvement takes four main forms: the Rent Acts, the subsidising of council house rents, the subsidy to owner-occupiers through tax reliefs on mortgages and the system of planning restrictions on housing land. Some of the motives for this intervention appear to have been: the avoidance of tenant 'exploitation' (Rent Acts), welfare support to poorer people but tied to housing to ensure no diversion into other expenditure (council rents), the building of a 'property-owning democracy' (mortgage relief), and the protection of the environment (planning). All are regarded as 'politically sensitive', i.e., big potential vote-winners or -losers. This political sensitivity is clearly illustrated by the way that even Mrs Thatcher's Government, although it has shown itself to be relatively brave in economic policy, has so far largely refused to tackle the central problems of the housing market.

In this chapter, we try to evaluate the economic inefficiency or waste ('welfare costs', in the economist's jargon) which arises from government intervention; then, after reviewing the detailed mechanisms by which it is implemented, we suggest ways in which they could be modified to diminish this inefficiency without abandoning any cherished political aims.

There are two main sources of waste because of current institutional arrangements:

a. the direct waste caused in the housing market itself by inducing people to over- or under-use different sorts of accommodation.
b. the indirect waste caused in the *labour* market (i.e., unemployment) by the *immobility* which comes about from intervention in housing.

* Written with Paul Ashton and Michael Peel. First published in *Economic Affairs*, Supplement, pp. 32–4, February–March 1986.

Direct waste is probably quite considerable but not for the reasons usually given. Of a total waste which we 'guesstimate' at a large figure of 5% of GDP, as much as 4½% of GDP is due to planning restrictions on housing. Yet this figure is certainly an over-estimate, because we have been unable to put a price on what people would pay to protect the environment (the Green Belt, etc.) If people had property rights in the environment, they would sell them to developers and a 'fair' (that is, market) price would be set for such protection; and the market would also reveal the 'right' amount of it, as decided by consumers. Although there are some problems in defining these rights, in creating a market for them, and in inducing people to reveal their preferences accurately for 'public goods' like clean air and attractive countryside, the present bureaucratic planning system is so deplorably inefficient that the solutions should be studied and pursued. Nevertheless, this sort of work is still in its infancy and we are, therefore, stuck with the present system for some time at least until more research has been completed.

The other ½% of GDP under (a) is the misallocation because of council house subsidies, mortgage tax relief and the Rent Acts. This distortion is 'not peanuts', although it is dwarfed by the effect of planning restrictions. Yet it is the sort of loss that, both because it is largely concealed (in the form of invisible 'lost consumer surplus') and because the solutions are politically difficult, may well not stimulate political action.

Not so the costs under (b). Clearly unemployment is such a serious political issue that, if it can be shown that housing reform can reduce unemployment, the issue will be seriously considered whatever its difficulties. It is well known (and fully documented by numerous statistical studies surveyed in our book) that the private rental sector is very important in enabling people to move jobs, and also that its size has been dramatically reduced by the cumulative operation of the Rent Acts, especially since they were extended to cover furnished accommodation in 1974, from 62% of the housing stock in 1945 to about 10% today. So it would not be surprising to find that by obstructing the movement of people from areas with high to those with low unemployment, the Rent Acts have raised both regional and national unemployment. A statistical analysis of regional unemployment since 1963 confirms this assumption. We estimate from this analysis that *national* unemployment has been raised by around 2¼% of the labour force by the Rent Acts. The formal value of this loss in economic resources to the nation is about 1% of GDP – but, of course, most people will be concerned primarily about the unemployment effect itself.

What can be done, in practical political terms, to remove this major obstacle?

Immobility is created by the large gap between the protected or subsidised tenancy, which is linked to the worker's staying in 'his' area, and the free-market tenancy which he must take if he moves to another area. This immobility in turn creates unemployment, because in the North wages are prevented from dropping sufficiently to create jobs for those who will not move.

Let us consider an idealised solution to this problem. Suppose all tenancies were at free-market rents under free-market conditions of tenure (i.e., some contractual basis agreed freely and solely between landlord and tenant). For the employed man in the North, housing will not then obstruct his decision to move: he will pay market rents wherever he is (minus whatever state rebate he may get in housing benefits).

What about the unemployed man? Under our present benefit system, his rent will be 100% rebated if he stays in the North, whereas he will only get a partial rebate if he takes work in the South. Under free-market rents his incentive to move would be greater than at subsidised or otherwise protected rents because free-market rents in the South would be lowered by deregulation. However, the comparison between his out-of-work income and his in-work income if he takes work in the North will be now much more favourable to his remaining unemployed, because his rents have gone up, with 100% subsidy if unemployed, but only a partial one if employed. Hence ironically, on its own, letting rents rise to free-market prices, while it should increase mobility among the unemployed, may well also increase unemployment in the North and will do so if the number of employed induced to leave (or not take) employment at low wages exceeds those induced to migrate to the South.

Since 1979 the Conservative Government has been following this policy on council house rents and, to the small extent it has loosened Rent Act restrictions, also in protected private tenancies, *it may have worsened the problem*.

Such are the complexities provoked by a system as heavily

intervened-in as in Britain's – but there is an answer, which is perfectly reasonable and politically acceptable: this solution is to introduce a ceiling on benefits as a percentage of previous net income in work. We have suggested this elsewhere (Minford *et al.*, 1985), setting it at 70%. Such a gap between income in and out of work is a form of pressure on people to take a new job at rather lower rates of pay than their last one if they cannot find one at the old rate. If they do so, the state will nevertheless, under our existing system (of which we would retain the principle but must improve the practice), support their in-work net income above a 'decent' minimum living standard.

With this ceiling in place, the unemployed man will now find that his unemployment benefits do not go up. His incentive to find work in the North will now be unchanged because he will still be 30% worse off out of work. Furthermore, his incentive to move to the South will now be considerably stronger because he now has to pay a larger proportion of the economic rent if he stays in the North.

A simple arithmetical example may be helpful here. Suppose in his previous job he was paid £100 (per week), with net pay at £80. His benefits under the ceiling are 70% of £80 = £56 per week. Suppose he could earn in the South £120, net pay of £95; but his rent would be £15 higher, and so he is not interested in moving South (any more than in taking another job in the North at £100).

Now his Northern rent goes up, because of deregulation, by £15. His out-of-work benefit will not change, remaining at 70% of his work income if he stays North. But it will now be only 59% of his work income if he goes South for a job (previously it was 70% if you allowed for the rent factor). His incentive to move and take a job in the South will thus have increased significantly.

The ceiling we have proposed is not the only way to create pressures on the unemployed to take available jobs at lower wages than before. Others exist – from 'moral' pressure, through 'work-fare' schemes, all the way to straight compulsion via cutting off benefits for job-refusal (the 'work-test' which legally ought to be applied to all unemployed under present rules). Let us assume that some such mechanism is functioning. Then we can pursue our main purpose which is to reduce the obstacles to mobility posed by housing regulations as such. Clearly, our argument implies that the rental sector should be freed from regulation entirely.

However, in practice some timetable is necessary. And what

respect should be given to the principle that 'retrospection' should be avoided? The easiest course would be first to announce that over the next five years the ceiling on regulated rents would be raised to free-market prices in five equal percentage instalments – with *all* regulation of rents to cease in 1990. As for security of tenure provisions enjoined by the courts, a two-year transitional period could be announced in which *existing* security would prevail. At the end of this period landlords and tenants would be expected to have freely negotiated contracts and the courts would no longer be involved in enforcing statutory 'security'.

Does this simple course – despite the 'precedent' set by the 1957 Rent Act – involve unconstitutional retrospection? For regulated tenants, regulation is both recent (1965 is the earliest date) and subject to a system of 'fair rent' adjudication, whereby rents are varied in accordance with a variety of statutory criteria which are subjectively assessed by rent officers. Rights, if any, in such regulatory benefits appear to be weak. A five-year phasing of rent increases and a two-year warning of security cessation appear adequate recognition of them.

For council tenants reform has only to follow existing policy to raise council rents to market prices, but over a similar period to that for regulated tenancies, so that by 1990 these rents too are at market prices. That this implicit policy does not violate council tenants' rights might be considered clear from its failure to be contested to date. Tenants who choose to buy their own houses are able to do so on most favourable terms, which might partially reflect their rights accumulated by years of tenure and partially the state's desire for them to become home-owners with a 'stake in society'. Yet should those who choose *not* to buy have their rights to tenure reflected in some way? The problem for them appears to be the same as that for regulated tenants: 'what the state giveth [at least relatively recently – via the 1980 Housing Act], the state may take away'. Their rights are comparatively weak. The good fortune of those who can buy is undeniable.

What of security of tenure for council tenants? Here we have seen there *are* statutory grounds (non-payment of rent, etc.) under which councils may evict tenants; but in some cases, suitable alternative accommodation must be provided, and the power of a council to evict even for 'gross underoccupation' is almost totally fettered. Council housing has developed a status of 'renter of last resort' for the poor, the old, the handicapped and the unfortunate. There would seem to be every reason to move people out of this last-resort housing as soon as they are capable of renting normally. Many of these people will buy their own house within the next five years. Those that then remain will largely be the difficult cases, unlikely to move in any case. However, we wish to ensure that those capable of moving are not deterred from doing so to their advantage by the existence of security of tenure (albeit at an economic rent) in their existing lodgings. This analysis points to an additional statutory ground for moving tenants who do not fall into the 'renter of last resort' category: namely, that they have the capacity to find alternative lodgings outside the council sector.

Our proposals are step-by-step in one sense, in that they embody transitional periods, and recognise existing legal rights. Even so, the announcement of such a programme for regulated tenants (not for council tenants, where we advocate merely an extension of existing policies) could create a storm of protest from housing lobbies and so on. The storm could be weathered – but it might be risky.

Are there other measures that would reach the same conclusion, if by a more roundabout route?

For regulated tenancies, one obvious variation would be to introduce a new criterion into the setting of 'fair rents' – that of scarcity. This single amendment would allow tribunals to raise rents towards market prices. Scarcity could be made a binding criterion (i.e., rents must not be below market prices) by a certain time – for example, 1990. A second series of variants could build on the innovation in the 1980 Housing Act (the assured tenancy and the shorthold), as well as on the licence agreement which has always been outside 'full' Rent Act protection. These categories should now be extended so as to deregulate *all* new tenancies and relets. This simple measure should instil confidence into existing and potential landlords – who at present are trapped in a legal minefield involving licences (unprotected) and tenancies (fully protected) – and stimulate the supply of new (unrestricted) lets. (The efficacy of such a measure would, to a large extent, depend on how landlords – and investors – assess the probability of a future government being elected with an opposite policy).

A third variant would allow the landlord to draw up these rent tenancies with a clause denying the tenant the right to go to the Rent

Officer for an assessment of a 'fair rent'. Since no landlord would be willing to let without such a clause, this would effectively place all new tenancies outside the Rent Acts' rent provisions. This measure would still leave the problem of repossessing existing regulated tenancies. If rents were at market rates it would be easy (a mere matter of contacting market agencies) for landlords to offer tenants 'comparable' accommodation at comparable prices where at present it is often impossible. A general mandatory ground for eviction, after the tenancy agreement has expired, could be made to be such an offer by the landlord. (At present, a landlord may only – at the court's discretion – obtain possession by providing 'suitable alternative accommodation' or a (similar) regulated residence – and the court must be satisfied that it is 'reasonable' to order possession.) This provision would be our fourth variant.

By these four variants existing rents would be raised where there was scarcity (i.e., market rents exceeded regulated rents), existing tenants could be evicted after their contract is up once market rents were reached, and new tenancies would be unrestricted.

These proposals are made to deal with mobility. They are all that is necessary to that end. Nevertheless, we noted earlier the other distortions in the housing market. These distortions arose not merely from the Rent Acts and council house rent subsidies, but also from the subsidy to mortgage interest via tax relief. Strictly speaking, this tax relief is also a distortion within the financial markets, since much lending on mortgage in effect is done for general financial purposes.

There is a well-known solution to this tangle: make saving tax-free, and tax only consumption. The tax-free allowance on your income will then be not the mortgage interest on your borrowing but your total *saving*; if you borrow, it will not affect your tax position unless you add to your consumption.

There are by now so many distortions in financial markets, because of the complex incidence of a variety of taxes and tax relief on financial transactions, that it is a hopeless task to estimate the costs. They may be small because of the efficiency of financial markets in avoiding tax; but they are nevertheless worth clearing away, if only because of the urgency of making the City of London as competitive as possible and to allow individuals to own shares on their own account without a loss of tax efficiency.

Reforms of this magnitude in the tax system will take some years to put into place. Nevertheless, they will come as soon as the atmosphere of crisis that surround tax revenues (because of their *shortage*) has subsided. Meanwhile, it is unlikely to be a high governmental priority to abolish mortgage tax relief. Its economic cost is small, and the political cost of abolition too high.

The proposals made in this chapter will reduce the living standards of those who use protected rental accommodation, whether council or private. These people are, for the most part, in lower-income groups. The distributional consequences of the proposals are therefore regressive.

As they stand, our proposals also have no revenue cost, because the higher rents will be paid by the renters themselves, under an assumption that out-of-work benefits are subject to a 70% ceiling and that housing benefits are fixed (being related to income).

In principle it is possible for the distributive consequences to be offset by higher housing benefits (although the 70% ceiling implies that only 70% of this addition accrues to the unemployed). Yet this restriction must be seen against a background in which the highest priority is being given to raising tax thresholds over the next four years, in order to reduce the tax burden on the low-paid; and a second priority is being attached to relieving the low-paid of National Insurance contributions as far as possible.

How much will our proposals cost renters? Assuming that rents rise to market rates by 1990 on all regulated and council properties, the cost to the average person on these properties would be about £11 per week spread over five years. If this Government's plans for tax cuts go through in the next four years, that average person – if he is earning £120 per week – could gain up to £16 per week in tax cuts.

These proposals considered, seen in the wider context, can therefore be seen, potentially at least, to pose no distributional threat, without raising housing benefits, given the large tax cuts planned by the Chancellor.[1] The proposals can therefore be considered primarily in their efficiency aspect.

The British housing market is in a mess because it is over-regulated, and this interference has serious effects on mobility, and so on unemployment. It *is* politically feasible to reform the regulatory system, particularly against the background of rising tax thresholds currently planned by the Government. This intention offers a major opportunity to reform the housing market, since at times when taxes have been rising it would have created excessive hardship. We have suggested ways in which it could be done without sweeping aside existing institutions, by building on the 1980 Housing Act, the first 'step' in the reform of housing law instituted by this Government. The step-by-step approach that has proved so successful in the reform of union law could be used here, too. It is time for the second step.

Notes

1. This conclusion is further strengthened if the suggestions we have made elsewhere for Negative Income Tax and public spending economies are followed up (Minford et al, 1985).

References

A.P.L.Minford, P. Ashton, M.Peel, D.Davies and A. Sprague (1985), *Unemployment – Cause and Cure*, Blackwell, Oxford, 2nd edn.

10. Centres and Peripheries: A Policy Perspective*

A Straw Man

There are ways of defining a 'regional problem' that make it unsolvable. For example, if the objective of regional policy is to eliminate regional discrepancies in income per head and to prevent regional emigration, then it may well be impossible to achieve. It would require regional subsidies to be sufficient to offset any inducement for firms to move away from one region to another. Yet not only would this be expensive to the taxpayers of the more fortunate region, it would require constant adjustment of subsidy rates as fortunes changed.

Why do I start with such a straw man? Because it seems to be what has traditionally been expected of regional policy: it should prevent swings of demand or cost advantage between regions creating either regional inequality or emigration. This is the same welfarism that we have seen at the level of individuals being written into policy at the regional level.

Yet both regional inequality and inter-regional migration should be entirely acceptable in a free society. The welfare safety net indeed is there to ensure that no individual slips into destitution: and welfare assistance such as supplementary benefits and housing benefit is calibrated to national standards, allowing for differences in regional costs. Yet, just as individual inequality is inevitable, so some regions may well contain higher concentrations of richer or poorer people. As for migration, again there seems no basis for the idea that regional or local populations must be preserved in aspic: subject to the protection of property rights in the environment, appropriate charging for infrastructure use, and other such public good elements, people should go where they have a mind to.

I take it then in what follows that there are limits to the taxpayer's

* First published in *Quarterly Economic Bulletin*, Liverpool Research Group in Macroeconomics, **8**, pp. 25–8, October 1987.

purse (usually the Southern taxpayer's) and that migration is a legitimate market mechanism. I now want to discuss the regional policy problem as the problem of relieving inter-regional mis-allocation of resources at minimum cost to the taxpayer. By inter-regional misallocation of resources, I mean that the resource is generating less net product in one region than it would if transferred to another.

Two Models of Regional Interaction

To make this quite concrete, let me set out two models or stylised pictures of what is going on in Britain today.

Model 1 is a properly functioning environment with no (or at least no easily identifiable) misallocation. Call it the market in people who own their own home and typically work in non-manual occupations; their productivity is such that they will not usually qualify for welfare benefits and if they are unemployed their benefits will be well below their usual pay.

Imagine two regions of this market which start out equal in every respect – then demand shifts from the South to the North. What will happen? There are two extreme possibilities.

If land, with planning permission, is plentifully available in the South (at some constant price of farming land), then wages will fall in the North and rise in the South; this will cause migration Southwards until wages are equal again. Housebuilding expands in the South and contracts in the North; land prices are unaffected by assumption. Figure 10.1 illustrates.

The other extreme case is for planning land to be absolutely limited. Then, as wages fall in the North and rise in the South, people attempt to migrate to the South. Yet this attempt only drives up the price of scarce land as the migrators try to buy houses. As house and land prices rise, business in the South has to face higher and higher costs; it has to pay more for its own business land and premises, and it has to pay still higher wages than before for its workers to compensate them for their higher housing costs. Conversely in the North, planning land which was previously scarce loses its scarcity value and falls in price; this means that business costs in the North, including wages, fall continuously. There is only one eventual upshot of this process. Real wages (after allowing for the effects of housing costs) are equalised between regions so

Figure 10.1 Non-manual markets with building land unrestricted in the South

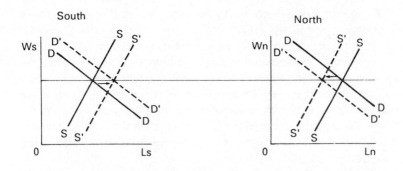

Figure 10.2 Non-manual markets with totally restricted building land in the South

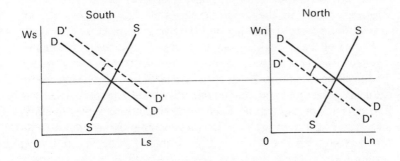

Figure 10.3 Manual markets with Rent Acts

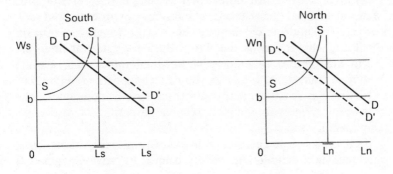

attempted migration is stopped: but costs in the South have risen, costs in the North have fallen, sufficiently to offset entirely the shift of conditions in favour of business in the South. In effect the business is driven back North because the South cannot accommodate it (see Figure 10.2).

It is important to realise that in both these extreme cases there is no regional misallocation, because in both cases the net marginal product of labour is equalised (i.e., net, after allowing for the costs imposed on the environment as reflected in planning restrictions on land). There is also no unemployment caused in either case. In the first case, migration restores regional equilibrium; in the second, relative cost differentials move to restore it and there is no migration.

In Britain the way this model works is probably closer to the second case as planning restrictions are quite tight in the South as a result of presumably legitimate environmental concerns. Planning is the only way we have of recognising these concerns, as creating property rights in the environment is not feasible because of transactions costs of defining them, trading them, etc.

How well is it working out in practice? We must distinguish between the very natural complaints of Northern houseowners about rising Southern house prices and their own falling house values, on the one hand, and on the other hand, the effectiveness of the mechanism for keeping down Northern non-manual unemployment and generating new businesses employing non-manual workers. As far as one can tell from limited disaggregated data, unemployment rates among non-manuals appear to be regionally much less differentiated than corresponding rates among manuals. Non-manual earnings differentials are also not very great (see Table 10.1) after allowing for differential housing costs. Certainly this seems plausible if one reflects that housing costs absorb about 13% of the typical budget, and the 'same house' costs roughly 2.5 times in the South what it does in the North. Businesses starting up in the North are tending to employ non-manual rather than manual labour. A highly tentative verdict based on poor data would be that, certainly relative to the manual labour market, the non-manual one is working roughly to eliminate regional disparities of real wages and unemployment.

That brings us to the second model, of manual workers living in rented accommodation, mostly council or private regulated.

Table 10.1 Wages and unemployment in the non-manual and manual labour markets

Region	NON-MANUAL		MANUAL	
	Real Wage 1986 (SE=100)[1]	Unemployment Rate 1983 (%)[2]	Real Wage 1986 (SE=100)[1]	Unemployment Rate 1983 (%)[2]
SE	100.0	3.2	100.0	9.7
EA	90.7	4.2	92.0	9.2
SW	88.1	3.8	89.5	9.6
Average for 'South'[3]	95.4	3.7	96.0	9.5
WM	93.5	5.5	91.9	17.3
EM	92.3	3.2	92.0	9.6
YH	94.6	5.0	92.7	14.6
NW	95.7	5.5	93.8	17.7
N	94.2	4.7	93.7	17.5
WL	92.3	3.8	90.9	17.1
SC	98.3	4.1	93.7	15.1
Average for 'North'[3]	94.4	4.5	92.6 (89.8)[4]	15.6

[1] Wages adjusted for purchasing power by 0.13 times differential in house prices.
[2] Labour force survey (large sample survey) for 1983, latest available with regional unemployment rates.
[3] Weighted by estimated shares (Source: Labour Force Survey) of non-manual and manual labour force respectively.
[4] Bracketed figure includes unemployed (estimated real living standard 70.8) with a weight of 0.15.

Their productivity being lower, they are typically eligible for benefits and if unemployed will receive not much less than their normal pay. This is an altogether more dismal, and I believe by now a very familiar, story. It is illustrated in Figure 10.3.

Imagine as before two regions initially equal, hit by the same demand shift from North to South. Wages rise in the South, and start to fall in the North. As they rise in the South, local labour becomes somewhat more fully employed; but there is a limit beyond which wages rise with little corresponding reduction of unemployment. As they fall in the North however they quite quickly reach the 'benefit floor' below which they are unattractive compared with benefits: there is little countervailing pressure on firms to create jobs, to offset the ones lost in the fall of demand. Unemployment rises by more than it falls in the South.

As for migration, this does not occur at all; it is not even attempted. For the regulated or council tenant requires a very substantial wage differential to compensate him for the difference between the rent on the black market lodgings available in the South and his sitting-tenant rent in the North. Such a differential is unlikely to occur when wages in the North are held up by benefits; migration is accordingly restricted.

In the second model, nothing happens to offset the inequality in real wages and unemployment opened up between North and South. In the first model, migration or attempted migration was the engine that forced away the inequality, either by people moving or by business moving back. In this second, that engine is stalled. The result is severe inter-regional misallocation as the marginal product of the employed Northerner is less than the employed Southerner, while there is also a rise in national unemployment, an additional source of waste.

The evidence of the inequalities under this model is over-whelming, as Table 10.1 shows, in disparities of manual unemployment rates, in the limited disparities of manual wages and yet in the continued differentials of real wages (council rents being kept closer together than market circumstances would dictate).

Policy Implications

With the aid of these two models, it is possible to sketch out a coherent policy package.

The first thing to notice is that basically we can leave the model 1 market alone. We should not worry about rising house and land prices in the South (and falling relatively in the North), for example. Let them rip! That is the market working, to drive business up North. About the only concession would be that the planners will naturally be forced by the increased scarcity value of their planned environment to consider the marginal uses of the scarce land again. Everything has its price, and no doubt parts of the environment have a price lower than other parts; local councils, realising the rates they can now levy on new businesses, so compensating local ratepayers for the marginal loss of amenity, will move along the appropriate trade-off.

The model 2 market cries out for policy changes, however. The full menu of the necessary changes is rather large and complex: I have set it out at length elsewhere in a book on Housing (Minford *et al*, 1987) and in the second edition of *Unemployment – Cause and Cure* (Minford *et al*, 1985). I cannot repeat it all here! Essentially, they consist of reforms to the benefit system and the Rent Acts to permit downward wage flexibility and mobility from North to South. Moves in both these directions are now underway, with the Restart programme on the one hand, and on the other, deregulation of new tenancies and related actions in the council sector.

Is this enough? It would certainly cost the taxpayer little or nothing.

It is not enough because of the way in which inner urban local authority finances work. A somewhat satirical characterisation would be as follows. The bulk of inner urban councils' electorates are manual workers or related to them. Most of them receive rate rebates, the unemployed 100% rebates. If the local authority raises personal rates, they pay little or nothing. If it raises business rates and businesses close, so that they become unemployed, they are sustained on supplementary benefit and are little if at all worse off. On the other hand, they benefit from local services. Hence they have a strong incentive to elect councils which will provide these services and pass the cost on either to central government in rate support grant or onto ratepayers.

This 'representation without taxation' in our big inner city population centres is the major problem of local government finance. It exacerbates the regional misallocation, because it adds to business costs in Northern cities. This creates a distortion in the model 2 market as it widens wage differentials and increases Northern unemployment. (In the model 1 market it results in still higher Southern land prices! This is not a distortion however.)

The problem is so severe that I believe it does justify drastic action. The idea of capping business rates (at some notional unified national level) is certainly a good one. A unified business rate, though an improvement, is perhaps less good; this forces low-spending responsible councils to raise their business rate in order effectively to subsidise high-spending metropolitan councils. It represents a hidden cost to the (Southern) taxpayer. When the market is already squeezing the South so hard via rising land prices, it levies an additional congestion tax and may appear a redundant cost. (Remember that rate revaluation will in any case dramatically change the pattern of rate support grant in favour of the North – appropriately so.) However, a case can be made for it because of the social costs of inequality of unemployment and real wages in the manual market; if the unified business rate speeds the removal of this cost, it will be justified.

The community charge is a further attempt to induce metropolitan responsibility by making the electorate pay for their services at least to some extent. I support this idea; indeed I can see little alternative.

Finally, there are all these development corporations on fairly small budgets which are attempting to break the stranglehold on private development of other public sector bodies, especially local authorities, in metropolitan areas. This can only be for the good, as again such development is resisted for the same reasons that inspire distortions on the rates.

A package along these lines offers real hope of breaking the logjam of immobility and unemployment among manual workers in the North which is the essence of our current regional problem. Break that and related problems – inner city decay and crime, regional inequalities of income – will fade also.

References

P. Minford, Michael Peel and Paul Ashton (1987), *The Housing Morass*, Institute of Economic Affairs.

P. Minford, Paul Ashton, Michael Peel, David Davies and Alison Sprague (1985), *Unemployment – Cause and Cure*, 2nd edn, Basil Blackwell.

11. Regional Policy and Market Forces: A Model and an Assessment*

In this chapter we describe regional developments over the last few decades in terms of a new regional model, based on the Heckscher-Ohlin Inter-regional trade model allowing for mobility of certain factors of production.

Introduction – The Theoretical Framework of Analysis

Regional behaviour will be influenced by the elements which vary regionally – its 'regionally avoidable costs'; these can be quite a small proportion of a firm's total costs, so that variations in them which are small in relation to total value added acquire a crucial significance in terms of regional location.

Capital and raw material costs are fixed in world markets. The costs of skilled labour, which, typically home-owning, is free to migrate anywhere in the country where rewards are more alluring, are determined nationally; there will be one going wage, adjusted for any differences in the cost or quality of life, for such workers across the country.

Prices are fixed regionally for those elements which cannot move from the region. Those are land with planning permission for non-agricultural use and unskilled labour (whose mobility is restricted by tenant subsidies and controls).

The prices of land and of (unskilled) labour are fixed by their marginal value in industrial use by firms competing in world markets. There is a wage rate and a land rental rate that will be just competitive for these firms if they establish locally.

Of these firms, manufacturing is more (unskilled-) labour-intensive than services. Then a decline in manufacturing prices

*Written with Peter Stoney. Summary of paper in *Proceedings of NEDO Conference on Regional Economics and Prospects in the UK*, March 1990.

relative to services prices will reduce wages and raise land rentals. So will a shift in technology away from unskilled labour, in favour of mechanisation. Both of these will produce unemployment as wages fall relative to unemployment benefits. They will also raise land prices relative to the reserve cost of agricultural land, and increase the pressure for development. These effects are national.

Transport costs or other locational cost disadvantages can alter relative land and labour prices in North and South. If the North's transport costs to the UK's main markets go up relative to the South, then the competitive wage and land price in the North goes down in proportion to the reduction in value-added this produces (net of capital, raw materials and skilled labour). This proportion is estimated to be 20–40%.

We have just sketched out the basics of our explanation for the rise in manual unemployment, especially in the North (hit by the double blow of falling relative manufacturing prices and rising relative transport costs); also for the large rise in relative land prices in the South. We can also explain urban dereliction as the result of inner urban land prices being driven down below the value of non-industrial use.

To these basics, we should add the roles of local authorities and unions. Local government raises taxes whose incidence falls variously on land rentals (business rates) and on the cost of skilled labour (personal rates). The former can drive the net price of land below its non-industrial use value, driving business out. The latter acts like a tax on the value-added available for land and unskilled labour (like transport costs above).

Unions operate in the protected sector, where competition from abroad is kept at bay and so wages can be marked up by monopoly unions. This sector includes government and non-traded goods and services such as electricity production and construction; also any parts of industry with quota protection against imports, such as the car industry and some electronics. In this sector, the only limit to the wages that can be set for an industry is the loss of jobs as the industry contracts. Union mark-ups reduce jobs and raise unemployment.

In the North, local authorities have pursued more aggressive rating policies and unions have been stronger than in the South.

A final factor is the size of the protected sector itself. After 1979, government policy was to reduce protection of industry and to cut the size of the public sector. While this enabled taxes to be cut and the economy as a whole to benefit, the contraction in the protected sector was particularly marked in the North (an obvious example being the coal industry, whose employment has more than halved, mostly in the North); this meant that people previously employed at high protected wages now found themselves faced with low-paid unskilled jobs, and many opted instead for benefits.

One might expect the share of the protected sector to remain broadly constant at relative prices; however, relative prices will stimulate relocation. As the cost of land and labour rise in the South because of the pressures driving the traded sector southwards, the protected sector which is not driven by the same pressures will react by relocating northwards those parts that are not directly parasitic on the traded sector.

Within the traded sector, the share of manufacturing will be set by the supply of unskilled labour relative to that of land, since manufacturing is about twice as manual-labour-intensive as services, and considerably less land-intensive. Even with high Northern unemployment reducing the supply of manual labour (as manual wages have dropped relative to benefits), the North has remained on this basis the natural location for manufacturing; as measures to bring back these unemployed into supply (for example, by worktesting and retraining, if necessary backed by benefit withdrawal) take effect, this advantage will be enhanced.

Regional Developments 1979–1989

The developments referred to in a general way above are quantified in our full paper – the North's reliance on manufacturing because of the high proportion of manual workers in its labour force, the collapse of the manufacturing terms of trade since 1955, and the substitution from manual labour. All these factors are national in impact on land and labour prices, though the North suffers disproportionately from them being more dependent on manufacturing and manual labour.

The key factor worsening the relative position of the North has been its increasing transport cost disadvantage.

Deep sea ship size has increased, rewarding concentration in routes on the Channel ports, with marginal loads to the North being sent by land. The poor competitiveness of Northern ports because of the restrictions and barriers to competition produced by the

Dock Labour Scheme has aggravated this problem on deep sea traffic; and has been largely responsible for the North's disadvantage on short sea traffic, now dominant in Britain's trade because of Europe.

It is estimated that these differential transport costs are typically imposing a 20–40% tax on Northern land and unskilled labour. This is the extent by which both wages and land rentals are driven down in the North.

Other factors with relative impacts on the North's costs and prices have been:

Northern union power may well have raised the overall Northern unemployment rate by around 1%.

Northern local authorities have raised personal rates more than in the South. This has contributed a further 7.5–15% tax on Northern land and unskilled labour prices, driving them down by this much.

High Northern business rates may also have raised Northern unemployment by around 1%.

Current and Future Policy

The Effect of Enacted Policy Measures

Local finance reform will remove the rating difficulties discussed above.

Housing reform should increase mobility among manual workers. Once manual labour can migrate, the only immobile regional factor, or regionally avoidable cost, is land. This will further widen land price differentials.

A return to the Beveridge principle that the dole is only payable to those who cannot help themselves either by taking an available job or going on training courses offered them, is now government policy. This will continue to lower the incentive to stay jobless, particularly strong among the manual unemployed.

The four trade union laws have, according to the most recent evidence, been having an effect on the union mark-up over non-union wages; since 1980 the mark-up has been steadily declining.

Deregulation and privatisation have substantially increased goods market competition within the protected sector. As health and education, and other parts of the public services, are exposed to market forces, this will continue.

Regional aid has been essentially abandoned – with good reason. The problem with it is that it was neither universal, in a typical Northern region or even area, nor permanent in the sense that a recipient in a marginal activity could rely on its repetition when the capital stock needed renewing.

Present policy is to use modest amounts of public money to facilitate market forces, given that planning procedures of possibly hostile local government and other distortions may stand in the way. Urban Development Corporations (UDCs) are part of this, as are discretionary grants and consultancy aid to new businesses by the Department of Trade and Industry (DTI), but UDCs must be sensitive to the comparative advantage of their sub-region.

Necessary Reforms in the Manual Labour Market and Related Areas

The present programme must continue vigorously to revive the Beveridge work-test procedures, fraud inspection, and compulsory training if on the dole with no other job prospect.

The rented sector needs to be freed as rapidly as possible by pushing council rents to market levels.

Union power remains a problem especially in the North. Besides further reduction in union immunities, competition should be increased within the protected sector, whether by contracting-out or privatisation or deregulation. Government departments should negotiate locally, insisting on value for money given local conditions.

The size of the protected sector in the North will increase through market forces as land prices in the South drive these businesses North. Government departments too should evaluate moving decisions in a commercial manner; if it pays them to move North they should do so.

Dock Labour Scheme abolition was necessary to eliminate the North's transport cost disadvantage. It has now occurred.

The shipping conferences should be referred to the Monopolies and Mergers Commission (MMC) over their deep sea container pricing practices which discriminate against Northern ports.

The Landbridge from the North through the Chunnel to the Continent and back is a promising idea under active study but it is not viable without the above opening up of competition.

Rail and air competition should also be enhanced, to allow the emergence of more competitive Northern facilities.

Planning consents are a sort of market in property rights in the environment; the local authority is a fairly cheap intermediary who releases these rights in return for expected benefits from development. Hence there is nothing wrong in principle with planning controls.

Development should proceed to the point at which the marginal gain to developer just equals the marginal loss to residents; this will happen if the developer has some mechanism to compensate the losers, for example, by offering some 'planning gain' to the local community. This could be achieved by an explicit auction of planning consents. Though this is politically unlikely to be feasible, planning gain rules could be made more flexible.

Current and Future Regional Trends

We consider regional prospects under the central Liverpool forecast of steady and by historical standards high growth (around 4% per annum). We also look at a pessimistic case of about 2.5% growth.

With supplies of land already in short supply in the Southern regions and much the same true of manual labour supplies, the strong growth we see in the UK economy can only be satisfied by spreading to the North where availability of both is plentiful. Land supplies in the North will be activated by rising land prices; in any case so great is the availability of land, that supply is likely to be highly responsive to quite small rises in price.

As for labour, underlying our optimism on unemployment is our view that manual workers will be compulsorily retrained under the Restart/ET programme; that benefits will be held constant in real terms and eligibility tests tightened; and that the growth in productivity will average 3–4% per annum. These factors will steadily increase the gap between manual wages and benefits.

Manual labour will also become more mobile with the greater flexibility in the rented sector and increasing home ownership. As this happens, manual wages will tend to be equalised in real terms across the country, just as non-manual wages are now; they will hence, in the very long term, cease to be regionally avoidable costs. Ultimately land prices will take on all the North–South locational (mainly transport) differential; only the differential will be wider because it is now on a narrower portion of value-added.

Some, but not massive, migration by manual workers will take place (limited by Southern land shortage). Instead more firms will migrate Northwards to take advantage of cheaper land and also (because of lower housing costs) cheaper wages.

Northward migration of business will be speeded by the spread of competition in transport, especially the ports. The Dock Labour Scheme has now gone and there is increasing cost consciousness among Northern shippers which could put pressure on Northern port managements to innovate.

Relative to the South, the North will continue to be dependent on manufacturing because of its large stock of manual labour, more so as full employment returns.

The size of the protected sector in the North is likely to rise at the expense of the South because of extensive relocation of government and industry overhead functions.

On the basis of these considerations, our projections for the Northern regions are that they will converge in performance on that of the Southern, up to the year 2000. Unemployment will by 1995 be generally low, and by 2000 the rate will be much the same for manual and non-manual workers in all regions. Land prices too will tend to equality across the country. Essentially, this outcome will have been the result of relying on market forces, with policy in the role of removing the obstacles and distortions to the market process.

12. How to De-politicise Local Government*

The merits of land- or property-based taxation and the role of local authorities, including their appropriate mode of finance, should be distinguished.

It may be that we should make more use of the Henry George land-tax methods in our national taxation; that is one issue and it is much bigger than local government finance, even if accidentally rates have been the main means of local taxation. It is an issue I want to leave on one side, to come back to it briefly at the end.

The primary issue of this article is what should local authorities do and how should they be paid for it? I shall argue that they should be regarded as clubs providing services and charging for them according to the service's characteristics. Some services are collective in nature and must be charged for by a general levy. Others are normal and either can be farmed out to private enterprise or the local authority can act like private enterprise and charge for them normally. One of the services is that of representation and interpretation of local wants; this is the planning function and requires special consideration.

This approach contrasts with the traditional view of local authorities as highly politicised mini-states, in which local government could achieve a mandate to redistribute income locally, for example, or to provide benefits and services in kind to favoured groups at the expense of the local taxpayer. There is no justification for this view in British constitutional history nor does it seem to have popular support.

Economic Efficiency

I shall argue that my approach is best for economic efficiency and end this part by discussing the reforms which are possible within this framework, and their benefits for employment and productivity.

*First published in *Economic Affairs*, pp. 12–16, October–November 1988.

The existing system of local government finance gives, as is well known, incentives to local government to provide services to client voting groups at the expense of the minority of full personal ratepayers, the business ratepayer, and the general taxpayers elsewhere. The community charge is designed to place the burden of financing *marginal* expenditure fully on those who benefit from it. Business has been taken entirely out of local finance through the unified business rate. Some 75% of local expenditure will now be paid for nationally, with about 25% falling on locals through the community charge.

The idea is that people will now get the amount of expenditure for which they are willing to pay – because extra spending will be pushed to the point at which the extra tax burden is willingly paid – and not one that someone else can be assumed to pay for. Yet the high proportion of nationally-subvented expenditure ensures a high degree of overall tax burden-sharing, related to income.

The involvement of the general taxpayer in local finance reflects the desire of politicians to equalise *per capita* provision of such services as schools, police and roads. Effectively, these are national services in which local government is an agent. It is these services that have catapulted local government into a powerful position politically. Contrast this with the development of local government in Germany or Switzerland. There the local power – whether the Land, state or the Canton – was primary and central government a later usurper. In Britain the central state was primary and involved local government in its own role, giving it delegated powers. Presumably, the development here reflects the evolution of a monarchical constitution into a centralised parliamentary democracy, whereas these other states were formed from federations of localities or principalities.

Distribution of the Local Tax Burden

Given our centralised constitution, it makes sense to ask how the overall tax burden is distributed. It does not make sense to ask how the local tax burden is distributed, because the central state has the power to override any local decision about its distribution of the tax burden. The debate on the community charge has often missed this fact. If the total tax burden is distributed acceptably, it makes no sense to look at the distributive effect of, say, the VAT on Mars

Bars; we would not think of making the tax borne by every commodity reflect its effects on the distribution of the tax burden. This would be a recipe for serious inefficiency in the allocation of resources.

The same goes for the Community Charge. It is efficient as it will be paid largely by those who benefit from the expenditures it will finance. Local government is being forced to act like a purveyor of collective Mars Bars, while the average tax burden is dealt with nationally.

This is not the place to discuss the provision of education, police and so on – but it is worth mentioning in passing that the principles of charging and privatisation apply to most of these services, as I have discussed elsewhere.

Let us focus here on the residual role of the local authority in providing purely local services, these collective Mars Bars. Many of these services are not collective in nature at all – that is, they can be charged for in a normal way without any loss of efficiency. For example, a local swimming pool can be charged for just as a golf club can, through a mixture of subscriptions and fees for services. Those who benefit can be individually identified by their desire to pay the subscription for the pool; their frequency of use will give rise to extra costs which can be recouped from them.

There are many such services that one can imagine local authorities charging for rather than financing by the Community Charge. Imagine how local democracy would work, using the insights of public choice theory. There is a floating local voter who weighs up the package of services he or she receives against the Community Charge. If the rival party out of power can promise a reduction in the charge without a diminution in the service, it stands to attract this voter. So it will propose to charge for those specific services that the floating voter may not want. At worst, if the floating voter does use these services, he or she will be no worse off, at best, if he does not use them, he will be better off.

Competing for Voters' Favours

The various parties will be driven, in spite of their ideological differences, to compete for this voter's favours; they will tend to move towards a common policy of charging or privatising specific services. Ideology will prevent a complete homogeneity of policy, but as we now see in national politics with the 'Labour Listening Party', the forces towards homogeneity are very powerful. This tendency is called in public choice theory the Median Voter Theorem. It is a key principle that predicts the de-politicisation and privatisation of local authority activity under the reformed system. No wonder one hears of activist local politicians who are thinking of retiring.

Technology places a limit on such charging. For example, it is probably just too expensive to design a club for bin services. Houses would have to be tagged according to which service they had paid for and houses that had not paid could create a health hazard. Road repairs, street lamps appear similarly to be examples of genuine local collective goods. One can see the Community Charge shrinking to cover just these minimalist functions of local government.

What of bus subsidies, a big local cost at present even after bus privatisation? These have two functions, redistributive and allocative. Allocatively, they induce people to use public transport rather than cars and so reduce the social costs of urban congestion. But this function can be discharged equally by taxing parking space, limiting it, or auctioning it off and penalising ferociously those who park illegally.

The redistributive function has been critical. It has been politically attractive to gain votes from the many bus users at the expense of the few full ratepayers. This policy is likely to be an early casualty of the Community Charge, because the floating voter, being typically of middle income, is likely to be a much less intensive bus-user than the average poorer user; therefore he will probably receive in subsidy less than he pays for it in Community Charge. Politicians will accordingly gain his vote by reducing it.

Planning Controls and the Green Belt

There is also a debate in progress about planning controls. The 'Green Belt brigade' want them to be rigidly enforced, the developers want them diluted. Is the local authority, here the vested planning authority, to use the environment or to frustrate market forces?

Here we have a major function of local government that will grow rather than wither. In effect the local people's property rights in their environment are exercised on their behalf by the authority. The costs of trading such rights individually, even if they could be clearly defined for individuals, appear to be prohibitive; indeed they could involve violence, for different groups might not be able to agree on terms of trade for allowing a new development on their street. Even without violence, there is the problem of the last house obstructing a major development; it pays massively to be in this position, to reap the potentially vast bribe for removing the obstruction. People will jockey for it in exhibiting unreasonable obstructiveness; the problems of preference revelation become impossibly hard.

Certainly, I know of no serious suggestions for allocating and trading rights to planning objections. Furthermore, the local authority can in principle represent local residents' views in a democratic manner. This is certainly not a perfect process but it may be difficult to find an alternative with legitimacy.

Suppose we accept the vesting of these property rights in the local authority. Then the work of Professor R H Coase showed that for efficient use of property rights to the maximum benefit of society, it was necessary to vest them clearly with one party only and make them tradeable. Graham Mather has recently suggested just such a scheme for auctioning planning consents, with the revenue going to the local authority as owner of the rights. He points out that already this is happening in a covert and therefore inefficient way, when authorities allow consent in return for the developer doing some local favour such as building a road. The inefficiency arises because it is sometimes not possible to find a local favour suitable or legitimate; and when one can be found, it may well not be as valuable as cash for free disposal.

With auctioning, the planning consent is traded at a price that compensates the local residents for the net extra amenity costs caused by the development. The developers will bid the auction price up to the point where it equals the excess profit from the development. Hence marginal private gain equals marginal social cost when the development goes ahead. Development is permitted – indeed actively encouraged – by the local authority until the marginal amenity costs are no longer compensated by the auction price, i.e., by the excess profit of the developer.

This is a workable market solution for the intense planning bottlenecks and controversies now plaguing the South of England in particular. The qualifications to the process are already built into planning procedures; these recognise that non-residents, as represented by the central government, also have certain rights. These rights include control of areas of exceptional natural beauty, wildfowl territory and similar important areas for the environment. Government restrictions can be placed in advance or on appeal. It seems unlikely that these super-rights could be auctionable. It is hard to imagine a legitimate sale, for example, of the right to damage the Lake District.

Urban Development Corporations

A particular aspect of new arrangements is the spread of Urban Development Corporations (UDCs), following the London Docklands and Merseyside experiments. The UDCs are mini local authorities for their designated areas, acting as planning authorities and collectors of service charges.

Since the local authority is reverting to its original basic function of planner and service provider, the UDC is quite legitimate if the property rights vested in it can be legitimately awarded to it – but these rights belong to the people in the area, as qualified by the wider national interest. Provided that the UDC is responsive to the interests of the ultimate right-holders, there is no problem. Of course these areas are selected on the basis of their degeneration and are recipients of special national largesse for other reasons; the local residents are invariably grateful for the monetary influx and this means that the key rights to be safeguarded are those of the general taxpayer. So little conflict arises; where the wider area has an overall plan of development, the UDCs must take reasonable account. In service provision, there is no problem, since the UDCs have no powers of taxation, and all services must be put out to competitive tender.

If legitimacy is no problem, what is the justification for such special local authorities? It lies in the obverse of the Green Belt justification. There is a national interest in obstructing development in the Green Belt; but no public body is needed to encourage it. In degenerate urban areas, again there is the national interest in revival; here a body is needed to avoid planning blight and streamline the injection of subsidy, the planning, the execution of works and the negotiating of change with existing interests. The last is particularly important. The Mersey Docks and Harbours Company, for example, successfully prevented development of the docks because of complex legal problems with central government, dock agreements and shareholder rights; only central government had the necessary powers while properly compensating the Company.

I have sketched out a world of shrinking, de-politicised local authorities, losing delegated powers in many areas, such as education, police and other basically central functions, to privatised operations dealing more directly with either the public or the government as its agent. They will tend to contract out and to charge for those services they retain rather than finance them by the Community Charge. They will retain the power to plan and could well be allowed to auction off planning consents, subject to the usual appeals and other safeguards. They will compete with each other and with UDCs in selected areas. It is a world in which the market will rule the local authorities rather than the other way about.

How will this affect regional problems of growth and unemployment? The reforms in local finance and related housing and labour markets are likely to be more powerful instruments of regional policy than the system of grants and loans that is being wound down. Essentially, the new policies harness and support market forces in the regional effort.

Already, we have a clear illustration of what market forces can do for regional equality if we look at the market for non-manual labour and its associated business activities. Non-manual workers are almost entirely home owners, free to move wherever their opportunities are best; their pay is also not close to unemployment benefits, so that if they become unemployed they are flexible in their search for a new job. The result is that non-manual wages are similar after allowing for relative housing costs; non-manual unemployment rates are also very similar everywhere. And there is an increasing influx of non-manual businesses to the 'North' seeking to escape from rising land costs in the South. So development is spreading more evenly in this part of the labour market. Regional policy is working through the market virtually unassisted, to push jobs where the non-manual labour is and away from the congested South.

The story is well-known to be different in the manual labour market, where unemployment is both concentrated and regionally diverse. Over half of such workers live in subsidised or rent-controlled rented accommodation, which restricts their mobility artificially. Many have productivity wages close to unemployment benefits. So the reforms must be judged by how well they tackle the problems of this market.

Unified Business Rate as a Congestion Tax

By taking away the local authority power to tax businesses, the reforms will remove a major disincentive to invest in the North, where business rates have been higher though the needs to attract business should have driven them lower. Some work I and my co-authors reported in *The Housing Morass* (Minford *et al*, 1987) suggests that these rates have contributed to differential Northern unemployment. The Unified Business Rate will go further and act as a congestion tax, especially as rateable values are revised; it will stimulate the process already occurring through land prices, but the beauty of it is that as development spreads the tax alters in incidence automatically.

Clearly, the complementary changes in rent deregulation and union power reduction are necessary to assist the freeing up of the manual labour market. Together with tougher attitudes to the work test conditions for benefit, these measures should improve the flow of manual labour to the South and the reduction of manual wages in the North, promoting local jobs.

The diminished role of local authorities in the provision and financing of services means that those ambitious for a land tax will not find much scope for their hopes in local authority finance. If a land tax is to come, it should be a national tax, like the abolished taxation of the imputed value of house ownerships ('Schedule A'). The Henry George proposal to tax land at its potential value has theoretical attractions; it is a pure lump sum tax, in no way penalising marginal uses. Yet its practical difficulties are enormous – for example, how is potential value to be objectively judged and will it not inevitably be influenced by actual value? How too are considerations of distribution to be brought in?

In any case, this is not the place to discuss it properly, since I have been dealing with local authority finance. As we have seen the desiderata for such finance are that it approximates closely to club finance; the beneficiaries pay a combination of subscription and fees for services. Property is not a natural measure of benefit for most of the local services involved. Many will be directly charged for as we argued; the residual will fall under the Community Charge which has the merit that benefits and payments roughly correspond for the relevant services.

The changes are large and significant. They are controversial because they cut across powerful vested interests. Yet they surely point us towards a more efficient deployment of functions and powers in this crucial area.

References

Patrick Minford, Michael Peel and Paul Ashton (1987), *The Housing Morass*, Hobart Paperback 25, Institute of Economic Affairs.

13. A Policy for the National Health Service*[1]

The National Health Service is in crisis. Yet those who call for more resources for it without reform carry little credibility. In 1947 the NHS boldly attempted to sever the connection between access to health care and the ability to pay. However, even some sympathetic academics (e.g., Le Grand and Titmuss) have documented its failure in this attempt. Unfortunately, it has failed expensively and is prone to chronic problems which cannot be solved simply by more funding.

The problems were inherent in the removal of health care from the market-place. If a commodity is offered free at the point of consumption, there will be excess demand; some rationing device must be found. The NHS uses several; some patients are not treated, some join waiting lists or go private, and more urgent cases are treated according to informal and often arbitrary priority schemes. Not only does this cause inefficiency in the allocation of resources, but it is also a cause of constant political embarrassment; the government is blamed for waiting lists and for particular failures of treatment, as recently we have seen with children in intensive care and constant claims by doctors of the inadequacy of resources.

On the supply side, there is monopoly power and politicisation of management, whose main object must be seen as coercing government and taxpayers to provide extra resources. Monitoring of costs by ministers is handicapped by lack of power over management, who have an interest in denying proper information for control and can engineer a headline-grabbing scandal of closed wards to frighten off too enthusiastic a search for economies.

Economic efficiency and political considerations both point to a greater role for the market, with government intervention reserved to ensure effective protection of the weak, the poor and the

* First published in *Economic Affairs*, pp. 21–8 (Part I), October–November 1988 and pp. 23–6, (Part II), December–January, 1989.

unfortunate. This article argues that this can best be achieved within a privately organised insurance system.

In 1984, I argued for privatisation of supply, charging for health-care supplies, compulsory basic health insurance, and direct cash help for those unable to afford this insurance (Minford, 1984). Individuals would then choose freely to spend extra private resources either directly on health-care supplies or indirectly through more expensive insurance. This solution I believe still offers the best prospect.

The practical questions are how precisely to arrange this eventual solution in detail and what steps can be taken to make it easier for politicians to introduce.

Background: The Health Industry

Health expenditure falls into three main categories. There is spending to maintain or promote good health; this is a wide spectrum covering diet, exercise, constructive leisure activities, preventative medicine, and anything else that forms part of a healthy life. While much ink has been spilt on the government's duty to spend on preventative health measures, beyond obvious things like free inoculations and public information campaigns, there is no case for intervention. Nevertheless, in a reformed NHS public health, hygiene and information on health issues would remain an important area of government activity.

The second category is care for those who are old or disabled or in some other way unable to look after themselves, but who do not require active medical assistance. There is already a substantial private sector and there is no good reason why the rest should not be privatised subject to safeguards against fraud and exploitation.

The idea of giving vouchers or cash help to those in need is also natural here; the gain would be that clients can shop around, and that they will find the most appropriate solution for their needs. Their own families may be in some cases the best source of home and help; the cash or voucher would not discriminate against this solution.

The last category is the NHS core-curative medicine dispensed by GPs and hospitals, both in the NHS and the private sector. This part is the most difficult to reform. In the Appendix to Part I, I list the traps awaiting the unwary reformer. The most dangerous is the morally charged nature of curative medicine; many feel it is wrong that an ill person should be denied treatment because he or she cannot afford it.

There is misunderstanding and confusion about the nature of most sorts of medical care. Some is urgent and unpredictable – such as accident medicine, but much of NHS work is elective. Most therapies are a complex bundle of skilled medical treatment, care and hotel conditions. This allows considerable flexibility and choice. Many people, and not only the rich, may wish to exercise choice over qualities of treatment. This would not mean, as some opponents of reform have argued, variation in *medical* standards, with poorer people getting inferior treatments; rather the non-essential elements, including timing, would naturally be tailored to individual choice.

The moral charge does not extend to waiting for certain periods or to being denied non-essential treatment, such as much cosmetic surgery, or to hotel conditions in hospital. This limitation on the universality principle fortunately gives some flexibility.

Politically, a major problem is the length of waiting times and waiting lists. As we shall see, the efficient economic solution will dramatically reduce, if not totally eliminate, this problem.

From a purely economic viewpoint, there are three main sets of problems. Efficient insurance and effective consumer choice require good information on claimant patients, on rival medical services, and control on the costs of satisfying insurance claims. Competition, efficient resource allocation and minimising the burden of taxation on incentives point to privatisation and charging. But finally, if direct help is given to those who cannot afford to pay directly or through insurance, it should not worsen the poverty trap.

I. A Reform Proposal

To satisfy the universality principle as seen by the typical taxpayer, a basic insurance contract should be devised, which provides essential curative medicine. It should define clearly what is expected to be paid for in different contingencies; presumably, from nothing for routine doctor's visits to all of bills for serious operations. But this aspect, the degree of co-insurance, would need to be carefully thought out, especially in the transition period. The contract would also specify maximum waiting times in these contingencies; again from long to short depending on the urgency of the treatment. In fact, as argued below, I expect waiting times to disappear as the industry organised itself to meet demand efficiently; waiting is essentially a feature of a planned and rationed health-care industry, but including maximum times in the contract would be a reassuring feature in the transition period.

The contract should then be priced, on the assumption that it is compulsory for the whole population (some will add to it, as we shall see). Compulsion is necessary to enable a fair actuarial premium to be charged, which requires a large pool of insured persons. It also ensures proper personal cover; health insurance can be compared to having third party motor insurance, in that it is a 'public good' that people should be obliged to purchase.

Payment of this insurance premium should replace one part of National Insurance contributions currently devoted to the NHS; the other part represents the implicit tax being paid to support the poor and those not insurable on normal terms. The precise way in which this support would be given, essentially as now, is dealt with later.

Some will wish to take out larger policies and will pay accordingly as they do now; only they will be able to contract out of, or convert, their basic policy and so pay only the extra cost of the policy enhancement, whereas at present they pay twice to some degree.

So far the proposal mirrors a number that are circulating, but more radical action is needed to make the new framework work much better than the old. Merely relabelling National Insurance and allowing partial contracting out of the NHS could mean that the NHS would be left with the poor and the less cheaply insured cases, so raising the average cost per case in the public sector. There would be improvement of some aspects, notably waiting times, and resources would flow into medicine through the private sector; fewer resources would be needed in the NHS because of the lower number of cases.

However, there could be difficulties politically in having the NHS seen as a lower-class service. Also, the service would still be bureaucratic and politicised, without competition either in the insurance process or the supply of the medical service. These problems are removed by the move to full private supply and insurance, to which we now turn. Besides competition, this will ensure that no one part of the insured population is concentrated with one company or in one part of the industry.

Accordingly, we now propose to hand over the operation of the basic insurance contracts to the private sector, as well as the bigger contracts which are already private. A competitive insurance industry would keep costs and premiums down by shopping around the medical sector and by competing on the premiums offered to the public. Premiums would be paid to these companies.

The government's role would be limited to that of policing the compulsory insurance and vetting policies for compliance with the compulsory minimum contract; this would included regulating competition between companies to ensure no creaming off good risks from a rival company's market. It could be argued that the state itself should remain as the provider of the basic insurance contract, since regulation would be complex in practice. Yet it should be possible to design rules of fair competition, much as is done in other areas raising complex issues; for example, takeovers and insider dealing, Lloyds underwriting, and the investment industry generally.

The precise details of contract design require careful attention and are not discussed in this chapter. Essentially, the basic contract implies not a single normal premium but a lifetime premium structure rising with age, with designated renewal dates corresponding to these age points; companies would compete by offering a complete schedule of premiums for each age group, and would have to accept anyone who applied. Those falling outside normal risk categories must also be covered on the schedules with a relevant price; as discussed later, the government will top up their premiums (just as now it pays for them directly) according to politically agreed criteria of social support. Regulation would in this way ensure that companies competed across the whole population, offering a complete service.

The Structure of the Medical Industry

We now turn to the structure of the medical industry itself. This has no need for public intervention, since the insurance contract has done all the necessary work. GP services are already private partnerships, but hospitals would need to be sold off to private organisations (including charities) in combinations that gave no group a monopoly in any region.

It is tempting to think of selling whole regions off as they stand. This would avoid breaking up current administrative units, with all their local expertise and information. The disadvantage would be the lack of competition within regions, which could be serious. Nevertheless, competition could be ensured by divesting each regional group of at least one major hospital (or possibly of one whole centrally placed district); the divested units would be sold separately to one or two major private firms operating across the country, no doubt already in the business of private sector medicine.

It is hard to predict what final structure would emerge from this sell-off – but probably, as in the USA, links would be formed between GP practices, hospitals and insurance companies to minimise administrative and monitoring costs. These links need not be ownership, however, they could be merely contractual. Probably, too, Health Maintenance Organisations would grow as in the US, offering the consumer the advantage of paying his or her GP a fee for health maintenance and not for treatment. In any case, subject to the control of regional monopoly, this restructuring is best left to the private sector to work out through market forces.

The break-up of the industry should ensure that firms negotiate with their own doctors, nurses and ancillaries as in a competitive labour market. Attempts might be made by some unions to exert monopoly labour power. However, the existing and new labour laws should be sufficient to break any such attempts; there is an international market in doctors, ancillaries are easily recruited from the unemployed, and there is a large potential supply of trainee nurses among non-working women. Below, I argue for the opening up of the medical schools to competition, to ensure free entry into the medical profession – ultimately the only way to break its monopoly power. Firms will also have strong incentives in the competitive environment to resist labour power, as the alternative is to go out of business.

Very likely the new arrangements would benefit workers in the industry without the exercise of any monopoly power, as the health-care business will undoubtedly expand rapidly once privatised. This is, contrary to what is often implied, clearly a good thing provided that the labour market is not protected from competition by union laws or restricted entry. The health industry is a potentially dynamic part of the economy (as in the USA) and it is not allowed currently to realise its potential for jobs and wealth.

Income Support and Exchequer Implications

The last element in this reform is the system of support for the poor upon whom the extra costs of the compulsory insurance contract would fall as an extra burden compared with their NHS-related National Insurance payments (including those made on their behalf by their employers). They would now also have to pay for those elements of health care not paid for by the insurance contract – for example, doctor's visits and medicines up to some modest level.

In my 1984 article, I argued that amounts should be added to supplementary benefit and to family credits to offset these extra payments; the extra costs in respect of children should be added to child benefit. This is still, I believe, the only practicable way. In that article I showed that it would not seriously worsen the poverty trap; the extra child benefit element involves no worsening at all, while the adult element does cause a modest worsening offset there by large rises in tax thresholds. Even this worsening can be avoided if

Figure 13.1 Income support for health illustrated

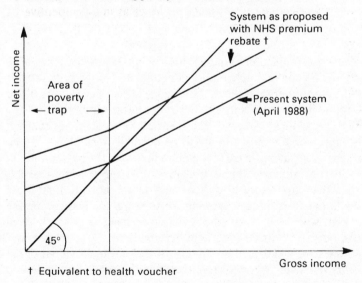

† Equivalent to health voucher

the extra family credit and supplementary benefit payments and National Insurance rebates are structured carefully to approximate to a voucher system. This involves subjecting the extra NHS-related supplement to the poor to withdrawal only when they qualify for the full NHS National Insurance rebate – see the illustration in Figure 13.1.

The reforms should yield a significant fiscal surplus which can be distributed in tax cuts or rising tax thresholds to achieve a positive improvement in incentives generally. While it is not possible to be precise about the arithmetic because there has not yet been a serious attempt to price the basic insurance contract or to assess the privatisation revenue, one can make up a schedule of public finance gains and losses as follows:

Gains: Recurrent saving of NHS budget.
             Privatisation sale revenues implying a recurrent saving of debt interest resulting from liquidating government stocks.

Losses: Reduction of National Insurance contributions by an amount equal to the cost of the basic insurance contract for the whole population (rebate of the NHS premium).

The cost of income support for the poor (defined as those currently receiving supplementary benefit and family credit) *equals* the difference between the cost of the basic insurance contract and the reduction in their National Insurance contributions.

Funding of those not covered by the new basic insurance contract – because already ill or too old to be normally insurable – can be thought of as paying an extra premium on top of the basic premium cost above. Much of this is transitional so the recurrent cost is mainly the extra interest on the public debt needed to fund these transitional costs, plus an amount for topping-up. This continuing payment will cover those who, even when insured privately from birth, begin with or develop above-normal risks. At each renewal date the state will top up premiums for those who move out of the normal risk category, with topping-up being regulated by agreed criteria (much along the lines of current sickness and disability benefits). The proposed system comprehensively covers the whole population as now.

The transition would be self-financing if the new system makes *no* efficiency gains; this is because one is simply giving people back the money they are currently paying so that they can pay for the same service privately and ensuring that the poor still get the service they are now getting at the same cost. The only change that costs extra money is the rebate to those already with private insurance, in so far as this insurance duplicates what is offered by the NHS. This element of duplication is likely to be quite small as existing private insurance tends to provide a supplementary service for the most part, leaving the acute and the expensive treatments to the NHS.

However, the point of the change is to establish a system of incentives to achieve greater efficiency. By introducing competition in supply and insurance, by allowing consumer choice, and not least by de-politicising management (so that it can take decisions free from media pressure on politicians to intervene), the efficiency gains could be large. This has been the experience so far in the privatisation programme. There are good reasons for believing the NHS to be an inefficient supplier and its obvious failure to satisfy consumers is unlikely to be entirely due to the fact that it is free at the point of delivery. There are obvious parallels on the supply side with the large de-nationalised industries like British Airways, British Steel and Austin Rover. On the demand side, the less close parallels are with education and local authority services (increasingly being charged for, especially with the introduction of the Community Charge). The essence of the market case is that we do not really know until the market has done its work in a way that no central planner can guess. In short, there are likely to be significant savings, available to raise tax thresholds and improve the poverty trap, or increase incentives generally through tax cuts.

How to Get There

The ideas outlined above have been designed for maximum flexibility in introduction; it is a privatisation-cum-insurance-voucher scheme. By using the National Insurance and income support system, greater flexibility is possible than with explicit vouchers (though these can still be used if politically their simplicity and transparency seem desirable). In such a sensitive area, a step-by-step approach seems inevitable.

From the public finance viewpoint, the privatisation revenue and the phasing of National Insurance rebates both create a source of financing to meet the largely transitional costs of those who will not be normally insurable.

Privatisation of hospitals can occur independently of the switch to private in place of state insurance. Privatisation could take place by region, starting perhaps with the prosperous Southern regions with large Conservative majorities.

Preparation for privatisation could begin at once with 'internal markets' whereby hospitals within the NHS become profit-centres competing with one another for the custom of Regional Health Authorities (RHAs); these in turn can spend their resources in hospitals outside their region. Restrictions on competition between GPs should be lifted.

Preparation would include proper accounting procedures in hospitals so that costs can be allocated across activities and patients. All patients should be charged according to their actual cost, making it possible then to charge other RHAs on a real basis.

Turning next to insurance, the estimated total costs of the NHS should be charged explicitly against the National Insurance fund; a part of National Insurance contributions should be earmarked as an NHS charge. This charge is to be thought of in two parts, the NHS premium and the NHS tax, and it would be helpful to make this clear so that people should not expect eventual rebates of the whole amount.

It would then be possible to proceed region by region. An RHA which had prepared full accounts and costings would be in a position to make actuarial calculations of insurance premiums for normal and high-risk categories of patient in its region. It would invite quotations from competing private insurance companies for its entire population in the first instance. It would then hand over its population to the successful company. People in that region would then be rebated their earmarked NHS premium; for those in high-risk categories the government would also credit them with the extra premium over normal. Those in the region on Family Credit and Supplementary Benefit would be topped up as described earlier.

One could imagine this as a second stage after the region had successfully privatised its supply side. The RHA would then be left as a private hospital-service company, with whatever commercial links it desired to GP partnerships.

The ultimate scheme leaves no room for tax relief, because there does not seem to be a case for subsidising health-care expenditure relative to other goods and services. Indeed, if anything the opposite is the case; we want people to remain healthy, so they should spend their money on prevention including healthy living, and the curing process should reflect its true expense to discourage careless illness.

Nor does tax relief play even a transitional role, for the same reason. It might seem attractive to give tax relief to private medical care in order to encourage people to increase their insurance and relieve the NHS of caring for them. But this would not, in practice, relieve the NHS of its role in caring for such people; the private sector is unable to cope in acute operative surgery or expensive treatments. Private insurance currently provides fast service for elective treatments, relying on the NHS for the rest. It is an add-on symbiotic service. People already are using this service precisely to speed up operations for which there are long NHS waiting times.

Giving tax relief would reduce waiting times for such operations, but it is a blunt instrument, not designed to mirror accurately the relative cost of private *versus* NHS care. It could develop into an unnecessarily large charge on the Exchequer, and would prove difficult ever to remove. Besides, there is a basic economic inefficiency in subsidising curative, as against, medicine.

An alternative proposal is to allow contracting-out of the NHS premium in return for joining a full private scheme. This is quite different, because it assumes that the private scheme would offer a *complete* service outside the NHS; the contracted-out insuree would forfeit entirely rights to NHS treatment, except at full cost. Since in our scheme here it is envisaged that the basic insurance contract would be competitively priced, the person who pays privately will get no advantage. There is no objection to allowing this sort of contracting-out early on. The contract will not undermine the capacity of an RHA to offer a large viable population to insurers, since they will already have people who have contracted-out on their policies, and can put them into the insurable pool.

The transitional movement towards the final pattern of provision can be expected to take a number of different routes. As the ideas and experience spread, the pace of change is naturally likely to speed up. The programme enables constructive action to be taken without political storms and yet goes in an appropriate direction for long-term change.

Political Issues and Government's Role

Once the new system is in place, government will have two main residual roles. It will regulate the content of the basic insurance contract (not its price which will be determined by competition) and will ensure that information from medical research flows freely and effectively through the population. Other information – about the effectiveness of individual doctors and hospitals, for example – is best left to the market, though the government as regulator of consumer standards generally will obviously take an interest in professional incompetence and fraud.

The role of medical education will need to be considered in the context of university reforms. It would make sense for the medical schools to be privatised and to charge fees, with the government acting solely as a provider of scholarships to worthy students. These schools would negotiate contracts with private hospitals to collaborate, much as now occurs in the NHS. By introducing competition in the schools, the restriction of entry into the medical profession, giving it its monopoly power, would be frustrated.

Waiting Times

The basic insurance contract was to specify all aspects of medical services to be made available and their refund structure. One aspect of great political significance is waiting times. Maximum waiting times are to be specified in the contract for different categories of illness. The NHS currently operates a policy of urgency ratings to regulate waiting times and practices vary widely around the regions and even within them. These disparities cause political embarrassment; indeed there is the suspicion that waiting times are manipulated to cause enough embarrassment to get additional resources.

The private sector gets its business currently from treatments that are not too expensive where patients would rather pay than wait the required NHS period. For such treatments NHS waiting time is determined by the marginal cost to patients of waiting relative to the cost of the private operation. For example, if a treatment costs £500 and the cost of waiting an extra week is £100, then the average waiting time will be five weeks.

Under the proposed new system, the NHS and the private sector will charge the same for equivalent services, so there will no longer be an incentive to wait for the NHS service. However, the NHS might opt to provide certain operations on a limited basis which involved waiting for beds to become free, and at a lower price (or insurance cost) than parts of the private sector which might offer the same service on demand. In the previous example, it might cost only £100 more to have the operation on demand rather than say in one week on the NHS; then the extra insurance will reflect that, so that NHS waiting time will drop to one week. Another way of putting this is that, if you go private now, you pay up to twice; in the new system you will not pay the basic premium if you opt out of the basic contract. In other words, the cost of waiting will fall to equal the true cost of *reducing* waiting, with a gain in consumer welfare and a probably sharp reduction in waiting time. Figure 13.2 illustrates this point.

It is likely that waiting lists as we know them will be entirely eliminated; indeed they are virtually unknown in the USA. The extra cost of providing a service essentially on demand subject to normal operational delays is probably quite small and waiting time would correspondingly be small too; the NHS operates with large queues, not because it saves much money, but because it is a necessary rationing device.

In setting the terms of the basic contract, waiting times will be set initially as a reassuring safeguard to reflect the average voter's trade-off between waiting for specified treatments and the cost to be paid, in the form of the minimum insurance fee plus the NHS support tax. Presumably the result will be similar to the average in the NHS today; non-urgent treatment will also be largely covered by more expensive policies that buy speed, leaving the basic policy to provide such treatment to those who prefer to wait. The political gain is that the maximum waiting times would be known and contracted for, so that any delinquent hospital would be disciplined. Furthermore, politicians would no longer be involved in policing delinquents; they would merely reflect popular feelings about the basic contract, pointing out the cost to those who want it expanded. Finally, the average voter would – as shown above – take out more enhanced insurance than now, have a much lower waiting time, and be better satisfied.

A private system might not entirely abolish waiting time but it

Figure 13.2　The demand for enhanced insurance under present and proposed systems

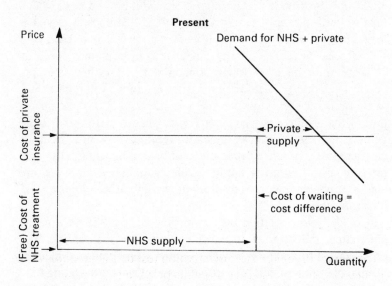

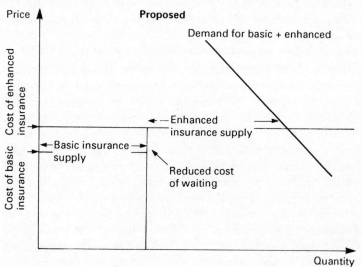

would efficiently price and regulate it. Average waiting times would fall sharply as a result of efficient pricing; while all including the poor would be guaranteed *maximum* waiting times by the explicit terms of the basic contract. Waiting would cease to be an issue for politicians.

A major aim of reform is to ensure that resources move into health care in response to people's demands. Again, just as with waiting time, the new system will, by bringing down the extra cost of buying improved service to the true extra cost, increase the demand for enhanced insurance for this purpose too – for example, to pay for more nursing care or better hotel services. At present the buyer of these extra services pays up to twice for them, a considerable disincentive. Here, too, we would see a closer correspondence between consumers' demands and health supplies.

Appendix to Part I   Traps in Health Reform

The free market arguments for privatisation rest on the monopoly power and resulting inefficiency of public provision, the denial of free choice to the consumer with bureaucratic choice inefficiently second-guessing consumer needs and creating queues. The current system also has the added burden of inefficiency from the incentive-reducing taxation needed to pay the cost of publicly provided health services.

Against this line of argument are ranged two main sets of arguments, which are the traps outlined in this Appendix.

First, it is argued that health care is a service that morally should be available equally. Waiting lists, with first-come first-served, not price, should be used to ration scarce resources. Political difficulties arise, reflecting these moral attitudes, if waiting times become excessively long for essential treatments.

These attitudes are inescapable. Any reform must not confront them or it will risk political destruction. They are subject to qualifications, and it is these qualifications that allow elements of a free-market solution as sketched in the current chapter.

It advocates the design of a basic health-care insurance policy, to be affordable by all, if necessary with income support. Essential, high cost and emergency services would be insured differently from low cost and inessential services. Acceptable waiting times will be defined in the light of necessity and cost. To ensure equality in essential health protection, the policy would be compulsory with the poor covered, paid for but unable to switch the money received into other forms of spending.

By definition, any voluntary spending above this minimum will be politically acceptable, since the voters will decide – if necessary they could do so by some form of direct consultation – on the characteristics of the basic contract; more they would not wish to pay for. But, of course, no one would be prevented from paying for more on his or her own account.

The second set of arguments relate to the possible inefficiency of the free market in health. It is said that information is inadequate for consumers to exercise proper choice, doctors have the information and must be regulated to prevent them abusing their powerful position.

In private health insurance, two main problems arise. First, people who are a poor risk conceal their true riskiness, and to protect themselves against this, insurance companies have to charge higher than normal premiums. In turn this discourages the people with normal risks so that a vicious circle develops, of excessive premiums being charged for the worst risks only. This 'adverse selection' problem can be solved by regulation, forcing a large population to insure so that premiums can be kept down.

Secondly, private insurance companies have trouble controlling the costs of claims, because doctors have an interest in inflating bills by, for example, over-prescribing or over-testing. The insured have no interest in limiting costs and may have an interest in inflating them in certain ways. This is 'moral hazard' in health insurance in its particularly dangerous form of 'third party effects'; insurance companies have difficulty in controlling doctors because of their information advantage.

These arguments have been deployed over the years by health economists eager to preserve the NHS, but they neglect the ability of free markets to produce market solutions. Doctors are hired by companies to check applicants; if doctors have better information they may well be able to deploy it effectively in this sort of screening, so limiting adverse selection. Consumers do not have professional information about the qualities of different doctors or hospitals but they can consult independent experts who make a living from such comparisons. Reputations for good treatment will become an important market force – just as for airline or drug safety. Third party moral hazard can be contained by insurance companies sending their customers to their own hospitals or by paying only according to their own competitive scale of charges.

Competition is a potent force in both the supply of health care and of insurance. Hospitals that are inadequate will eventually go out of business, as will insurance companies that do not ensure minimum cost in satisfying claims. Much has been made of the explosion of health-care costs in the USA; but this has come about largely because of the growth of Medicare and Medicaid, both state programmes where cost control by the state insurer has not been subject to the disciplines of competition. The private sector in the USA has produced a variety of competitive innovations, including the Health Maintenance Organisations designed to protect people against doctors' over-treatment in fee-for-service, and the vertical integration of insurance, doctors and hospitals in particular companies such as Humana. The power of the American Medical Association has been broken, not by government, but by these private developments. The US health system is no model but it does exhibit interesting features, that a free market here could certainly imitate. (The issue of malpractice suits is a US problem which is as potentially important here, NHS or no; its resolution requires the courts to take into account the full social costs of their settlements. Awards that are too high act as a tax on the whole health-care sector, because they induce doctors to over-test and over-prescribe to protect themselves, with the effect that the cost of malpractice insurance soars.)

These problems should by no means be dismissed, but for the most part they can be dealt with by the market. Regulation may also have a role to play as a last resort. We have seen in any case that compulsory basic insurance, included in our proposal for other reasons, compensates automatically any adverse selection for basic care. No doubt too the government will continue to exercise powers of consumer standard inspection in the medical as in other areas. A little regulation to allow markets to work is preferable to a totally controlled, centralised organisation like the NHS.

To conclude, there are indeed traps for the unwary health reformer but they can be skirted round with a little care.

II. The National Health Service – Options for Immediate Action

The NHS already has had one review, that of Mr (now Sir) Roy Griffiths in 1983.[2] He, it will be recalled, recommended that the NHS needed more management, but that the basic structure was sound. The government took Sir Roy's advice, and applied it, appointing managers to all Health Authorities. Yet today the problems are as bad as ever. The approach, of shoring up the existing structure, has manifestly failed.

The reason that it failed is obvious. First, there was no competition to spur producers to better efforts; instead, the existing vested interests – doctors, nurses, administrators and ancillaries – continued to share power and resources. They and their unions had an understanding, and the new managers, lacking powers to break this consensus, could at best go along; in most cases, they were recruited from the existing ranks of doctors and administrators.

Secondly, the consumer was given no say in the allocation of resources. In particular, GPs at the gateway to the NHS held a monopoly of access to NHS resources, apart from the desperate measure increasingly tried by consumers, of going direct to hospital casualty departments, with long waits and no guarantee of any better service. The result has been an increasing remoteness of the NHS from patients' demands, poor quality service and excessive waiting times.

The consumer's impotence also ensured that the cosy consensus among producers was under no threat from outside, except from their political masters; but they, of course, were easily dealt with by the producers, who resisted attempts to discipline them by cutting services most likely to cause indignation among politicians and newspapers.

Waiting lists are the issue that causes most controversy in the NHS. They have been used with great effect by the producer lobbies to demand more money. Yet the irony is, as we shall discuss below, that these lists are the result of the NHS's monolithic planning structure and insensitivity to consumer demands; and that they cannot be removed without changing the system itself, any more than Soviet queues for groceries can be removed without allowing market forces to operate.

A Cautious Model of Change

The current review must recommend genuine change in the system, if it is not to fail like its predecessor. And the signs are that Mr Clarke, the Treasury and Number 10 have seen this point, for all the bland reassurance in Clarke's speech at the Conservative Party conference.

The most obvious means of achieving competition and choice are privatisation and allowing the consumer to opt out, but equivalent alternatives with a less radical appearance are also possible and under active consideration.

The current front runner in the NHS review is an 'internal market' (that is, NHS units should compete among themselves for patients) with GPs 'holding the budget' for their patients. This means that GPs would choose and pay the hospitals and consultants on their patients' behalf. The government would then refund GPs like an insurance company, monitoring their bills against best-practice costs elsewhere.

True competition within the NHS would be ensured by letting GPs use private hospitals, homes, consultants and other services. This is equivalent to opting-out but it is being done by GPs, rather than the consumer personally. The effect is the same, to enable NHS waiting lists to be reduced by transferring patients to the private sector with an NHS credit. (To produce exactly the same effect, GPs must be cash-limited on each patient according to some NHS-entitlement formula: anything over that, whether spent in the NHS or the private sector, must be paid for by the patient, unless on income support.)

So far so good, but there is a major problem. GPs are a closed shop, notoriously uncompetitive and protected by their trade union, the British Medical Association. Resources have been thrown at them (doubled since the war, up 50% since 1978), yet standards have dropped by all available measures. Home visiting has halved in the last twenty years, use of locums has risen by a third in the last ten, and hospital 'emergency' cases which bypass the GP have risen by two-thirds since 1965.

The variations in referral rates (the worst fifth 400% higher than the best fifth) and in prescribing (with an 80% differential between best and worst region) tell the same story of huge deviations from best practice across the country. Another symptom is that a quarter of GPs spend less than 30 hours a week on the job. But if, like Yvonne Gibson, patients try to get their rights, they are refused by NHS GPs as problem patients.[3]

It will not be much use having GPs doing the shopping around if they themselves are under no competitive pressure; they will simply go for good incomes and a quiet life.

Under full opting-out, the consumer could switch from his NHS GP to a private GP, so ensuring true competition between as well as with NHS GPs. Something equivalent should be included in the new proposals. A simple device would be to allow patients to switch to a private GP and transfer to him their NHS drugs and hospital budget with them: patients could also transfer to him the current NHS charge for GP services (or 'capitation fee'). To make sure this produces genuine competition, the capitation fee should be set as low as possible (to cover no more than the most efficient no-frills service available): and NHS GPs should be allowed to charge for extra services, just like their private counterparts.

Though the BMA would object to this effective new system, hardworking individual doctors have much to gain and there are obvious attractions to the consumer. The proposals would be both a giant step forward and attractive to politicians.

There are many other variants of this scheme one could pursue to introduce competition and consumer choice. Indeed, many of the suggestions for reform published in the past months have been much of this type.[4]

Other economists have supported the particular GP model that is now central to the review.[5]

All these proposals have been influenced by the highly successful experience of the Health Maintenance Organisations (HMOs) in the USA, reflected in Professor Alain Enthoven's proposals to introduce them in an 'internal market' within the NHS.[6] The fact remains that we are dealing here with, not so much an internal market, as a total market to include the private sector, since in practice only the use of the private sector with its freedom of entry can ensure sufficient competition.

These proposals mainly differ in the extent of consumer choice. Some envisage the consumer opting-out of his NHS GP service into private practice, whereas others, such as Enthoven's, do not. As I have argued above, the GP sector requires the competition that only genuine consumer choice between them can ensure.

Two other sets of proposals, David Green's *Everyone a Private Patient*[7] and Ray Whitney's *National Health Crisis*[8] are more radical than these, in that like my blueprint in the last *Economic Affairs* (Part I above) they envisage private insurance and government income support. However, they too strongly endorse the HMO model as the likely market development under competition.

So the current of opinion is running strongly in favour of changes that will produce real competition across the health sector, with the government footing the bill for any opting into the private sector that GPs decided to do. Assuming that the review accepts the consumer's right to opt for an alternative to his NHS GP, we have here a viable model of competition and consumer choice, but one that avoids the trappings of 'radicalism'.

Some Objections

In what follows, I want to deal with some of the arguments advanced by those hostile to such a release of market forces upon the NHS.

Health care is a special product the market cannot handle   Health economists who support the NHS make a lot of play with the special nature of health care as a product: they argue that because it involves insurance and because doctors know more than patients, normal market mechanisms cannot work. Yet other products have the same characteristics and we would not dream of more than lightly regulating them; house rebuilding, for example, where we take out house insurance and builders know far more than we do, yet the market rules. Markets find ways of dealing with insurance and information problems.

This is shown not least by the world's biggest health-care market, that of the United States.[9] This market was finally freed of doctor monopoly power by a 1982 Supreme Court decision against the American Medical Association, declaring that AMA boycotts of the new 'Health Maintenance Organisations' were illegal. These HMOs and similar companies offer the services of doctors and hospitals to consumers in novel ways that compete with the traditional visit to the doctor for a fee followed by possible referral and covered by separate insurance.

For example, the HMO company will offer to insure you for your health problems for a fixed subscription, provided you go to their doctors and hospitals. However, by putting the insurance company and the doctors together they cut out the padding of costs in insurance claims. By shopping around for doctors and hospitals, they cut the basic costs as well. Finally, like house builders they advertise their own strengths and their competitors' weaknesses, so that the consumer has sufficient information about comparative performance to make a reasonable choice on quality and price.

Such failures in the American market system as there were can now be seen to be due to over-regulation which encouraged the monopoly power of the doctors: it had the effect of preventing the growth of a true market, such as has now grown up with remarkable rapidity since the monopoly was broken. So a market solution for the NHS – with its curbing of inefficiency and waiting lists and its provision of consumer choice – would work.

The NHS reduces waste in health spending   According to some economists, the NHS is an excellent instrument for curbing wasteful health expenditure.[10] They argue cynically that curative medicine 'is largely ineffective' and preventive medicine little better, so that the problem of health care is that of stopping people spending on it as far as possible, while satisfying their need for '(an often illusory) reassurance'. The authentic voice of the planner!

However, this view is not without flaws. First, there is its contempt for the consumer's preferences; yet who is to judge a person's need to spend money on health care and reassurance, including even the taking of 'unnecessary' tests, other than that person himself or herself? It is right to be concerned about waste by doctors whose spending and prescribing patterns are out of control: but the competition of the HMOs just discussed takes care of this.

Secondly, the manifest variation in hospital and GP performance across the country (cited above) and the evidence of surveys of consumer dissatisfaction belie these authors' claims of efficiency.

Yet, third, the Achilles' Heel of the NHS efficiency claim is waiting lists. We do not know exactly what the 0.75 million people waiting for NHS operations are suffering by way of loss in earning power or enjoyment of life; let alone what the millions of them lose waiting in NHS surgeries, outpatient clinics and so on. However, a figure of £2 billion per year of pure waste, about 0.5% of GDP, can be justified.

Time will be spent waiting for an NHS operation until its cost is just equal to the cost of going private. The average waiting time for NHS operations is just over four months and the average acute operation costs about £700; hence the cost of waiting four months is £700, or £40 per week. This cost is equal to welfare or income foregone. It can be thought of as the extra income, or welfare, obtained if the operation is brought forward by the waiting period of four months. Notice that £40 per week is about one-fifth of the average weekly wage, suggesting that people when pre-operative and waiting are on average about 20% less productive or happy than they are after the operation.

If this cost is multiplied by the 750,000 people waiting for NHS operations, the total annual cost rises to £1.5 billion, plus whatever is due to other NHS queues, perhaps £2 billion in all.

Waiting lists can be dealt with by spending more on the NHS   This is the cry of the NHS administrator, and indeed it is also a trap into which politicians too easily fall – as witnessed by last year's Conservative party conference, when promises were made to cut waiting lists by concentrating resources on them; needless to say, the promises cannot be kept, in spite of heroic efforts by the NHS and ministers.

Waiting lists are equal to average waiting time (set by the cost of going private as above) multiplied by the rate at which people are operated on. If the NHS can only handle a few people at a time then there will only be a few people in the queue; the rest will go private. But if the NHS becomes bigger and quicker, the waiting lists will grow, as more people join them from the private sector.

It is rather as if on a crowded beach on a hot summer day, an ice cream man appears and a queue forms. It soon reaches ten minutes in length, and many on the beach decide to do without, but now a second and a third ice cream man comes. Of course there are now three ten-minute queues formed along the beach. Waiting lists have risen in proportion to supply.

Thus we obtain the NHS waiting-list paradox. More spending equals longer lists, not to speak of more political ammunition for the critics.

Opting-out as under these proposals, however concealed, will be expensive to the Treasury   Waiting lists are the core of the failure of the NHS, but the bureaucrats say that they will eliminate waiting lists by greater efficiency and that there is no need to change the system in any radical way. How wrong they are!

The main enemy of opting-out has been the Treasury's expenditure division, which begrudges the £0.4 billion direct cost of opting-out (as those with existing private insurance get their NHS money back). Yet a rise in the tax base of £2 billion will yield the Treasury around £0.8 billion in extra taxes at current rates. To this can be added NHS cost reductions from introducing competition, which cannot be estimated but could well, judging by the gains from contracting out by health and local authorities, be of the order of 20%. By contrast, existing policies promise a continuous drain on revenues, as the inexorable demands for NHS supplementation proceed. Mr Lawson should over-rule the mandarins.

A related concern of the Treasury is with the timing of private sector expansion. That the private sector would expand rapidly under opting-out is in little doubt.

Regression analysis of data since 1962 suggests that the long run response of private hospital demand to a 1% fall in the cost gap versus the NHS would be a rise of 3.8%, with a 0.94% rise in the first year. Suppose that opting-out reduced the cost gap by 50% on average, this would imply a 50% expansion in the private sector in the year opting-out began with a 200% expansion in the long run and about 150% in five years. The equivalent contraction in the NHS would be about one-tenth of these percentages; about 5% immediately rising eventually to 20%.

The Treasury's concern is that the NHS could not in practice contract at this speed, so that there would not be the appropriate saving of public resources, and that total medical spending would rise, putting upward pressure on costs. Yet with the long leads involved in NHS reform, this concern looks misplaced; one need only look at the way electricity privatisation is being prepared for, now, eighteen months ahead of enactment, with the public sector generators cutting back plans and the new private boards already commissioning new private generating capacity. If the NHS is privatised at least partially on the supply side, then unneeded NHS resources could be sold or transferred to the private sector. Finally, it is not likely that there would be much if any expansion in total demand for medical services; eliminating queues does not alter demand in a steady state, it merely clears a backlog. The Treasury is quite mistaken.

Tax relief is preferable to opting-out Tax relief has been floated as an alternative to opting-out. However, it is inferior (if better than nothing on the demand side). Opting-out works by reducing the price differential between the NHS cost and the private cost. Strictly speaking, if the NHS service is valued properly, it eliminates the differential by giving the consumer exactly what he gets by value from the NHS as spending power in the private sector. Tax relief goes in the same direction. But it is not so exactly targeted on the differential and so it is less efficient – that is, it achieves less economic benefit per pound of tax revenue. First, it is worth more to a taxpayer than to a non- or low-taxpayer; and more to a high-rate taxpayer than a standard-rate taxpayer. Secondly, it is related to the amount spent privately, regardless of the value of what is provided by the NHS; yet opting-out would rightly give nothing if the NHS did not provide the service at all, and little if it provided it in small degree and with very long delays. Whereas if the NHS provided it routinely but with some delay, opting-out would give nearly the whole cost of the service. Tax relief subsidises cosmetic surgery as much as hernia operations; opting-out gives spending power for hernias but none for the cosmetic surgery. Finally, tax relief suffers from a longer-term problem which does not affect opting-out. If in time the NHS becomes more market-orientated and charges more fully for its services, giving rebates or assistance to the poor and chronically sick, then opting-out payments will decline as the differential of NHS v. private cost declines; but tax relief will be seen as for health expenditure, and it will be hard to withdraw. We risk then ending up with tax relief for health-care spending in general, when logic dictates if anything a tax advantage for preventative spending and preferably no tax subsidies at all.

These arguments reveal incidentally that tax relief would be less popular than opting-out because the latter's benefits are more widely spread and also bring non-essential operations for painful conditions within the reach of many ordinary people.

These proposals will provoke a political hornets' nest On the contrary, they will allow many ordinary people locked into waiting lists to get private treatment; as much of a master-stroke as was the sale of council houses to their grateful tenants. A political running sore would, as then, be transformed into a political running mate.

To understand the political and economic significance of waiting lists, it helps to think about the queues for basic groceries in the heyday of Stalinist Russia. (Those who would appreciate a really vivid picture should read *Galina*, the autobiography of the famous Russian soprano, Galina Vishnevskaya.)[11] For the ordinary Russian, the only way to acquire these groceries was to join a separate queue for each; he or she would spend most of each day queueing, just to get together the raw material for the evening meal. Exhausted by this process, they would have little energy left for constructive activity. But equally, this system rendered them helpless in the face of the party bureaucracy who controlled even the ration books.

Yet the politician who can offer citizens control of their medical services stands to reap an enormous reward. They will turn round and say 'Thank you; nobody before you told me this was possible. I will never vote again for the party that kept me in bondage'.

These proposals will create a two-tier health system   Since there is already a flourishing private sector, we already have two tiers (or more) of health-care provision. Allowing people to opt-out of state provision at cost would extend private medicine to the majority of the population and create a genuine health-care market for millions of ordinary people.

The market can be made to work in health care without sacrificing the interests of the poor and the chronically sick. The NHS gives them spurious equality by sacrificing the interest of the mass of ordinary people. It is an illogical waste.

Notes

1. This is a personal paper; no responsibility attaches to other individuals or to institutions providing me with financial or research assistance. I would however like to thank my colleague Richard Stevenson for excellent comments and Paul Ashton for diligent research assistance; and Dennis Boyles, Michael Grylls and George Margetts amongst others for helpful advice.
2. (Sir) Roy Griffiths, *Report to the Secretary of State for Social Services*, NHS Management Inquiry, 6 October 1983.
3. *Daily Telegraph*, 11 October 1988, p.17.

4. Examples include: Michael Goldsmith and David Willetts, *Managed Health Care: A New System for a Better Health Service*, Centre for Policy Studies, 1988: Madsen Pirie and Eamonn Butler, *Health Management Units: the Operation of an Internal Market Within the National Health Service*, Adam Smith Institute, 1988.
5. Nicholas Bosanquet 'GPs as Firms, Creating an Internal Market for Primary Care', *Public Money*, March 1986, pp.65–68.
6. Alain Enthoven, *Reflections on the Management of the National Health Service*, Nuffield Provisional Hospital Trust, 1985.
7. David Green, *Everyone a Private Patient*, Institute of Economic Affairs, Hobart Paperback 77, 1988.
8. Ray Whitney, *National Health Crisis*, Shepheard-Walwyn, 1988.
9. See the accounts of the US market in chapter 3 of David Green, *op. cit.*, and of chapter 8 of Ray Whitney, *op. cit.*
10. Notably, Nicholas Barr, Howard Glennester and Julian Le Grand, *Reform and the National Health Service*, Discussion Paper 32, The Welfare State Programme, Suntory-Toyota International Centre for Economics and Related Disciplines, LSE, May 1988.
11. Galina Vishnevskaya, *Galina*, Sceptre Books, Hodder & Stoughton, 1984.

References

P.Minford (1984), 'State Expenditure: A Study in Waste', Supplement to *Economic Affairs*, April/June.

14. Higher Education – A Simple Solution*

In all the chaos that has attended state secondary education, the plight of higher education has gone largely unnoticed. Yet in many ways the problems are more serious; for it is on higher education that we rely to produce the stream of managers and innovators who will take us into the 21st century. Of course, *entrepreneurs* are born, not created by education; but a host of less creative but necessary generators of wealth reach their full effectiveness only after higher training of the mind, whether it is in classics, English, or engineering. It is graduates who have the necessary flexibility of mind to assess changing environments, to know what tools to use in responding to them, and above all to be able to recognise when they are out of their depth and whom to call on for help.

Now all this is at risk. Higher education in Britain is in crisis, partly because of the bureaucratic morass it sank into after the Robbins expansion, and partly because the necessary pressure for greater efficiency has been applied without sufficient thought about the *framework* within which institutions could appropriately respond.

Let me illustrate. If a 'company doctor' told an ailing company it must improve its performance but did not suggest either expanding its sales or making any staff redundant, that 'doctor' would be fired. Yet that is precisely what the government has done to universities and polytechnics. Home student numbers have been restricted by quota, and tenure of lecturers has been retained; but funding has been cut. The only chink of flexibility has been to allow freedom to recruit foreign students at economic fee levels. Universities have responded in the only way possible. They have been recruiting heavily in foreign markets, forced by sheer necessity often to fill up with students of dubious quality in many cases. And they have cut back departments whose staff has left; high turnover subjects and

*First published in *Higher Education – Freedom and Finance*, IEA Education Unit, pp. 6–10, March 1988.

departments have been decimated by 'natural wastage'. Meanwhile, low turnover areas emerge unscathed. The resulting contraction seems naturally to be biased towards reducing the quality of staff, since there is some correlation between quality and mobility.

Brave talk nowadays of 'academic plans' to 'restructure' into necessary 'priority' areas is just that – brave, but empty; the universities cannot do it, because of simple arithmetic. Those who ought to go will not go; therefore those areas that ought to expand cannot obtain resources. The government created a Frankenstein's monster after Robbins; you cannot improve such a monster by chopping off its working parts.

Possible Action: Free Universities to Recruit Domestic Fee-Paying Students

A starting point is to recognise that higher education brings substantial returns in an advanced society and that returns are 'private', that is they are reaped by the graduate personally in the form of higher earnings. This means that many potential students would willingly pay for higher education if they could get it; for example in the USA 40% of 18–24 year olds are receiving higher education, and most of the universities charge economic fees, many being actually private. Here only 7% of the same age group are in higher education because the state has taken over this area and restricted the number of places. The result is a loss of welfare and economic efficiency, at which we can only hazard a guess, but which is likely to be substantial.

In Britain, the state has stepped in because of a concern that some who would benefit could not afford university. However, the result has been less than inspiring. The many who could afford university now get subsidised unnecessarily, so creating a large middle-class lobby for university funding, and many who would be willing to pay are unable to go because they cannot achieve the artificially high 'A' Level grades. Finally, one may ask how many cannot afford an education which increases their future earnings by more than its cost? Would they not be willing to take out a loan for such a proposition.

Suppose that there are some who would be put off higher education. One can imagine a system of state scholarships taking the form either of outright grants or of loan subsidies, limited by exam performance and means-testing to just such poor deserving students. No doubt, too, the middle-class lobby would put up such howls of rage if grants were withdrawn wholesale at once, that some transitional package would have to be devised to placate it; at the most this could preserve grants on the present scale and no more for some period, then be gradually scaled down. Given where we start from, it would be utopian to assume we could get to a restricted scholarships system in one bound.

Yet now consider how to deal with those currently excluded from higher education. Let universities be allowed to treat them as they now treat foreign students, namely to offer to take them at economic fees. This would make universities compete to offer attractive courses to those who would enjoy a return from them, i.e. benefit from a university education. We already have an example of what this can do: the University of Buckingham is Britain's only private university, offering courses on a full fee-paying basis. It is now thriving, and its students are able in most of the subjects it offers to take a full degree in two years, because this is an obvious way to reduce the cost of higher education while maintaining its benefits; to maintain its research output the university gives lecturers terms off, equivalent to the summer vacation, so there is a gain to students without loss to the lecturers, made possible by the efficiency from a competitive private operation.

By broadening the universities' markets beyond foreign students to include domestic residents, hitherto excluded by government rationing, we would not just be benefiting domestic students and the economy, but improving the universities' own efficiency, as they competed to bring in the extra students. We would also be solving the recurring headache of university financial crisis. The extra freedom for universities would enable them to earn extra revenues by redeploying staff who would otherwise be redundant but remain, because tenured, on the universities' books. Whatever may be said about tenure, retrospective over-ruling of people's rights is against our unwritten constitution; it was sound instinct that kept Mrs Thatcher and Sir Keith Joseph from such a step. So, apart from new staff where universities are bound to be circumspect in awarding tenured contracts, the abolition of tenure offers no solution; in any case tenured contracts are often necessary to induce people into academic careers from which they will find it difficult to switch to commercial jobs. As for buying out tenure, that would be hopelessly expensive; the compensation needed for an academic in a subject with no commercial use is very large.

The irony of all this is precisely that higher education ought to be, and would naturally be, one of our fastest expanding service sectors. Only the government is preventing that. Once it took its restrictions off, resources in universities would become fully employed and would probably have to expand further in many areas of high demand.

The Role of Government Councils for Research and Higher Education

Suppose we moved in this direction, freeing universities and polytechnics to compete for British students' personal investment in their own intellectual capital. Is there then a role for state institutions like the University Grants Committee (or its successor to be, the University Funding Council) and the Research Councils?

The Research Councils are easily dealt with. Research is a 'public' good because it produces new knowledge whose dissemination should be as wide as possible; taxpayers form a sort of club to fund this activity, on the basis that its fruits will be made available to the public. The case in principle is clear; the details are for the taxpayers' political representatives to argue out. Councils of some sort are needed to administer the programme of funding on behalf of the taxpayers but with the necessary advice from professionals in the field; risks that these councils may be dominated by a professional clique must be countered by broad representation of the taxpayers' interest and diverse professional expertise, policed by the powerful system of 'peer review'.

The University Grants Committee is another matter. At present it acts as a lobby for the universities on the one hand, and on the other as the universities' paymaster. With my proposed system, universities would become less and less dependent on government funding, so returning to their position before Robbins. The government would pay only for scholarships, and it would no doubt wish to specify in what areas these should be held; the UGC would have a role in advising on this and in administering the scheme. There seems to be no logic in the UGC handling, as it does at present under the so-called 'dual-funding' system, a large part of the money the taxpayer gives for research; the Research Councils have recently been closely involved in allocating this, and they might as well deal with it in its entirety.

This would appear to diminish the UGC's role, or that of its successor body the UFC, to a 'mere' provider of student scholarship money. Yet this money is likely to be considerable for some time to come, and even after a transitional period, it may well not be negligible. So it is a source of great leverage to the UGC under present arrangements by which it awards money to each university according to its own secret criteria.

The trouble about these arrangements is that they centralise power in a bureaucracy which can too easily be 'captured' by a group of clients, or just plain corrupted. If the market has its faults, they are as nothing compared with these. Anyone who has watched the recent UGC exercise in allocation cannot but be struck by its arbitrariness and vulnerability to who precisely is whose friend at court; for example who can say why Salford – a university emphasising many of the technologies in high industrial demand – was cut so drastically in 1981, other than that it had no allies on the UGC? A related problem is that the academic priorities urged on universities by the UGC are set by self-interested Committee members; how tempting for them to urge (no doubt quite un- consciously) the type of approach pursued by their own institution and to try to close down the approaches of close rivals. It is virtually impossible for even the most disinterested civil servant to police this sort of thing; for whom is he to rely on? Who is not personally interested? His best hope is to call in advisers from abroad; but even that is not immune to academic politics. Academics are clever people; not the least of their abilities is that of convincing themselves that what they do personally is of supreme importance and can only be done the way they do it. Schools of them naturally band together for protection and to inflict maximum damage on their rivals; because of their personal conviction such damage is meted out with a peculiar ruthlessness and arrogance.

Can we devise an alternative market-based allocation mechan- ism? In fact it is easy to do. Student scholarships are won by bright students; why not let them decide where to study? If the UGC has good information about the relative merits of universities by subject, let it be published; from then on, market providers of information will have the incentive to update it to satisfy students who wish to make the best choice. So it surely makes sense to limit the UGC's role to that of a channel for money to deserving students. This is not abolition of the UGC; but it is effective abolition of its extremely damaging current powers.

Conclusion

The higher education crisis can be solved by freeing universities and polytechnics to recruit domestic students at economic fees. This would stimulate them to compete, cut costs and expand, so generating more income and utilising their tenured staff effectively. The essence of this solution is so simple and yet so potentially effective that one naturally wonders why it has not been pursued before. The reason presumably lies in the grip that privileged middle-class voters and bureaucrats have had on higher education. Its expansion under competition would threaten the privileges of the middle class to obtain grants and to command salaries, the higher for the restrictions on other potential graduates. Competition threatens the bureaucrats' power to allocate funds. Beating such interest groups requires, first, that ordinary people understand how they are being duped and exploited; and second, that their key representatives mobilise these ordinary people's voting power to override these special interests. Oddly enough, in all this university staff have been innocent and ineffective; they are too weak to take industrial action and too unloved and intellectual to present a good popular case. The irony is that it is in the general interest that they are properly utilised in what should be one of the nation's most dynamic industries.

15. What is the Effect on Tax Revenue of Cutting Top Rates of Tax?*

In recent months, the statistics on the income tax revenue raised from people paying top rates have yielded (mainly in Parliamentary questions) the astonishing fact that these revenues have risen faster than the average, in spite of quite hefty cuts in the rates. The top 1%, whose tax bill in 1985/6 was cut by £1.5 billion (as compared with under the 1978/9 indexed tax regime), increased their tax contributions by 7.1% more than the average between 1978/9 and 1985/6; thus they not only recouped the £1.5 billion, they also added the equivalent of another £0.3 billion to their contribution. The top 5%, whose tax bill was cut £2.5 billion in 1985/6 (and whose marginal tax rate dropped on average from 50% to 45%), increased their tax contribution by 11.3% in this period, adding another £3 billion onto their recouped £2.5 billion.

These startling facts, on the face of it, point to a 'supply-side' explanation, based on people reacting positively to cuts in tax rates; such has been the general interpretation, for example with the *Sunday Times* and the *Wall Street Journal* adopting it in strongly worded editorials. However, dissenting voices have been raised; the most detailed rebuttal came from Peter Kellner in *The Independent* of November 17th. We have been trying to piece together the various bits of evidence; in this chapter we give an account of our preliminary findings.

It is a matter of arithmetic that for all this to occur these tax payers must have generated a higher increase in taxable income than the average; to be precise, the top 1% 11.8% higher, and the top 5% 14.7% higher (up to 84/5).

The rest of the arithmetic is that the tax burden on the average tax payer has also been cut by higher thresholds and cuts in the basic

*Written with Paul Ashton. First published in *Quarterly Economic Bulletin*, Liverpool Research Group in Macroeconomics, **8**, 1, pp. 31–2, March 1987.

rate; also rising unemployment, as Kellner points out, has lowered the tax take. However, this part of the arithmetic does not really interest us; we are concerned with the *income reaction* to cuts in tax rates.

The question is: was the rise in income due to the fall in marginal tax rates or was it the result of other causes? Some other candidates suggested by Kellner are:

1. that average incomes were depressed by rising unemployment;
2. that top incomes were boosted by the surge in *unearned income*, from stock market dividends and interest (capital gains tax is not included in these figures), and
3. that a sharp rise in demand for top people's services drove up their relative pay rates.

Yet the influence of unemployment is very small: had we used the *median* income, on which unemployment will have no significant influence, in place of average income, average top incomes would have risen 3% less relative to the average.

It is *not* unearned income. In fact, the opposite. Earned income of the top 1% increased (up to 1983/4) by 10% *more* than unearned income (for the top 5% there was no difference).

Is it top pay rates? The evidence is that these have risen a little more than average pay, but only a little: the very top managers (Group 1 of the occupational classification) have seen their earnings other than performance-related bonuses rise 1.7% more than the average in the last six years; for the next layer of executives (Group 2, represented mainly by consultants and marketing executives) the relative rise was 5.4%.

Together, these account for none of the top 1%'s relative rise in incomes, and for only just over half of the top 5%'s; leaving the rest to be explained by tax rates. Not surprisingly perhaps, because of the more dramatic change in their tax rates, this suggests that the top 1%'s behaviour is more affected by tax rates than that of the top 5%.

However, can we identify any *positive* evidence of harder work, less tax avoidance, or less 'brain drain', that could be generating this response? There is some exciting evidence of the first two. Performance-related pay among Group 1 and 2 employees has taken off; for Group 1 this pay has increased 121% faster than for all employees and for Group 2 142% faster; this has been due not merely to higher rates of bonus per person receiving it, but also to the spread of performance-related pay to people who previously just received salaries. This suggests not merely that people are working harder but also that they are being paid increasingly for performance, something that was not tax-efficient with marginal tax rates of up to 83% (or 98% on profits from share options).

As for migration, what Kellner did not do was control for effects other than tax rates. If you examine net professional and managerial migration *relative* to net emigration by manual and clerical, you find that since 1979 there has been an extraordinarily sharp turnaround. Professionals have begun to *immigrate* in large numbers (0.5% of employment in 1985), having been net emigrants during the 1970s (for example by 0.3% of employment in 1976). The turnaround in manual and clerical workers' migration is much less; from -0.1% of employment in 1976 to +0.01% in 1985. Both were, of course, affected by recession as you would expect; but the point is in the trend, which again seems to show the effect of tax rates.

Up to now we have been assuming that, other things being equal, top people's income would have kept pace with the average. Yet, it is almost certain that, without the change in the environment we have identified, top incomes would have fallen relative to the average. From 1970/1 to 1978/9 the income of the top percentile fell by 17.8% relative to the average; that of the top 5% fell by 9.6 percentage points. Though we cannot be sure without another careful investigation of why these falls occurred, that long-standing trend (a continuation from the previous 20 years of rising marginal tax rates) would very likely have continued had tax rates not fallen. The true rise in taxable income due to the rate changes would be as much as one-fifth for the top 5% and one-third for the top percentile. The tax yield of that extra income would be over £3 billion (against a 'cost' from cutting higher rate taxes of £2 billion); the extra productive value put into the economy we cannot estimate precisely, but it could well be of the same order (around 1% of GDP). The case rests for more of the same.

16. A Positive Theory of Rights*

What is a man's right? Does he have a right to a job? Does he have a right to enjoy clean air? To be spared loud noises by passers-by in the middle of the night? To commit suicide? To pass his property on to his children without penal taxation? To be protected against theft and physical threats? To have a vote? To vote in a referendum on some major issue – or on all issues? To have any religious beliefs he pleases? To have *any* beliefs? To avoid fighting as a conscript for his country on any grounds, on grounds of 'conscientious objection', or not at all?[1]

What is immediately clear when one asks these questions about randomly chosen 'rights' is that the answers where they are agreed differ across countries – even within parts of some countries – and have differed over time within the same country; and also that the answers are not, in many cases, agreed at all in many places.

Considerations of morality may well be associated with particular rights at a particular time and place, but 'what is morally right' and 'what is right' are different classes of things. It may be my right, say because it is within the province of my 'private life', to break a promise to my children, but it may equally well not be morally right to do so. It may be morally right for me to help someone to commit suicide, but I may not have a right to do so. Hence the title of this essay: I seek not a 'normative' but a 'positive' theory of rights.

Suppose a man wishes to establish what his rights are; how does he set about doing so? The answer to this is quite straightforward. He must find out how *the law* stands. His rights are what the law permits and enforces. Just to be quite clear about this, let me answer, in order, the questions posed in our first paragraph; my answers will be tentative (I am not a lawyer and, in any case, they may need to be tested in a court) and special to the UK today (even in some cases, *England* today).

He does *not* have a right to a job; he cannot force anyone, any corporation, or the state to provide him with one. He may offer

---

* Written in 1987. Previously unpublished.

himself for any job that is, or he thinks may be, available, that is all.

He has some – limited – right to enjoy clean air. If his neighbour, for example, has a large and smoky bonfire in a 'smokeless zone', he can stop him. But if a factory belches forth smoke which upsets him, he can do nothing about it, provided that it is operating within the law restricting emissions; if it is exceeding these restricted levels, he may draw the attention to the Department of the Environment officials to it and they *may* bring a case against the factory. He cannot compel them to.

Loud noises are like the smoky bonfire.

The law allows him to commit suicide without any sanctions on his inheritors.

He must pay penal taxation on his inheritance (unless he can avoid Capital Transfer Tax by signing it away very far in advance of his death).

He is *not* protected against theft and physical threats (i.e., the state does not provide burglar alarms and bodyguards). However, these are criminal actions and, if these acts occur, they may provoke retaliation by state prosecutors against the criminals.

He does have a vote (compare Singapore, South Africa or 17th century Britain).

There need be no referendum on any issue (compare Switzerland) but if there is, he has a vote.

He may hold any beliefs, including religious ones (but he may not *practise* certain acts required in some religious beliefs, such as human sacrifice) – compare Spain under the Inquisition.

He may not avoid fighting as a conscript except on grounds of 'conscientious objection' which are defined quite narrowly, principally limited to religious objection.

'The law' in fact is nothing other than the definition of 'man's rights'. It is a comprehensive 'statement' of what a man may and may not do; what acts are 'criminally wrong', what are 'civil wrongs'. The law defines these rights quantitatively too; if wrongs occur, then it specifies the severity of punishments and the extent of damages to wronged persons.

This is not to say that the law is necessarily written down anywhere so that it is clear at all points of time. It may have to be discovered by a court case, testing it or establishing it in a new case not covered by precedent or Act of Parliament.

We can take this much further. The way in which the law is

discovered by a man who wishes to know his rights differs widely across time and place. In many early states, the monarch 'dispensed justice' – i.e., made the law; in the 'Wild West' the sheriff was the 'law in action'; in a 'police state', the police have wide powers of detention and punishment and, in effect, make the law over acts falling within the scope of these powers.

But wait. We have suddenly moved from a discussion of the law (man's rights) in the UK today to speaking of 'summary justice' such as that of monarchs, sheriffs and police chiefs, as if it too were 'the law'. Can we not drive a wedge between the law ('proper justice') and the 'arbitrary' decisions of such people?

Suppose I am a member of a remote tribe. The chief is the chief administrator, the judge and the head of the police in this tribe. I steal, cook and eat a fellow tribesman's chickens. I am caught, brought before the chief, the chief agrees with accusers that I did it, and sends me to be flogged (twenty strokes), also to repay my fellow tribesmen double the number of chickens I took.

That is 'the law' in that tribe. I did what was not 'my right' to do, I infringed the law. Yet it was dispensed by a single person who was the unique head of government, judiciary and police. Suppose he had decided I did not do it – even though I did it, plain as a pikestaff (the bones were found in my rubbish, say) – and let me off. Or suppose, worse, he agreed I did it, but let me off, stating that this action is admissible.

It would still be the law. Other tribesmen might not like it and might try to change it, either by remonstrating with the chief or even trying to depose him, but as long as they do not succeed, his word *is* the law. How do we tell that it is so? The reason is plain; he has the power to enforce his word.

Let us make things worse still. Suppose I was a close relative, a brother, of the chief. He agreed I did it but he let me off because I was his close relative (he even says so, such as 'I cannot have my brothers, on whom I rely for support, punished like other ordinary people'). Then the next week, he punished another unrelated chicken-stealer with twenty strokes, etc.

We would say 'there is one law for the chief's brothers, another for the rest'. But note: *it is still the law*. (Even if it was not before, he has now changed it, and it is.)

Whether this chief would survive for long is an interesting but quite separate matter, which is highly relevant for our enquiry; but later. For now we simply notice that, as long as he has the power to enforce his wishes, his word is the law.

Now take the police chief case. Suppose now there are familiarly courts and judges, independent of the executive and the police. But there is an emergency law in operation, that for certain suspected offences (as suspected by them) the police may detain, interrogate and sentence without trial. If I am detained, etc., under this law, no matter how unreasonable the police chief's interrogation and sentence may be, it is the law.

There is another situation. Suppose there is no emergency law, but the police chief acts just the same way towards me, hoping that he will get away with it, perhaps because I am frightened and will not make a fuss. I now do make a fuss; I enlist a lawyer and bring a case against the police for unfair detention, etc. The judges of course award in my favour. The police chief is infringing the law.

Yet, what if I *am* intimidated (as everyone else is)? And the police chief gets away with it – repeatedly?

Here, I and others are failing to enforce our rights. The law is not being enforced. In its place, the actions of the police chief are in force, but if our rights are not enforced, their existence is qualified. In this and similar situations, we have to draw a distinction between what is technically the law and what is the practice (the 'law de facto'?).

Is this the wedge we were seeking? Not really. Though it is true that our police chief is operating unlawfully and his decisions are 'arbitrary', it is only helpful if there are the means at hand – even eventually – to prevent his operations and reassert the technical law. Suppose there is no such prospect. Then a man's rights not to be dealt with as he pleases by this police chief would be known to be unenforceable. Here we would refer to the law as it operates in practice, rights as they exist in practice – and we would not mention the technical law, now in desuetude (just as we do not refer to the Sabbath Day Observance Laws). These are now 'the law', 'man's rights'.

If the means are there to put a stop to this police chief's operations – say, because someone is willing to put himself at severe risk by taking him to court – then the technical law still has potential force. We have here competition between *two* 'laws'; we do not know which law will prevail, the police chief's or the other (society's, technical) law. There is uncertainty about what the law is (not about what technical law, but about what law in practice, is).

We can see this if we imagine how this clash might occur and be resolved. First possibility: the brave man goes to court but after two days of the trial, he suddenly disappears without trace and the case is dismissed for lack of a plaintiff. The police chief's law now prevails. Second possibility: the brave man survives and wins the case, the police chief is humiliated, and the technical law prevails. Either way, there is now a prevailing law and defined rights.

To sum up this introductory argument then, a man's 'rights' – or 'the law' – are those things he is permitted to do by the civil power, whatever that may be. That civil power can take many forms, from the autocratic whim of a sole ruler all the way to the complex and divided powers of a modern democracy.

Our enquiry could now take two directions. First we could ask: what is good law? What rights *ought* a man to have? And similar questions which, among other things, involve the morality of different laws/rights. Second, we could ask: what sort of civil power *will* occur, permitting what sort of rights? What are the sources of civil power? And similar questions concerned with the causality of different laws/rights.

We shall take the second direction, that of causality. Causality is logically prior to morality, for what is good must be conditioned by what is possible. For example, death cannot be bad or good; it simply is inevitable and the 'morality' of it does not arise. Nor will it be any use decrying a particular form of power or state, if it cannot be avoided. Furthermore, before we recommend that a particular form should occur, we must know how it could be brought into being, what difficulties this would involve, etc.

Many authors have considered what states, rights and laws *ought* to be. Our contribution, such as it is, will be to speculate only on what states are, are likely to be, and why.

The Basis of Civil Power

Civil power, henceforth power for short, is the subject of much art, particularly drama, usually describing the evils produced for those wielding it, as well as for those over whom it is wielded. 'Power corrupts; absolute power corrupts absolutely', we have been told.

In *The Ring of the Nibelungen*, Richard Wagner allegorises power in the ring forged from the Rheingold; gods, dwarves, giants and men struggle for possession of the ring. Originally, it is won from its keepers in the Rhine by the swearing of an unnatural oath ('to forswear love'). Then it is stolen from the winner; this illegitimate act brings a curse on the ring, which dominates the story to its ending in the destruction of the old world and the power of the old gods. The ring returns to its keepers in the Rhine, and the world to a new beginning. The implication is that power, seized unnaturally from its dormant state in nature, falls into the wrong hands and causes great evil, ultimately destroying itself and all who attempt to control it; only a state of nature, in which power is *not* wielded – at least in a manner that involves 'domination', whatever that may be – will cause no harm and survive.

Contrast this vision with that of Thomas Hobbes: in the state of nature life is 'nasty, brutish, and short'. Power is necessary to prevent men from killing and thieving from each other. Men give it to some man or body of men for this purpose.

Robert Nozick's argument follows the same lines as Hobbes'. Men surrender some of their 'natural rights' (i.e., they submit to a civil power) in order to achieve protection for their remaining rights.

There are three questions we would like to answer about power:

1. Must it exist at all, and if so, why?
2. What type of person or group will hold it and why?
3. How much power will he or they have, and why?

The first question is one to which many great minds have addressed themselves: namely, the existence of power or the 'state' at all and its reasons. The widespread answer that has emerged has been the theory of the social contract, as set out, for example, in Nozick and summarised above.

The second and third questions have been addressed less, and less systematically. Clearly they form a large part of the subject matter of history; but historians have preferred (perhaps rightly) to chronicle the particular and not to seek general explanations. Political theorists too have tended to concentrate on the answers for given institutions, mostly in modern times those of democracy and, in earlier times, those of monarchy (in Greek times those of the 'city state'). One general theory has been proposed by Michael Oakeshott. He argues that if a society is composed for the most part of independent-minded people who prize their self-fulfilment, it will tend to be a 'societas' where the citizens have submitted merely to a set of rules in the pursuit of their own interests. If it is composed of people who value security above self-fulfilment, it will tend to be a 'universitas'; here the citizens regard the state as the active provider of common economic and physical security. To Oakeshott, the nature of the state thus derives from the character of its citizens. We shall consider this seminal idea further below.

We shall attempt to find general answers. These will necessarily be about long-run tendencies, not particular ('short-run') situations. We shall try to formulate 'laws' of the form: such and such will happen 'in the end' under such and such (rather general) conditions. This type of theorising is common in economics when 'equilibrium outcomes' are investigated – i.e., outcomes, which once arrived at, are self-perpetuating (as distinct from others which are self-destructive). We shall also have something to say – though probably rather sketchy – about whether these equilibrium outcomes are likely to be arrived at and, if so, how; what in economics is commonly described as 'stability analysis' (i.e., will the political system be driven towards the 'stable', self-perpetuating state or away from it into a series of self-destructive states?).

The Conditions for Power to Emerge

The question: 'must power exist?' is generally taken to be co-extensive with 'can a state of nature (in which there is no power) be self-perpetuating?' We shall see later that the questions are not coextensive but we shall start as if they are.

The usual answer to the latter question is: 'no; a state of nature cannot survive.'

But this does not seem to be correct.[2]

Let us begin by constructing a counter-example. Imagine a community of smallholders. Each, with his family, farms his own plot. With given sized plots, each farms this plot to the point where the extra crops yielded by a given extra effort (a diminishing output) just equals the pain of that extra effort.

Each is concerned to protect his possessions, so he buys weapons, dogs, etc., sufficient to deter any other farmer from thieving or taking forcibly from him.

Now we seem to get in a difficulty. Must he not guard against a combination, by all the others, to despoil him and divide up his possessions between them? That indeed he must do. For, if he does not, the others have an incentive to pick him off.

This is the worst aggression (internally within the community) he can face. So he arms himself sufficiently to deal with it.

He may do this in various ways. He may buy powerful enough weaponry, for himself and his family to operate. Or he may enter into a private alliance with other farmers (at most, half of them would be enough) for mutual defence in this contingency. Or he may enter into an alliance with a few farmers and invest in (less powerful) weaponry.

How will such an alliance be 'policed' by its members? It is policed by itself; each member comes to the help of a threatened member because if he fails to do so, the agreement is that he will cease to obtain the help of the alliance. With such an agreement, it pays no member to avoid helping the threatened member; for, if he helps, he is one of many risking little, whereas if he does not, he loses the help of the others and risks being threatened himself without help. Since it pays each to behave so, then the others will expect this behaviour from each other; they will then have confidence in the agreement. Therefore the agreement will be kept and expected by all to be kept, so providing security.

Exactly how large such alliances will be, will depend on the costs of forming them relative to the costs of defending oneself through weaponry alone. Technology and geography will have much to do with it. Suppose there is a super-automatic machine-gun-cum-mortar which, in the hands of one family, can rapidly destroy a large attacking force from a place (a 'hardened' shelter say) which cannot be reciprocally attacked by that force. Suppose too that farms are separated by large distances across mountainous country. Then alliances will be minimal, weaponry will be the principal defence of our farmer.

We have described a community in which the members exercise mutual deterrence via a combination of alliances and domestic weaponry. There is no 'power' so far in this community; it is in a state of nature.

We must now consider the *external* aspects of the community. Suppose now there is a 'community' in a contiguous region; to make it meaningful, suppose that it is separated by a large mountain range so that contact is rare and difficult. How does our original farmer react to this? Does he say, 'Now, not only could all the farmers in my community gang up on me, but so could they *plus* those in the next community'? How would he modify his defence plan?

He will argue that the members of the other community will also be in a state of mutual deterrence. They will therefore have no incentive to attack each other, but they will have an incentive to join and attack members of his community, including him, if those members are inadequately defended against such a concerted attack. His own alliance-cum-weaponry is designed to counter an internal threat; the agreement does not cover external threat (it could not because the chances of defeat are too great for the members to have an incentive to deliver help, rather than to surrender or combine with the attacking outsiders).

He must now install further defences. This time, the maximum threat is of all the members of the other community plus those members of his own community who are not in his alliance, plus at worst (under pressure from such strength) even members of his own alliance.

Can this massive threat be countered without *power*? Surely it can. For he needs merely to supplement his alliance and weapons with a super-alliance between the alliances within his community. (Grant that technology is unlikely to provide weaponry sufficient for him alone to take on the maximum threat described in the last paragraph.) This super-alliance is an agreement about external threat only; it is subject to the same policing as that of the single alliance. This super-alliance may also specify additional weaponry to be held by members of each alliance.

The super-alliance agreement specifies that if any alliance is attacked by an 'outsider', the other alliances will come to their aid.

We now have specified mutual deterrence, both between members of a community, and between communities. Our state of nature is governed *by the principle of mutual deterrence*.

There is no 'power' in this set-up; no president, no council, no-one who can give orders to anyone else. There is therefore no 'state', only a state of nature in which the balance of terror keeps the peace. (There is however 'law' as we shall see.)

Compare with this idealised equilibrium the present state of international relations. Here too there is no international government or 'power'. The peace is kept, if it is kept, by mutual deterrence of nations.[3]

Figure 16.1   Alliance configurations illustrated

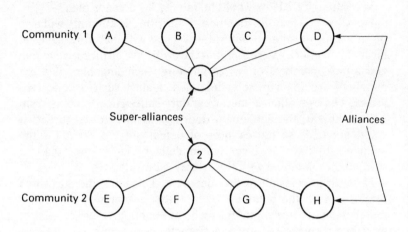

A, B, C, D = *groups of citizens forming alliances in Community 1*
E, F, G, H = *groups of citizens forming alliances in Community 2*
1, 2 = *super-alliances of A, B, C, D and E, F, G, H*

According to Locke, there are 'inconveniences of the state of nature', which lead men to create a civil power. What are they? After all, *nations* can coexist, without an international civil power, with alliances (NATO, Warsaw Pact, CENTO, etc.), and through mutual deterrence; why cannot *individuals*?

The parallel is striking. Think of NATO as a 'super-alliance' of a western 'community'; within it, there are various alliances of nations for the defence of particular interests (think of the Franco-German alliance over the nature of the Common Market). In the event of war within Europe itself, one can think of implicit alliances that would be called on (historically, there is plenty to go on). One may analyse the 'Eastern Bloc' similarly: the Warsaw Pact is[4] a 'super-alliance', and within the Bloc there are various implicit or explicit alliances.

As far as one can see, this international set-up is self-perpetuating. There is no pressure in the system for an international civil power. Such international institutions as there are (the UN, the World Bank, the IMF, and so on) have no power to *bind* any nation, at least in their own right; only if they are backed by the power of the larger nations composing them and not opposed by other large nations, is there any element of compulsion (e.g., the UK/French/Israeli withdrawal from Suez was compelled by US action, supported by the USSR), hence the compulsion comes from the nations not these institutions.

But we go too fast. One may grant that several super-alliances do not have to become one state. Yet, is there a tendency for a super-alliance such as NATO to become a state? NATO has a command headquarters which houses a bureaucracy for the co-ordination of the actions by member nations in the event of war; this includes preparation for war, exercises and so on. NATO has one 'super-power' in it, the USA, and several lesser powers, two of them with nuclear strike capacity. Is it then more than an alliance? Does it have a government – the USA perhaps acting through NATO command? Clearly not. If an attempt were to be made to impose such 'government' on the other members of NATO, they would combine in an alliance to prevent it; indeed, some have seen the EEC as just such a countervailing political force within the Western Bloc.

The case of the Warsaw Pact is an instructive contrast. Here the super-power within the Pact, the USSR, clearly constitutes a sort of government; opposition from other nations has been crushed by it. They are under effective occupation by Soviet forces, etc. This sort of civil power – that achieved by conquest and repression – will be a major object of our enquiry. Suffice it to say that the Warsaw Pact case shows that a super-alliance of nations *can* be (effectively) a state; but it is no part of my purpose to argue against this, either for nationals or for individuals. It is obvious enough after all! We are surrounded by examples of civil power! My purpose here has been to argue that, at least at the level of nations, it is not *inevitable* that a super-alliance becomes a state; the NATO example sees to that.

Let us return to the individual in the state of nature. My argument is that it is *possible to imagine* a community where a state of nature is an equilibrium state. This community consists of a set of alliances, within a super-alliance (of alliances); the alliances mutually deter individual acts of aggression, the super-alliance deters external acts of aggression.

To fix this state in our mind's eye as an equilibrium, let us depict the life of a typical farmer. He goes about his private business, working his plot of land (his 'ranch'), going to market to buy tools, animals and materials, and to sell his produce. In these activities, he knows that if his possessions are stolen or he is attacked, he has his weapons and his alliance to call on.

Suppose this community is fairly recent; then he will go about his business with some trepidation. When he goes to remote parts of his property or away to market, he may go well-armed and take his most ferocious dog with him, or even only go with his grown-up son or a neighbour.

However, suppose the community has been going a long time (he was born into it). People have *learned* that it does not pay to rob or attack because the results are unpleasant: restitution and retribution exerted by the victim's allies. Our farmer now has a sense of security. He will go about his business with little protection (only enough for the outside chance that some fool or newcomer who does not understand the set-up will go for him) or even none at all (he may decide to give in if attacked, secure in the knowledge that his allies will get his property back for him later).

We seem to have here, if not a Utopia, at least some sort of Arcadia. Farmers go about their business protected only by 'deterrence'. There are no private armies on the streets or out in the ranches; our farmers do not ride shotgun everywhere. There is but a stock of weaponry at home, to be used in mutual action by an alliance if one of its members is robbed or attacked. Our farmers own things in the state of nature which they turn into other things (produce) and voluntarily exchange with others for things they need.

This vision is said by Locke to be fraught with 'inconveniences'. The most detailed attack on it has been launched by Nozick, who argues that our alliances or 'mutual protective associations' will tend to give way to one *dominant* protective association (a 'government' or 'state'). The inconveniences he details are:

1. everyone in our 'alliance' is on call to serve and how will it be decided who shall serve?

2. any member may call out his allies by saying he has been wronged; he may do so in order to aggress on a neighbour.
3. members may dispute between each other; how can the alliance deal with this?

He says (1) will be solved by *hiring* people to perform the protective function.

(2) will be solved by the alliance following a certain *procedure* to establish whether it should act after a complaint.

(3) may be solved by non-intervention; but this 'would bring discord' and so a procedure would also emerge for this, to establish which member was correct and should be upheld by the alliance.

If (1) – (3) happened, Nozick argues, then alliances would differ in the quality and price of the 'service' they offered to members. Members would shop around, eventually joining the 'best', i.e., that which followed the 'most impartial' procedures and employed the least cost/most effective protective force. Thus, we would have protective firms offering

1. competing private armies
2. competing private courts for members' disputes and for deciding which complaints against non-members to pursue.

Nozick imagines the competitive process between several such firms. He presumes that they have each attracted a reasonable clientele by offering 'competitive' value; i.e., the service of each is forced by competition to be equivalent in value, but then he asks what happens if clients belonging to different firms have conflicting aims? There are three possibilities

1. the firms fight and one always wins; it then gets all the clients, it is dominant.
2. they fight and one firm wins battles centred in one geographical area, the other in another area. Each then becomes dominant in one geographical area.
3. they fight regularly and each wins roughly an equal number of times. To avoid this costly procedure for random wins, they set up a third party to decide on conflicting claims, this being a cheap procedure with an equally random outcome (the third party would have to be random in decision between the two firms, to be acceptable).

(1) produces a dominant firm in a 'united' super-alliance. (2) produces a dominant firm in each alliance. (3) produces equal firms subject to a federal appeals court within the super-alliance, upheld jointly by them. In all cases, people in a geographical area are under a 'common system that judges between their competing claims and *enforces* their rights'. The reason for this monopoly emerging is that protection is *relative*; it 'depends upon how strong others are'. This common system Nozick calls the 'ultra-minimal state'.

Nozick's argument is not convincing. Let us go back to the original inconveniences he lists.

Consider (2) – the member who tries to call the alliance out for unreal 'wrongs'. This is a trivial problem. The agreement setting up the alliance would have to have specified what constituted the grounds for action. Nozick's answer is correct but implied already. Any agreement must be *about* something; in this case a properly specified agreement will say, explicitly or implicitly, what is agreed when: a member could not call out the alliance for a ground not specified in it.

(3) is the same. The agreement may either treat intermember disputes as not within its province, or specify a procedure for deterring them. The former is the most likely; and it by no means follows that it will weaken the alliance, for each member in dispute still has the same incentive to join any alliance action (the incentive being to preserve his own right to alliance help). Two members can perfectly well prosecute a private quarrel and still bury it temporarily for a common cause.

As for (1), it is *possible* that the alliance will hire specialised people (as well as buying weapons, dogs, etc.); but it is by no means necessary. For such hiring carries costs; there are overheads of maintaining a specialised force and there are problems of incentives. How much must you pay a hireling to ensure he protects you

a. when his life may be endangered by it
b. when he may be bribed by your enemy to come over to his side at the critical moment?

Protection is indeed a special product; its purchase involves severe problems of 'moral hazard' (if you pay him by results, he may be dead before he can be paid, and if you pay him in advance, why should he stay and fight?). Its specialness implies that, in our state of nature, reliable protection if unlikely to be so provided, and is probably better provided by a *roster* of well-motivated alliance members.

However, suppose these problems can be overcome and the alliance hires some people as part of their defence (they will be unlikely to repose more than part in their hands). These people will be under the full control of the alliance. They are not a 'firm' but 'factors of production'. This means, unlike in Nozick's example, they cannot offer their services elsewhere *and* work for the alliance; such a conflict of interest would reduce the protection they offer.

Now we may replicate Nozick's 'competitive process'. Each alliance has its resources and procedures and faces the others. For an alliance to be effective it must deter at a reasonable cost; otherwise its members will desert it. Thus, competition *will* ensure comparable deterrence and resource cost.

Deterrence implies that a wrong to a member must result in unacceptable damage to the wrongdoer; 'unacceptable' means 'high relative to the gain to the wrongdoer'. Suppose that each alliance achieves this competitive deterrence level at a reasonable resource cost. Notice that this does not mean each is as strong in *attack* as the others are in *defence*; the deterrent implies attack is very costly to the attacker even if equally strong as a defender. So a *slightly* stronger defence organisation would not effectively *challenge* other ones by provoking quarrels with its members (as Nozick appears to suggest) and so achieve dominance by 'winning battles'.

Suppose that each alliance agrees about what is a right and what is a wrong (its procedures lay it down). Then any member of an alliance creating a wrong will be penalised by his *own* alliance in order to avoid provoking the deterrent (costly for them all); this alliance will go to the other and say 'look, we are very sorry for the behaviour of our member; we have disciplined him and here is restitution and compensation for your member. Please do not attack us with your deterrent'. Members of each alliance will have a strong incentive not to wrong members of other alliances.

Deterrence will in this situation mean no battles, and wrongs (occurring, say, by accident or because of a bad member trying his luck) automatically righted by the wrongdoing side.

Now take Nozick's 'crunch case' – the alliances conflict in their assessment of what is a wrong/right for their members. Will they *ever* do battle over such a thing? No, they will not, because by definition the deterrent exacts greater costs than the gains from the wrong. Rather than battle with large costs to both sides, they will make an agreement about what *is* to be decided as right and wrong, on a procedure as Nozick suggests (it need not be a court but simply an ad hoc meeting to bargain over each case) – or there could be a monthly 'clearing' meeting to bargain over outstanding cases.

What do we have other than a set of *voluntary* agreements by individuals? They join *alliances* but are free not to do so. Those alliances are 'bound by' (i.e., create incentives to carry out) agreements which specify rights and wrongs (and procedures for resolving them if necessary).

How many will there be? Will there be different alliances for protecting against different wrongs? We do not know. Answers to the first question depend upon the costs of forming and preserving alliances (geography, mainly?) and the costs of firepower (technology, mainly?). They will also depend (following Oakeshott) on the 'independence' of the people; but we must assume about any people that they would rather have more freedom than less, and therefore belong to a smaller alliance than a larger, since the larger the alliance the more rights they will have to concede to others in return for others' taking up obligations on their behalf. Maximum freedom would be obtained in an 'alliance' of only oneself and one's family, provided technology and geography (a farm in a sheltered valley, plus some devastating rocketry inside the walls?) permitted this to give security.

To the second question (the variety of alliances), the answer depends upon how varied are the activities of the farmers; one can imagine sheep farmers having different protective alliances from corn farmers, for example. There need be no 'dominant' alliance at all, in any geographical (or other type of) area. We have a community of several or many contiguous (possibly interspersed) alliances, naturally deterring and coexisting. It is a community of 'neighbourhood/interest group' coalitions, each prevented from attacking the other by the fear of mutual decimation.

Have we, though, introduced an 'ultra-minimal state' by the backdoor? For have we not derived a common (i.e., implemented) system of wrongs and rights; that is, either a common concept of wrong or, where differences exist, agreement on how to resolve them? What is more, have we not seen that members of each alliance will be forced by their own agreements to obey this common system? (This applies just as much to the man who is not in an alliance but is on his own; he can be treated as a one-man alliance.)

Yes and no. We have actually derived the 'common law', as it is called in the UK, but *not* a state of *any* sort. We have here a collection of free citizens who *in* the state of nature submit to, indeed create, a common law to bind themselves by. There is no civil power anywhere, only their own voluntary agreements policed by themselves, to force the implementation of that law.

This result is similar to Nozick's – in that, all accept a 'common system that judges between their competing claims' and their rights are enforced – yet it is also crucially different – in that, there is no 'dominant enforcement agency', no government. We have, to repeat, derived a common law, which is enforced, but no state, no monopolist, to enforce it; there is no power in our community.

This result of ours, in contrast to Nozick's, implies that we do not face the problem of why the 'state' (the 'dominant natural protection association') extends its protection to those who do not 'join' it. Nozick solves this problem by appealing to the *morality* of the state's behaviour. Yet there seems to be no reason why a state will actually behave morally. Therefore it is unsatisfactory as an explanation of why the law extends to all.

In our state of nature (restrictive as it is so far), we have already established that the law extended to all automatically. Those who remain on their own, forming their own individual defence system, obey the same incentives as an alliance, and they will voluntarily co-operate in the 'clearing house' exercise between alliances for the cases where concepts of right and wrong differ. This 'clearing house' may well come to look very like a 'court', as repeated bargaining by the various alliances gives rise to a set of agreed criteria which can be most cheaply applied by a hired nominee whose job depends on the strict interpretation, without partiality, of those criteria: in other words, a judge.

Ownership

Have we glided over a possible difficulty, by assuming each farmer owns certain things and that this is clearly known by all? Ownership itself is a 'right' (a 'property right') and we cannot assume that it will be generally agreed any more than other 'rights' and 'wrongs'. We need to demonstrate that our assumption was valid.

The extent of ownership also extends over life and limb and personal services. What rights does a man have to dispose of his own services (as opposed to being a slave)? Or those of members of his family? Were we wrong to assume implicitly that a man disposed of his services according to his own wishes and that his family's services were disposed according to some private intra-family agreement?

The answer is strictly that we should not have presupposed *any* rights at all in our discussion. Our doing so was simply an expositional device to take our readers with us in the early stages of the argument. One could re-read putting inverted commas round words like 'own' and 'his', to make it clear that these words would be clarified later.

We are now able to clarify them for our narrow case. We have seen that in the state of nature for our community (i.e., the group of people who happen to be in this geographical area) each farmer protects himself and what he desires to 'own' (including the full use of his own services) as *best he can*. The *result* is a common law *defining* what are rights and wrongs; that common law will consist of

a. the rights and wrongs commonly agreed by every alliance
b. a procedure (clearing house/court) to extend the area of agreement according to certain criteria to matters of dispute.

Does this imply a man will actually own what he desires to own? We do not know. It may or it may not. Strength – including the ability to join strong alliances – will be an important deterrent. The 'strength' involved need not be one-dimensional, simply that of strength in self-defence. A variety of skills can be bargaining counters in achieving ownership rights; for example, a weak, unaggressive farmer skilled in assessing the future course of the weather will be able to make himself useful to those whom he would wish to ally himself with, in exchange for a share of their strength and aggression.

This is a brutal conclusion, that there are no 'inalienable' rights in nature. One's property, whether one is a slave or not, whether as a wife one has the right to influence family decisions, these things and all other rights are the result of the complex interpla ᐧ of persons' bargaining power within the community, resulting in the alliances and the system of common law we have described. The law conceals the fundamentals of naked strength.

Remember that we are defining rights not in any moral sense: morality is not our concern at this stage. We are defining them, as we explained from the outset, in the legal sense.

Do the Indians of the Western United States have a 'right' to the land they once occupied? Did Israel have a right to the lands the Jews once occupied? Do Palestinians have a right to the West Bank? Does Argentina have a right to the Falklands? Did negroes have the right to be freed from slavery?

The logic of our argument can shed light on these questions. What they have in common is that they are all questions about the ability of those with a claim to a right to enforce their claim. The questions can be paraphrased: 'whose writ runs for these disputed lands, etc?' Some of them have been settled (by events), some are still disputed and events will yet tell us.

Widening the Argument

Our argument so far has been strictly confined to the development of a narrow case, a *counter-example* to the idea that the state of nature cannot be self-perpetuating. That narrow case was a geographical area peopled by farmers with a rather primitive technology. The case yielded the result that within this area there would be alliances, linked into super-alliances (communities for self-defence purposes), and that there would be a common law enforced by the people themselves acting within the agreements that formed the alliances. We distinguished the features of this result from those that others have alleged about the state of nature, especially Nozick with whom our agreement has the closest affinity.

But can our argument be generalised, or at least widened in applicability beyond this rather special and probably untypical society?

We have been trying for our narrow case to give an 'invisible hand' explanation of the law, as Nozick puts it. In other words, our argument has taken the form:

1. assume nothing about these farmers, except their initial geo-graphical location, their initial knowledge (technology), and

their initial supply of capital (tools, weapons, etc.)
2. demonstrate that they would be organised (after a time, from whatever initial state) into a common law, not because anyone or any group intended to produce such an outcome but just by the promptings of their own individual interests.

Thus for our narrow case, the state of nature includes law as one of the manifestations of 'natural', 'unhindered' activity by individuals. This state of nature is an equilibrium (i.e., self-perpetuating). It is reached from any initial state in which there are no constraints (other than endowments and geography) on persons' actions (i.e., from any 'natural' initial stage); it is therefore stable within an unconstrained world, i.e., within the set of states of nature.

Would a similar set of statements be possible for *any* set of people, in *any* initial geographical location, with *any* initial knowledge and capital endowment? There was nothing in our argument that hinged on the people being 'farmers', or on *where* they were located (plains, mountains), or on what weapons they had access to, or on what tools (with what strength and capability) they would use for their avocations, or on what knowledge they possessed. We did say that these things would affect the size of alliances (whether, for example, someone could securely go it alone without an alliance at all) and no doubt also the nature of the agreements (for example, if fences can be mended by a remotely placed device at low cost and with speed, then breaking fences would not be a violation of rights that would be punished severely if at all by an alliance).

It was in fact quite easy to explain our argument in terms of farms (ranches) and so on because we all have a common and coherent mental picture (whether derived from Hollywood, from Kipling, from experience or whatever) of simple agrarian societies. Many of us would find it hard to follow the same steps if we were talking about computer operators, lawyers, bankers and so on 'realistically coexisting' in a complex modern city; they would be too complex, for some unfamiliar, and for many hard to imagine shorn of the frequently found constraints on natural activity (whether tyrannical emperors or big city bureaucrats).

In case the reader is unpersuaded, let us set down an imagined scene in just such a modern city, Londago, but *without* such constraints. Our hero, the local barber, lives in a high rise block of flats in Londago; it is guarded by a neighbourhood police force which mounts a 24-hour patrol around the area. Periodically he takes his turn in a roster of 'officers' of this force, to keep an eye on the activities of the hired security men who are unskilled and low paid. His barber shop is in another part of town to which he travels by subway; the subway fare includes an element to pay for subway security (a system of alarms, closed circuit TV and patrols). Arriving at his shop, he enters another neighbourhood protection zone to which he also pays dues; this being mainly a commercial neighbourhood, the technology of protection here is heavier than at home (more like the subway system) with more emphasis on alarms than patrols. Yet, again he may contribute to a roster of 'officers' of the patrol force. His customers generally pay their accounts and if they complain about the quality of his haircut or any products he sells, he will generally pay them off (even for some barely justified complaints, for the sake of business goodwill). If a customer perseveres in not paying an account after the usual two or three demands spaced at monthly intervals, the commercial zone police in which he has a share will take up the case, approaching the customer directly in the first instance. Usually this is enough but on occasions where nothing happens, the zone police refer the case to the customer's zone police force. The case then is usually referred by the two forces to a local arbitration house with which many of these forces have a contract for settlement of disputes.

Our various zone police forces have at times considered a merger into a full-time professional force to do all duties, since the barber and some others have complained half-seriously about the hours spent in tedious and 'unproductive' protection duties. They have turned the idea down because of the fear that such a force could get out of control of its citizens, perhaps be corrupted by enemies, and even attempt to pursue the interests of its own commanders to acquire property and power. Nevertheless, various zone forces have merged into larger forces to save costs, taking a risk on these other aspects.

And so on. The features we found in our simple agrarian state of nature reproduce themselves here in a more complex form. Our argument is perfectly general for the explanation of law emerging within a state of nature.

Accounting for Other States

However, we are still far from a full explanation of rights. That 'the law will emerge from a state of nature of whatever form' is a useful statement. But we wish to know also:

a.   why are forms of *power* also found, side by side with the law, in many societies?

b.   can this power emerge from a state of nature? i.e., is there an 'invisible hand' explanation of power?

c.   is an 'invisible hand' explanation of power and/or the law a *complete* explanation? In other words, would such a combination of power and the law emerge (over time) *whatever* the initial stage, including 'unnatural' ones (for example, would law and freedom as in our farming society emerge if the society started out under the domination of one ranch-owner and his henchmen imposing their will as the law?). This is to ask whether the equilibrium we describe is globally stable, or only locally stable (i.e., only within the set of 'natural' states).

Let us begin by attempting an invisible hand explanation of power.

Return to our simple agrarian case; but view it now as illustrative of our wider argument. Suppose that for a farmer to leave his farm and do a roster spell on police patrol, or a longer period (a year?) as an army regular, is very costly; say farming requires continuous attendance or else these spells of patrol duty occur at crucial periods. Then, though the farmer will realise the risks of transferring police and army activities to an independent unit, he will be willing to run these risks to save the high costs of his personal involvement. There will also be gains in efficiency from specialisation in security/army work (as Nozick above).

Each farmers' alliance will no doubt set up a 'police council' to supervise the alliance police force. The alliances will set up an 'army council' to supervise the super-alliance's army. The members of these councils will now have civil power, as will the operational heads of the police and army. Thus, 'power' will come about because of economic costs/benefits; it too will in fact be part then of the state of nature. It is delegated by the citizens to individuals in order to economise on functions they previously had to share out among themselves as 'amateurs'. The citizens then devise ways to limit the abuse of power by these individuals.

How far will this creation of civil power go? How concentrated will it be, in other words? Again this will be a matter of economics. *Power is the outcome of economic specialisation in the exercise of the protective functions of the law.*

Our answers to the first two questions (a) and (b) above can then be derived from this general hypothesis. Power emerges – i.e., people are vested with power – because it is cheaper, even after allowing for the risks and difficulties of supervising their exercise of it, to give them power than for all to engage in the protective function. The varieties of power forms occur because of the variety of costs and benefits attaching to the exercise of the protective function.

Let us consider just two examples of power forms.

In the Athens of the 5th century BC the citizens gave power to an elected leader but controlled his power by a system of frequent referenda on council issues. The citizens gathered in the market-place and voted, after listening to the arguments from their leader and the opposition. This was a cost-effective action because it was physically possible for all citizens to gather together to enforce this highly participative form of control, while for efficiency they needed a single leader to organise the military and other functions of a highly civilised and advanced city state. The idea of federating with other Greek city states and creating federal power did not appeal to the Athenians; they merely had a 'super-alliance' with them in case of external threat (invoked notably in the Persian invasion). The economic gains from amalgamating these states' military forces (already formidable) into one did not offset the loss in control that would be implied with the technology of those days; with the rugged geography of Greece, it was hard for the citizens of Athens to check what was going on in Thrace and vice versa. A federal army and navy would be costly to check on and there would be a risk of it becoming an uncontrolled force. Notice in this example how the technology of communications enters crucially into the calculations.

Now consider the case of Tsarist Russia, a country of plains interrupted only at the Urals, a mountain range in any case of easy traversability. Nomad tribes of horsemen moved freely across this expanse of plain. As long as they alone constituted the population, they remained in tribal units, with a tribal power structure (i.e., very limited power for the leader, with constant and visible checking from his fellow-tribesmen). With no external threats except from other marauding tribes, federal power was unnecessary; super-alliances with other friendly tribes were enough, if that. Yet, of course, as settled agricultural communities grew up in the west of Russia, the settlers required effective defence against these roaming tribesmen. As settlers busy in the fields, their effectiveness against surprise attack could only be purchased by costly sacrifice of time in the fields. Furthermore, to counteract an invasion from afar by large groups of horsemen would require a super-alliance with rapid response times, with the technology of the horse operating in the geography of the steppe. Coordination of separate communities' military units against such invasion would be expensive indeed. A federal force offered the cheapest solution; hence the central ruler or chief, the Tsar. As for citizen supervision, the federal state of Russia is so far flung that formal referenda on voting would have been costly. Checks on the Tsar's power were provided first by sheer distance; no Tsar could keep effective control against their will of countries a thousand miles from Moscow. Secondly, by the 'contestability' of the Tsar's power by 'pretenders' who could capitalise on discontent.

In answering our first two questions, we have argued that there is no general bar to the existence of *power in a state of nature*. Power emerges in a state of nature for economic reasons; it is consistent with individual agents' voluntary agreement and simply a convenient extension of the mechanisms of their alliances. When power is of this form we will call it 'natural' power or 'power in a state of nature'.

This brings us to the hardest of our three questions. Suppose we can in this way show that, if the economics dictate it, a state of nature will yield power as well as law and that it will yield it in different forms suited to the tastes, technology and constraints of the citizens. Can we also show that a non-natural state would yield the same power in the same form? Suppose, as in the story of the Ring, something goes wrong; power falls into the wrong hands and is abused, with the citizens' sanction being overridden. Clearly this is possible, for the citizens recognise the *risk*; every so often the chances of abuse will be actually realised.

Let us now imagine the two states: the equilibrium (or 'natural') state where citizens are content, and the non-natural state which is *any* other. We now need to define rather carefully the 'contentment' involved in the equilibrium state. It is what economists know of as the 'core'; it is a state such that no coalition of citizens can be created which desires to, and can, prevent it in any aspect. Contentment of a citizen therefore consists in this knowledge that he cannot change the state, by joining any coalition (including of course acting on his own, this being a coalition of one).

By this *definition*, we have implicitly answered our question. The equilibrium state results from the state of nature; that is to say, a state of nature will always turn into the equilibrium state. A non-natural state must be one in which *some* coalition could and wishes to frustrate it. It will therefore not survive, for that coalition will frustrate it.

But answering via a definition is not enough.

We need to show that the power of coalitions to frustrate does not alter in such a volatile manner that the 'core' is a volatile concept and so of trivial use.

What I now assert, as an empirical hypothesis, is that the power of citizens' coalitions to frustrate is derived from their power in the state of nature. I refer to this as the 'fundamental' power distribution. I argue that the *actual* power distribution will be forced eventually to conform to the fundamental power distribution. This comes about through the activity of competitive intermediaries, the supply of whom is inexhaustible. They will perceive the profit from organising a blocking coalition of citizens, using their fundamental power.

What then is the 'power of citizens in a state of nature'? If this hypothesis is to be genuinely testable, as opposed to merely a restatement of a definition, then this concept must be carefully delineated. (What follows was written before the recent overthrow of the Marcos regime in the Philippines by a largely unarmed proletariat with the help of overseas, especially US, moral support and some specific backing well short of physical intervention.)

What we require is a concept of power to which neither initial conditions nor capital stock contribute. For these two elements are arbitrary and can be changed by human effort. Remember too that skills, mental and physical, are acquired and therefore must be included in 'capital stock' (they are 'human' capital).

If these elements are stripped away when we consider any set of citizens (not necessarily all of the same 'country', for a 'country' is already a particular power structure, which may not be 'fundamental'), we are left with their individual natural capacities, the technology available to them (we will assume that any technology anywhere that can be applied in their situation is 'available', in the sense that if it is technology, i.e., 'known', then it can be acquired at some cost by them or by their intermediary), and the natural constraints of their environment.

Suppose these elements can be listed in some necessarily incomplete way (for 'capacities', for example, is the set of all possible states to which our citizen may attain), can we make any sense of the concept of their power? What I have in mind is the result of a social optimisation plan by an intermediary, or 'political entrepreneur', looking at this situation. Such an intermediary will assess the possibilities of improving the welfare of a set of citizens, compute the costs (including his own required profit), and then sell the plan to the citizens, if he feels it is worth pursuing.

In this plan, there will be a cost in blocking the existing power structure – the initial conditions. However, the capital stock that needs to be used in the plan will *cost* the same whether the citizens have it or not; if they do not have it and must acquire it, then its cost is obvious (it is the interest and maintenance expense of leasing it for the time required), but if they do have it, then they must divert it from its existing use, where it earns an economic return, to its use in the plan. Either way, the economic cost is the same. So capital stock held by the citizens does not affect the plan's profitability.

The problem with the way we have set up the plan is that its viability may depend on the initial conditions. If the existing power structure is repressive, then the costs of blocking it may be very high and make an otherwise profitable plan unprofitable. Yet our concept of 'fundamental' power rules out the role of initial conditions.

To deal with this problem formally, we use a technical trick from economics: we discuss shortly what this 'means' in practice. Formally, we will assume that the economy in which our citizens are placed is in steady state with a zero real (marginal) rate of return on capital (i.e., the capital stock is invested up to the point where an additional unit of capital yields no extra return), its citizens have a zero rate of time preference (i.e., they value the welfare of their descendants equally with their own), and so does our political entrepreneur. This implies that if the plan yields a steady *flow* of profit, year in, year out, without counting capital costs or the once-for-all costs of blocking the existing power structure, then it is profitable to undertake.

To put this now into practical, human terms, this means that, if a group of citizens can be shown, a steady (permanent) future for themselves *or* their descendants that will be more attractive than a steady continuation of their present state, they will embrace it in spite of the transitory costs and turmoil required to bring the new state about. These costs and turmoil include:

1. the diversion of capital stock
2. the acquisition, at cost, of necessary technology
3. the effort, bloodshed or cost, required to block the existing state.

This is of course 'unrealistic': rates of time preference and real rates of return on capital are generally positive. So at any actual point of time, such a plan may not be embraced because these latter costs, when set against the *discounted* benefits of the future v. the present, make the plan unattractive. The current set of citizens in effect will shrug their shoulders and *put it off*; 'our descendants', they may say to themselves, 'will perhaps have a real chance, but we do not'.

However, this unrealism is necessary to define clearly the notion of 'fundamental power'. For what we have done is to define an opportunity waiting to happen when discount rates, etc., permit. *Chance* will eventually cause it to happen because

a. discount rates have a statistical distribution which includes zero
b. the costs of blocking a given power structure also have a distribution: in other words, power structures have periods of weakness as well as strength
c. costs of technology vary over time; indeed steadily fall as knowledge accumulates.

Hence, though the chance of the fundamental power being asserted at any given point of time is small, it is positive and therefore the chances of it being asserted at *some* point in time tend to certainty over the indefinite future.

It may be objected that the tyrant who has usurped or hijacked power will always have an incentive to bribe the outside intermediary to back off. This is true. It might seem that in a bribery competition between tyrant and revolutionaries the tyrant must come off best. For he can offer a substantial slice of the country's GDP without cutting into his own personal fortune, merely by oppressing his people more. The revolutionaries however must reduce their own supporters' returns to produce their bribe, since *all* the people will recapture their rights after the tyrant's overthrow; their ability to 'tax' their supporters will be limited therefore. Whatever they can raise by *voluntary* contributions, furthermore, can surely be topped by the tyrant with compulsory contributions. Better, therefore, for the revolutionaries to stop negotiations with an intermediary, since that way the tyrant too will stop and not require these supererogatory extractions from the populace.

The key objection to this line of argument is that there is an infinite supply of intermediaries at some 'price' representing the return on their activities (supplying technology, organising weapons, shipments, etc.). Suppose this price to be a not inconsiderable £y. The revolutionaries approach A offering £y. A seeks £y times 1.01 from the tyrant who buys him off. The revolutionaries, losing A, offer their £y to B. He too is bought off by the tyrant, who has now paid out £y times 2.02. The revolutionaries continue down the list until eventually the tyrant's resources are exhausted and they get an intermediary; the tyrant cannot win this game and unless foolish, therefore, is unlikely to engage in a bribery competition at all.

What if the tyrant seeing his predicament puts himself under the protection of a greater power in return for policy subservience (e.g., Husak and the USSR in Czechoslovakia)? This does not actually change the problem but merely transfers it to the greater power which must deploy its resources to combat the revolutionaries. Because it may have greater resources, this may put off the critical time of overthrow, but that is all (think here of Russian difficulties in Afghanistan).

To conclude, then, I must emphasise: this hypothesis does *not* predict that at any given time power is disposed according to its fundamental distribution. Rather, it predicts that over a (possibly very long) period it tends towards this distribution. That this distribution is not volatile should be clear; for it does not depend on initial conditions or capital costs or the cost of acquiring available technology, all of which will vary continuously. It does depend on the preferences of the citizens, on the natural constraints of their environment, and on the available technology. These latter will of course change; nothing is immutable nor, therefore, is the fundamental distribution itself immutable, but the changes in these are likely to be very gradual, and so we can think of this distribution as following some slowly moving trend. Actual power distributions, if they are different from this, *may* from time to time change discontinuously as volatile elements trigger a blocking coalition; or they too may converge continuously on the fundamental distribution as the *threat* of these coalitions is perceived by the temporarily dominant coalition.

What we have done, in effect, is to define the core with reference to a steady state world; the *dynamics* by which it is reached we have left rather vague, noting that they depend on (a) chance (b) anticipation of such chances, but we have shown that it *must* be eventually reached because of the cumulative statistical probability that a blocking coalition will be mounted. Our world is determined by the preferences of the citizens (as in Oakeshott's theory) interacting with technology and natural constraints.

Some Tentative Illustrations

a.   The Past – French Revolution v. British Evolution

In these two cases we seem to see illustrations of the two possible dynamics. In the French case, circumstances occurred by chance – a famine, a weak regime – to trigger a blocking coalition – an assertion complete with bloodshed and massive dislocation. In the British case, power was yielded gradually over a period of rapid industrialisation to the 'working masses', as it was perceived that they would otherwise eventually seize it.

Of course, this 'potted history' by a non-historian will provoke professional historians' utter disgust. Nevertheless, it is striking that both French and British histories led to the same eventual power structure, namely representative democracy. Could one perhaps chart the progress of other 'old' countries (i.e., with a couple of centuries in which the dynamics we have spoken of could work themselves out) in these terms also? The countries of Western Europe, North America and the ancient kingdom of Japan have all emerged as representative democracies. Has this system par excellence the qualities to avoid blocking overthrow, and instead to permit evolutionary blocking? Will this system itself mutate towards 'greater freedom', e.g., towards a 'libertarian' state? These, and related questions are 'empirical' questions, whose answers could shed light on the validity of our hypothesis. We cannot pursue them here.

b.   The Eastern Bloc: a puzzle?[5]

There is one group of countries that appears at least to pose a severe problem for our hypothesis: the Communist countries of the Eastern bloc and China. For here are repressive regimes whose citizens do not – so one would believe – willingly consent to them, and yet they have survived for 40 years, in some cases for longer (the Soviet Union for about 70 years). Can this be consistent with the prediction that power will tend eventually towards its fundamental distribution?

As defenders of the hypothesis, we could take one of two routes. We could assert that the citizens *do* truly (in the main) consent: that there is no group large enough to overthrow the system which has the (long-term) incentive to do so.

Or we could assert that they do not and that eventually these regimes *will* be overthrown; how long it would take we probably would not be wise to predict.

On the face of it, the latter route appears the most honest – in effect being the hypothesis, neither at this stage confirmed nor falsified for these cases – yet for the traditionally imperial and far-flung countries of the Soviet Union and China, it is tempting to take the first route (as implicitly we did earlier) and draw attention to the clear continuity between imperial past and Communist present. For Eastern Europe, the parallels with the dissolutions of earlier empires – Roman, British, French, Italian, etc. – appear striking. Indeed, already the rumblings of separation in Eastern Europe may well be growing louder. Notice that by contrast with the Soviet bloc, the USA has no *empire*; it does of course have allied states, for some of which the description 'client state' might be more appropriate. But, at least in principle, it is not committed to direct control and, if one client government fails, it has the possibility of wooing another.

c. South Africa and Apartheid

Must the fundamental distribution of power be at variance with its current distribution in South Africa? It might seem that the answer is obviously: yes. That indeed is what 'liberal' opinion in Britain, for example, holds.

Yet consider our earlier definition. If white rule in South Africa were overthrown by a black coalition, would this lead to a better existence for black people? How would this compare with continued white rule and economic growth, for those same people?

White rule is a means of assuring those whose capital is invested (massively) in South Africa that their capital and its returns will not be expropriated. (For better or worse, those capitalists associate black rule with expropriation; and, indeed, the recent history of Africa bears them out.) Thus economic activity, in which these people provide the capital, the management skills, and the entrepreneurship, is generated, with consequent employment (at wages higher than elsewhere in Africa) for blacks.

Hence for the majority of blacks who have the power, assisted by outside political entrepreneurs, to overthrow white rule, the problem is to balance up the economic loss against the gains of political rights (absence of pass laws, preservation of personal dignity, immunity from random search, etc.). This is not an easy trade-off.

An outside observer with little knowledge might wonder whether a rational white regime would not improve the trade-off with no significant loss of economic security for capitalists, by conceding on apartheid, pass laws and so forth,[6] but here we must stop an interesting empirical speculation.

Conclusions

I have argued that 'rights', in the sense of 'I have a right. . . .', derive from what is enforceable, that is the (active) law of the land. Power to enforce the law will normally be vested in specialised agencies because of economic constraints, though it need not be in principle; such civil power will be subject to a structure of checks. 'Power structure' in turn tends towards a fundamental distribution; we have identified this as that which no blocking coalition would (ultimately) prevent. This is also the 'state of nature', in the sense that it will occur (in time) 'naturally', 'inevitably'; notice that in this state of nature civil power – including a 'state' – can exist, and typically will, because of economic constraints. However, at a given point of time, even very early in history (in some 'natural' period?), there is no necessity that such a state of nature or equilibrium *will* occur; some of our argument earlier in this essay was couched in terms of a pastoral society in which the plausibility of the state of nature occurring at all times was made to be as great as possible.

That presentation was useful in developing my case; but we can now see that it was somewhat misleading. The 'hijacking' of power can occur at any time; the rules of chance dictate that it too may occur, in *any* society at any time. However, chance too dictates that the fundamental power distribution must reassert itself, discontinuously (when the hijacker's powers are temporarily weak) or gradually (as the hijacker recognises the inevitable and graciously yields up over time the reins of power).

I began by refusing to discuss morality, arguing that rights in the sense discussed were not derived from morality; what is morally right is not necessarily 'a right', nor is 'a right' necessarily morally right. I end by reflecting briefly on possible connections between rights and morality. Notice first that the fundamental power distribution is, if our hypothesis is correct, *inevitable*. Therefore, like nature, it *is*. The 'rights' it gives (or will eventually give) are also inevitable; one could reasonably call them 'natural rights' (but perhaps should not because of the varieties of this phrase's usage). In that sense they are 'primary', fixed points, beyond control, beyond the vagaries of custom and, dare we say, morals. This implies that what is morally right is dominated by these (fundamental) rights; just as if lightning strikes someone, it is an accident and not wrong even though that person may have a moral right to survive to old age. For example, two people may have differing views on the morality of redistributive taxation; one may say 'taxation is theft' and argue in favour of voluntary giving to the poor, the other may argue that it is everyone's duty and so they should be compelled by taxation to do so. This question, however, will be settled by the evolution of power; the moral discussion will be dominated, will be irrelevant. It is of course possible – even probable, I would venture – that, once the nature of these evolved rights has become apparent, they come to be dignified also by the status of moral rightness; but, if so, that is, so to speak, merely a decoration and in no way indicates their derivation or basis. I conclude by arguing, therefore, that the domain of morals – that language of undoubted authority which it is not our purpose here to explore – is a domain within, and subordinate to, that of fundamental rights.

Notes

1. I have benefited from comments made at seminars of the Oxford Hayek Society and of Liverpool students; I thank Dale Benest particularly for pressing me on the question of tyrant bribery.
2. I have recently (after writing this) benefited from reading Anthony de Jasay's *The State* which pursues a similar line of argument.
3. Again, de Jasay makes this point.
4. Now (1990) 'was'.
5. The puzzle has by now been dramatically resolved.
6. The recent actions of De Klerk confirm that rationality prevails.

References

Thomas Hobbes (1651), *Leviathan*.

John Locke (1690), *The Two Treatises of Government*.

Anthony de Jasay (1985), *The State*, Blackwell.

Robert Nozick (1974), *Anarchy, State and Utopia*, Basic Books and Blackwell.

Michael Oakeshott (1975), *On Human Conduct* (essay 'On the character of a modern European State'), Oxford University Press.

Richard Wagner (1876), *Der Ring des Nibelungen*, cycle of four operas.

17. Comments on Sir Geoffrey Howe's Vision of Conservatism, 1983*

The Chancellor's sketch of future Conservative strategy is at once encouraging and tantalising. It is encouraging because up to now there has been very little serious discussion of the *details* to be found in a second Thatcher term; a lot of general statements, yes, but few specific propositions. Such discussion must take place now – and before General Election fever sets in – for the programme to be implemented smoothly and rapidly after the Election. There can be no excuse this time for lack of preparation.

It is tantalising because Sir Geoffrey's propositions are neither clear nor specific. The reason appears to be that the debate within the Conservative party on the big issues outstanding is only just beginning.

But if there is to be progress in the debate, there must be more precision in public as well as within Consevative Central Office. What I propose to do in these few pages is to spell out these issues, set out some possible solutions, and infer from Sir Geoffrey's text how far he seems to have moved towards them.

The liberal Conservative vision of the good society is one in which people are free to pursue their individual interests, while government sets the framework of law, order and defence, provides a stable currency, prevents monopoly practices, raises taxes that interfere as little as possible with incentives, spends on goods and services that cannot efficiently be bought privately, and ensures that less fortunate members of society are cared for when they truly cannot help themselves. Redistribution and equality are not part of that vision; the concept of welfare spending is most easily summarised rather as that of a 'safety net'. Yet this concept does embrace the idea that there are certain critical goods and services which all people must be enabled to have, if they cannot or will not acquire

* First published in *Economic Affairs*, pp. 94–7, January 1983.

them by their own efforts, notably certain standards of education and health. Leaving aside in this context law, order and defence, let us consider these elements in turn.

Stable Currency

The one unqualified success story of Mrs Thatcher's Government is the dramatic reduction in inflation – likely to be running 4% or below this year. There can surely by now be no serious argument that this was brought about by a substantial reduction in public sector borrowing and money supply growth. The PSBR adjusted for the cyclical effects on revenues and spending was running at around 6% of GDP when the Government came to power; it has now been reduced to less than ½%. Growth in the (probably largely un-distorted) monetary base was running at 13–15%; in the year to September 1982 it grew only about 2%. The corresponding growth in M1 has dropped from 15–20% to 7%. Growth in Sterling M3 we know has been severely distorted by institutional factors, but growth of the widest monetary aggregate (PSL 2) has dropped from around 14% to 8%.

The next Thatcher Government must restore internal currency *stability* (zero inflation). It can do this by holding throughout its term of office the cyclically adjusted Public Sector Borrowing Requirement at its current near-zero level and by holding the growth rate of the monetary base, in particular, within a range of 2–5%. With these policies, I would expect currency stability by 1985 at the latest. (Incidentally, they would imply very likely a gradual appreciation of the exchange rate, since internal currency stability is not yet a serious aim, let alone prospect, in most other OECD countries.)

The Chancellor's text is encouragingly strong on the need for price stability, and the record suggests that the policies he has in mind would not be significantly different from these. But they should be spelt out, at the latest in a new 'financial strategy' soon after the election, and preferably before, in the manifesto.

Monopoly Practices

Considerable concentrations of monopoly power are still to be found in this country; in the goods market, public sector industries (in the broadest sense, from health and education, through electricity generation and coal), and in the labour market unions, wield substantial monopoly power. The socialist philosophy that set up the public sector monopolies and backed the growth of union power had it that the first would act as responsible agents for the social good while unions would promote the interests of the work force at large.

Bitter experience has shown us in Britain that, on the contrary, public sector monopolies collude with their workforce to maximise transfers from the taxpayer per unit of output, and that unions act cynically to improve wages and working conditions of their members, disregarding the severe side-effects on people they do not represent, whether in other unions, in non-union jobs, the un-employed, or future generations.

a.   Public Sector

Public sector monopoly power in the provision of goods and services needs therefore to be removed. Sir Geoffrey recognises this explicitly ('State ownership . . . should be displaced . . . by the . . . market'), and notes some steps already taken or in the pipeline, privatisation and references to the Monopolies Commission among them.

But there is a lack of detail on the way ahead. Education vouchers, student loans, more charging for 'social provision', 'more' privatisation are mentioned. Yet few of these ideas have been carefully worked out in public statements by Conservative politicians. Ill-thought-out, but plausible-sounding objections (such as 'education vouchers will cause children now getting a bad education to be worse off because good schools will not expand while bad schools will be deprived of resources', to paraphrase a recent contribution by the Headmaster of Westminster School), proliferate in these circumstances, as do emotional objections ('the principle of health provision for all is under attack', recently heard from some Conservative MPs over the Cabinet Think Tank's Report). What is required is a complete and detailed list of proposed steps to the removal of each public sector monopoly. Since these steps will be designed to increase the efficiency of *provision* of goods and services, without prejudice to how their purchase is financed (below), they should be widely welcomed once clearly explained.

Some senior Conservative politicians seem to feel that a full public debate of such proposals now could be damaging to their chances of adoption. Consequently any proposals that may exist have been suppressed and are half-seen through a penumbra of leaked reports, even though everyone must know that discussion of the Conservative manifesto is raging over them. But such proposals are an electoral asset to the Conservatives: the people are longing for a lead in these matters and will move strongly behind them in a proper public debate, so making both the manifesto easier to formulate and the proposals easier to implement after the election. The British have become more ready to accept the market over a wider range of economic activities than the Conservatives seem to have realised.

b. The Unions

Here again there is a fund of popular sympathy for this Government's approach and much to be gained by setting out a full programme of future reform. The 1982 Employment Act of Mr Tebbit – what a pity it was not the 1980 Act – restricts union immunities to direct action only, an immense step forward. My fear is that this will not be enough, first, because many firms – probably the overwhelming majority – will be intimidated from suing unions for damages; secondly, because immunities for direct action still confer an immense amount of power. Secret ballots – apparently to be introduced – will be helpful but will not solve these problems.

There is a necessity for a public agent, preferably independent of ministers, to enforce reductions in labour monopoly power; a Labour Monopolies Commission could fulfil this role investigating both sides of the labour market, unions and firms, as necessary. As for the remaining immunities, if monopoly power is against the public interest, then in all logic they should be removed. These two steps should be sufficient to finish off the job of union reform. As I have argued before in this book ('Unions Destroy a Million Jobs', *Economic Affairs*, January 1982), the evidence suggests this would massively reduce unemployment. The Howe text is clearly sympathetic to this line of argument but extremely coy on the further steps to be taken.

Taxes, the Welfare State and Unemployment

I leave till last the most intractable area of all: the tax and benefit system and its role in creating and sustaining unemployment. The liberal Conservative wishes to ensure education and health for all (and also, as noted earlier, that it is provided efficiently, without monopoly power), and he wishes to safeguard the welfare of the less fortunate members of society, in line, as Sir Geoffrey Howe argues, with the view of the majority of British people.

When we come to the mechanics of doing this efficiently, we get into difficult territory. By contrast, the issues we have already dealt with – inflation, public sector monopolies, unions – are all perceived as ones in which the people have tended to move towards the liberal Conservative viewpoint, partly because of experience with our acute problems since the war, but also because there has been a massive amount of literature explaining the problems to the people.

The British are extremely charitable people (this has been well documented, for example in the famous sociological analysis of blood donorship across a number of countries, R. Titmuss' *The Gift Relationship*). If some people fall on hard times, others wish to help. The benefit system is designed to provide minimum standards of living for the sick, the unemployed and the disabled. It is the social expression of this charitable instinct.

Unfortunately, this system has produced marginal tax rates in the range of 60–100% both on the act of entering officially recorded jobs and on recorded earnings within recorded jobs, for a disturbingly large number of people at the lower end of the pay scale. These 'poverty' and 'unemployment traps' have by now been widely publicised – for example, and pre-eminently, in *Why Work?* by Ralph Howell assisted by Mrs Hermione Parker (Conservative Political Centre, 1981) and recently in Mrs Parker's IEA Research Monograph, *The Moral Hazard of Social Benefits* – after a decade in which official efforts were stupidly made to minimise the size of the problem.

The effect of these tax rates is to create large-scale unemployment among the lower-paid. The mechanism by which this occurs is often misunderstood and misrepresented. It is *not* (as some would have it) because the unemployed are 'scroungers' or 'don't want to work' – manifestly the vast bulk of the unemployed are honest people who desperately want a decent job. It *is* because the minimum wage at which jobs – any job – can reasonably be taken by people is strongly influenced by the benefit rate. After all, it would clearly be absurd, if only for the sake of one's family, to take a job paying *less* than benefits; and to take a job paying only marginally more may also seem fairly unattractive when one can do useful things at home and even earn some small amounts legally while claiming benefits. In short, the benefit rate puts a floor beneath wages – and puts upward pressure on them as it rises – and so destroys jobs.

This point – which is obvious enough – does now appear to be gaining fairly widespread acceptance. But some of the solutions proposed are unrealistic because they involve large rises in general taxation (for example, if the standard rate were raised substantially, this would enable one to lower marginal tax rates on the lower-paid without lowering benefits). At any rate a liberal Conservative would not wish to pursue redistributive solutions of this type; and it seems doubtful that there would be a majority for them in this country.

Yet solution there must be because of the waste of resources and the social problems created by unemployment. In several issues of the *Quarterly Economic Bulletin* of the Liverpool Research Group in Macroeconomics, since October 1981, I have suggested the institution of a ceiling on the ratio of unemployment benefits to the previous net income of the unemployed. Such a ceiling exists in many European countries (e.g., Germany, France, Italy and Denmark), and it seems both just and a matter of commonsense. This would deal with the unemployment trap, by making low-paid jobs attractive again; a ceiling of say 70% should reduce unemployment substantially (about ¾ million on our calculations). Unavoidably, it would reduce the income of the previously lowest-paid unemployed; this is an unhappy side-effect, but it could be softened by introducing the scheme at a time when taxes generally were being cut so that the 'previous net income' was rising.

Raising tax thresholds and child benefits, as general savings within the PSBR are available, would be the most helpful of the feasible tax-cut proposals for this problem; judging from his November statement, the Chancellor clearly has accepted this logic.

Another measure that would be helpful would be stiffer conditionality on benefits: the refusal of a job, even one at lower wages than benefits, could be made a condition of denying benefit after some period of unemployment, say, six months. After all, there is already in existence a 'negative income tax' for lower-paid workers, albeit in the imperfect form of the Family Income Supplement, but this could be improved.

The poverty trap, too, requires such an improvement for its solution. Some interim moves towards this could be made within the next few years; paying FIS on *net*, as opposed to gross, income and abolition of means-tested 'passported benefits' would be two. A full system indeed has to await computerisation of the tax system, not due till the late 1980s. But again, the solution – unless it is to require a substantial rise in general taxation – will require some fall in the living standards of the poorest families, and again this side-effect could be softened by timing the reforms to coincide with falling tax rates.

Sir Geoffrey has not mentioned any possible solutions to these problems other than the desire to raise tax thresholds. This is less than candid; there is no doubt that a solution that goes well beyond raising tax thresholds is necessary if we are to reduce unemployment significantly. The sooner the public debate starts, so that people can make up their minds on what sort of system they want, the sooner the British problem of the 1980s – unemployment – can move towards a solution.

Conclusions

The principles we have been discussing are laudable in themselves, but they are also popular: if buying votes is a necessary accompaniment of parliamentary democracy, it may be that Sir Geoffrey Howe and his friends could buy more properly-won votes by offering lower taxes and more choice in economic life than by the tired old technique of more government expenditure at the expense of innocent taxpayers.

Sir Geoffrey's agenda for liberal Conservatism is therefore a fine *start* to the necessary public debate about the programme of Mrs Thatcher's next government. Yet, as the debate goes on and public interest is aroused, it will be necessary to supply nuts and bolts, chapter and verse. This is, after all, a major programme of reform. The people will need to be persuaded that, besides the fine principles, the mechanisms are in good working order.

18. Mrs Thatcher's Economic Reform Programme – Past, Present and Future*

Politicians sell products in the political market-place. That market is changing continuously with evolving tastes and technology. Sometimes the same old product will succeed with some repackaging, like Butskellism in the 1950s and 1960s. Sometimes a political entrepreneur will perceive, or think he perceives, an opportunity for a new product to topple the reigning monopoly. Such is the story of the Thatcher reform programme, at heart an economic reform programme.

Looking back on three elections, it is tempting to see inevitability in Mrs Thatcher's success, arguing from the interests of the skilled working classes, the *de facto* floating voters. But though I am no political scientist, I am impressed with the failure of political scientists to see any such alleged inevitability before the event. I do not hold it against them, any more than I hold it against skilled investment analysts that they did not predict the rise and rise of Amstrad and Mr Alan Sugar, a more familiar type of entrepreneur. The truth surely is that there is a discovery process in political, as in normal, markets: the successful entrepreneur has the intuition to guess what *may* sell and to build on any initial successes with more of the same, while closing down his failures swiftly so as to cut losses.

I leave to political scientists the hard task of piecing together just why the Thatcher product sold so well in 1980s Britain; why working-class voters plumped for more economic freedom instead of more social insurance, and why the middle classes did not embrace the Alliance middle way as many Tory strategists deeply feared. My job in this essay is to describe the product, how it has evolved, what it has become, and how it may develop in the future.

* First published in *Thatcherism* (ed. R. Skidelsky), pp. 93–106, Chatto and Windus, 1988.

Yet first I must allay concern about my choice of metaphor. If this is a product, are politicians mere salesmen out for more money? Of course not. The metaphor is precise. Politicians, like business entrepreneurs, are moved by an invisible hand to satisfy the common good; their motives are various and irrelevant. The rewards of success may take many different forms: money, power, satisfaction in being credited with helping one's fellowmen, a place in history, and so on. The same is true of business rewards: it is mere pastiche to suppose businessmen get rewards solely from money; think of the Chicago founders of museums and opera houses, enjoying the plaudits of grateful citizens. The main thing is that the rewards should be very large and variable to attract the best for the tasks involved.

Much has been written and spoken about Mrs Thatcher's and Keith (now Lord) Joseph's vision of a social market economy. Joseph's inspiration seems to have been not Victorian Britain, as is so often said, but the West Germany of the 1950s under Ludwig Erhard. Yet that particular vision has never been widely shared by Mrs Thatcher's allies; and we now see only too clearly that the German example is unattractively corporatist and flawed by massive regulation.

Since Mrs Thatcher's political judgements have guided the whole enterprise, it is relevant to ask what she has had in *her* mind as a guiding vision. True to her character as a woman of action, she has never been so unprofessional as to write it down or describe it too precisely. But my impression from her many interviews is of a world in which *small* businesses could compete freely for the favours of the individual *family* consumer; in this world the state keeps law and order, including the elements of a *moral* order to protect family decency, and provides succour to the genuinely unfortunate who cannot help themselves.

The vision of the small business freely competing to topple the corporate goliaths is basically Austrian, Schumpeter's arena of creative destruction; and it is clearly the antithesis of corporatism. Yet the passionate concern with the decent family consumer surely owes much to her father's shop in Grantham, surviving by satisfying ordinary people's needs efficiently. The philosophy of helping (only) the deserving poor is not so much New Right as the folk wisdom of the British families whom Miss Roberts helped to serve; for them independence was the *sine qua non* of happiness and self-respect, and charity was wrung from the housekeeping budget.

Such an ideal was far from both the reality of the late 1970s and the ideals of its dominant centrist coalition. Nor was it in the form of a product that the British electorate would conceivably buy as an alternative to the existing system, mediocre as its results obviously were. Imagine the problems. It was a vision easily damned as *simpliste* by the intellectuals to whom traditionally the electorate looked for guidance. There were no role models elsewhere in the developed world. The United States under Carter was committed to moving in the direction of the British welfare state, and everywhere in Europe corporatism was supreme. Within Britain, vested interests were ready to pounce on any encroachment of privilege and were powerful in key parts of the Tory establishment; and there was an opposition recently in power and expecting its imminent return, determined not merely to oppose but even to reverse change. Parallels drawn with New Zealand or the United States, where similar revolutions have occurred, are misleading. In New Zealand the opposition was powerless to oppose the wearing of what should have been its own clothes, and the reformers had plenty of overseas examples to follow. The US presidential system makes reform easier to initiate and more difficult to sustain; the President may get a clear folk mandate but Congress is designed to obstruct and diffuse its implementation. The difficulties of creating reform in Britain were unique.

The problem Mrs Thatcher faced was where to start and how to develop support for a programme of change that was as yet barely understood, let alone demanded enthusiastically enough to overcome the powers of defending interests. Mancur Olson has made a centrepiece of his theory of the decline of nations the power of these interests to frustrate those of the ordinary small man; his argument, widely accepted by public choice theorists, is that the small man will not care about the imperceptible increment to his tax bill needed to satisfy the vested interest group, whereas of course the group members care passionately about the sizeable increase in their welfare. It follows that a political entrepreneur who wishes to advance by reducing these vested interests has to mobilise the small man in spite of his modest stake in any individual issue – a task that according to public choice theory should be attempted only by those determined to fail. Mrs Thatcher was compelled to attempt this task of political aggregation.

This has to be understood to make sense of what followed. Some of Mrs Thatcher's closest advisers, not to speak of many critics both sympathetic and hostile, were frustrated by her frequent failures to make large, logically coherent reforms in the many areas she tackled to some degree; by the absence of any grand master-design; and by some positively counter-productive deviations from the logical path of reform. The truth is that as a political entrepreneur with finely honed instincts for her trade she probably could not do otherwise.

Her chosen method has been the 'step-by-step' approach, whereby problems were picked off in order of urgency and solubility, while others were prepared for future full attention with minor measures, often experimental in nature. So in her first two terms we have seen three major campaigns: the defeat of inflation, the curbing of union power, and privatisation, *in that order*.

In 1979–82 the fight against inflation dominated all else; monetarism and the Public Sector Borrowing Requirement reached their apogee in political debate, and economic expertise about them flourished in unlikely parts of the *Guardian* and the *Daily Telegraph* alike. During this phase, taxes were even raised in the notorious 1981 budget to establish anti-inflationary credibility; this measure badly worsened the supply side and incentives but it did succeed in its objective. Given that public expenditure proved resistant to further cuts after the easy ones on capital account, it had to be done. In our recent econometric reconstruction of this period, Kent Matthews and I concluded that this tax rise brought inflation expectations down decisively, much in line with Sir Alan Walters' assessment that it was a turning-point in establishing financial confidence.

The medium-term financial strategy was designed to create credibility for a four-year programme of *gradual* reductions in money supply growth and in the PSBR as a fraction of national income. By announcing long-term targets that it would therefore find embarrassing to miss, the government, so the idea went, was committing itself, like Odysseus binding himself to the mast before passing the Sirens; hence markets would expect the targets to *be* met, and reflation would cease to be seen as a relevant option.

Events turned out differently. The government tried very hard to meet its targets; but the markets never really believed they would – and have not fully done so until quite recently, perhaps as recently as 1986. The reasons in retrospect are not difficult to locate in the political economy of making such targets stick when powerful vested interests, including senior Tories, did not want them to.

This failure of credibility increases the *costliness* of counter-inflation policy. Matthews and I estimated the cumulative cost in unemployment by 1984 at one million, because policy was systematically tighter than expected.

At the same time, the *gradualism* policy was converted to *de facto* shock tactics because of the error in choosing £M3 as the target variable for money.[1] Because of banking deregulation £M3 turned out to be a misleading indicator. It overshot its target badly, the government tried to claw it back, and in the process delivered a very sharp monetary squeeze in 1980 and 1981: M0, the only remaining reliable indicator, fell from 13 per cent to nearly zero growth in just over two years. Inflation, of course, fell very sharply as a result.

It is rather like a general who announces he will crush the enemy with the gradual pressure of an infantry attack. The enemy does not believe he will attack at all. He does, but his commands are misinterpreted and activate the tanks and heavy shelling. The effects are devastating: the battle is won, but the casualties are high. How much better if we could rewrite it: he threatens the tanks, the enemy believes the threat and, when the tanks duly appear, surrenders – a victory with no casualties.

But I hasten to add that the analogy is also correct in suggesting that gradualism was unlikely to succeed, just as an infantry attack would be too feeble against a stubborn enemy; also that the move to shock tactics (the tanks of our analogy) while initiated by a mistake was then deliberately followed through in what amounted to a tactical revision for good reasons. Matthews and I judged that inflation expectations would have declined too slowly under gradualism to impress the electorate with counter-inflationary results, while nevertheless the long series of negative fiscal and monetary shocks so precipitated would have raised unemployment significantly; all this when unemployment was rising anyway. That judgement is a political one, but it seems secure; Mrs Thatcher and her Chancellor were embattled in their pursuit of 'monetarist' policies, and failure to bring inflation down decisively while unemployment was rising powerfully would surely have given unanswerable strength to their critics. It follows that gradualism was unsound as a strategy from a political viewpoint whatever its merits in the laboratory, and that its revision on the ground into shock tactics was necessary.

So the inflation battle, like so many battles in history, did not go according to plan, and the plan itself could have been improved. But it was won, and paved the way for the next campaign – against union power.

The union measure of Mr James Prior in 1980 had been a toe-in-the-water affair, which caused union leaders little loss of sleep. Yet, weakened by recession in their manufacturing heartland, they were unable to resist the two major Acts brought in by Mr Tebbit; these dramatically removed their immunities from common law tort action for damages, except for 'primary' strikes sanctioned by a majority in secret ballot.

Allocating responsibility for the reduction in unions' powers between the recession, the firmer policing of pickets as in the coal strike of 1983–4, and these Acts is difficult; all were essential in the change. But it is clear that the Tebbit Acts achieved *permanent* change where the other events alone would have had a merely temporary effect; their importance lay in facilitating the introduction of these Acts, which altered the relative financial costs of strikes to firms and unions.

Matthews and I attributed much of the sharp growth in productivity since 1979 (roughly quadrupled in manufacturing and doubled in the economy as a whole from the miserable 1 per cent or so per annum during the 1973–9 business cycle) to the decline in union power. Working practices have been transformed in the majority of industries, particularly but not only in manufacturing. While overmanning has been all but eliminated in manufacturing such as steel, cars, glass and chemicals, service industries such as newspapers, cleaning and, increasingly, financial services are also slimming down. The new service industries, such as computer software and biotechnology, are in any case not easily unionised, and so not held back in the application of new techniques.

This brings us naturally to the last major campaign of the first two terms: privatisation. Though initially this was just a side-show, the sale of council houses was one of those political products that sold so well that it begged for a follow-up: in political terms share ownership was the natural sequel. When so much in the shop-window is austere, like inflation-fighting, or confrontational, like union law, there is a particular need for softer-edged merchandise with sure appeal. This privatisation provided, in a way well explained by Cento Veljanovski.

The main successes from a purely economic viewpoint have to date been in the commercial disciplining of large public sector money-losers like British Airways, British Steel and British Coal, and the freeing of management from political interference in already promising public firms like Jaguar and Amersham. It is natural to credit privatisation with these effects even on the not-yet-privatised, as their managements either aimed for or feared entry to the private sector with much the same result. The gain has been in substituting shareholder for government monitoring of management, with improved managerial clarity of objectives, incentives and performance; surely this too contributed to the productivity surge, even if it cannot be quantified in a macro model.

What there has not been to date is any increase in competition, and so consumer power to discipline price and quality. Competition has either been judged to be adequate (British Airways, Jaguar, for example) or been replaced by regulation (British Telecom and British Gas most obviously). The reason is political: the power of managements to make or break this sensitive new political product. Mrs Thatcher chose to keep the managements on her side and go for the immediate gains in improved managerial performance we have noted. The problem is that once these gains have been made progress is slow or even backwards, as has been illustrated by Gas and Telecom. Regulation, however able in the short term (as exemplified by Professor Bryan Carsberg at Oftel), is no long-term substitute for consumer power as has been well attested by experience in the USA.

Yet there is no reason to write off this aspect now. The BT duopoly comes up for review in 1990 and technology will make possible a sideways move to greater competition from cable, satellite and other modes of message transfer. The CEGB is to be privatised around then also, which will allow the injection of a new competitive regime across energy. Managements will and are already fighting these developments, but the boot is now much more on the government's foot, with privatisation a settled programme.

I have reviewed the three major set-piece campaigns of the first two terms. But around these there has been much other activity, either related mopping up, in military parlance, or preparations for future campaigns.

Deregulation in the private sector, decontrol and contracting-out have been the natural accompaniment to privatisation. Though privatisation has had the limelight, real additional competition has been achieved by all this; for example in buses, long- and short-distance, in the stock exchange, in local authority operations, and in capital markets with the abolition of exchange controls.

The productivity miracle is surely also partly owed to this. So it must be too to the decline in marginal tax rates on the average earner (down from 49 per cent in 1979 to 45% today – after the 1988 Budget and allowing for VAT and national insurance charges on both employers and employees), on the top earner (from 83 per cent to 40 per cent), and on the corporation (down from 52 per cent to 35 per cent).

Yet, while we have examined the activity devoted to fighting inflation, and raising productivity via the supply side programme on unions, privatisation, deregulation and tax cuts, we have said nothing about unemployment. A stable financial order and greater efficiency is all to the good, but an efficient *economy* must also utilise *all* its human resources properly. It is in this field of unemployment that Mrs Thatcher has been slowest to engage battle, indulging in much preparation and experimentation before taking the field proper.

Analysis available to her early on indicated that the problem of unemployment was one of incentives: getting people to take the jobs that were or could become available rather than those no longer available that they were used to and preferred, usually using out-moded skills but then commanding better pay than these alternatives.

Matthews and I calculated that by 1980 the *equilibrium* unemployment rate (towards which actual unemployment was naturally tending) was already 3.1 million. This is a measure of the incentives problem Mrs Thatcher had to deal with. Our analysis therefore suggests that the sharp rise of about 2 million in unemployment from 1979 to 1983 can be fully accounted for by the elimination of overmanning, as the actual employment 'caught up with' this equilibrium rate; in other words, had Mrs Thatcher's government done *nothing* and no other shock had occurred, unemployment would have risen this much anyway.

Of course, both policy and other shocks did occur which had effects in both directions. But the point is that if inflationary and interventional 'fixes' were to be ruled out by other policy objectives, there could only be one way to cure this unemployment: that of reforming labour market incentives. Under such reform, the unemployed would opt for lower-paid jobs outside union protection while union powers to hold up their members' wages above market-clearing rates would be curbed, so that by these twin pressures wages would fall across both union and non-union sectors, creating new jobs.

The problem was political. To create such incentives meant tampering with the benefit system, or expensive tax reform, or curbing union powers to push for wage increases in excess of productivity increases. Benefits were widely felt to protect those in genuine need. Expensive tax subsidies like the basic income guarantee were ruled out by cost and also would make incentives worse for ordinary workers. And union members on whom Mrs Thatcher relied for votes would not welcome wage curbs, much as they had supported productivity gains.

The search has been on for a viable political approach to this problem. It has been spearheaded by the Treasury looking at tax reforms, the Department of Health and Social Security pursuing benefit reform, and the Department of Employment investigating job-creation methods. Along the way numerous useful changes have been made: Mr Fowler's reforms of the state earnings related pension scheme and the poverty trap, the cuts in tax rates and restructuring of national insurance charges, and the corporate tax reforms that have massively swollen tax revenues in an impressive supply side experiment. But until quite recently a coherent strategy for unemployment had not emerged.

That has now changed because of the success of the Restart programme initiated by Lord Young. It is no coincidence that unemployment began its steady fall in August 1986, one month after Restart went national. Backed by the ultimate sanction of benefit withdrawal for those failing the work-test enshrined in the original Beveridge laws, Restart produced a large 'melt factor' as numbers withdrew from the register rather than come to interview. Some have said this represents a fiddling of the figures. Surely the truth is rather that the figures have been shown to be phoney, swollen by those either not wanting a job on reasonable terms or actually doing a job while claiming. This is not really a surprise, because the labour force survey had been saying for three years that around a million claimants either had work or were not genuinely seeking it.

If a problem is defined by a statistic, then a legitimate part of its solution is the refinement of the statistic. But Restart has done more than this. While offering positive help to the unemployed, it also defined their obligations in return for social support. This was a beginning in tackling the incentives problem, because in principle at least now a job had to be taken if available on pain of benefit loss. It therefore limited benefit, while not denying it to any in genuine need; incentives were tackled without shocking ordinary people's caring instincts. Thus more people are now taking places on the community programme and the training schemes available. The rate of placement by Restart in jobs or training places is also around 5 per cent, which, though still depressingly low, is an improvement for the long-term unemployed who previously were apparently stuck in this state.

Restart is now being built upon, basically by increasing the element of compulsion. The below-eighteens *must* now take a YTS place or go off benefit. The morality of this is unassailable, since anyone receiving state help should presumably in return contribute whatever little they can. This principle will no doubt be extended to older workers in time, in the manner of US workfare, and the Swedish or Swiss benefit systems. Meanwhile it seems likely that the Chancellor intends quite sweeping personal tax reforms that will take large numbers in time out of the poverty trap.

The strategy is being completed on the union wage side by the new union bill now going through Parliament. This attenuates to virtual disappearance the remaining immunities, since unions will be stripped of the power to discipline those *members* who cross picket lines. Firms will be able to break even wage strikes by engaging disaffected union workers to help supervise non-union untrained ones. Under this new barrage it is possible that unions will cease to be monopoly agents and revert to their common law role of friendly societies providing insurance, legal assistance and communication channels with managers.

Other elements of the incentives problem are being tackled in the new 'inner cities' bills now also before Parliament. Rent de-regulation will lower the cost for a migrant worker of rented accommodation in the South East, and so facilitate mobility of unskilled unemployed from North to South. The rate reforms will push business from congested regions to unemployment black spots, both through the unified business rate and because the poll tax will limit the local domestic tax burden on incoming managers and skilled workers in these black spots. Education reform – if it is built upon boldly – offers the eventual prospect of higher productivity in these places' labour forces; because benefits are low relative to skilled wages, this improves incentives and job prospects.

What I have just described is the fourth campaign getting into gear as we go into this third term, its focus being on unemployment generally, and particularly in our inner cities. This brings our account up to date. But what of the future?

When this latest wave of legislation is in place, whatever its adventures in the House of Lords, a stock-taking will reveal areas still in need of reform. There is the NHS, an anomaly in a largely privatised ex-public sector. Education will be seen to be patchily touched, and the rest of an impatient electorate will ask how their supposed new freedom of choice can be exercised. We will still have large regulated private monopolies failing to deliver satisfaction. Even if the Chancellor has done all that I expect he will, there will still be excessively high top rates of tax, the confiscatory inheritance tax, and numerous privileged savings outlets featherbedding sleepy institutions. Mrs Thatcher's reform seam is far from exhausted; indeed it is obvious that, though much improved, the British economy could, by merely catching up with the best overseas practice, raise productivity sharply again. Some of that gain is already in the pipeline; but the rest is dependent on completing the process of reform.

Looking back on this process, it can be seen that it does conform to a path towards the vision I sketched earlier. Money is being returned to consumers to allow them greater choice; producers are generally being exposed to greater competition and, where competition is still lacking, to greater monitoring pressure. The poor *are* being protected – as the statistics clearly show, the share of the bottom 20 per cent of households in income after tax and all benefits including health and education has remained basically unchanged between 1979 and 1985, the latest year available – but less through universal provision, and more through selective help. I described such a strategy in a paper in the spring of 1984 when policy was somewhat in the doldrums after the 1983 election on a thin manifesto. I argued that through the better utilisation of resources that would result, the public finances would find themselves with increasing surpluses, so allowing the transformation to accelerate. Utopian as it seemed to many at the time, that strategy has gradually been implemented and has been paying off in those terms, as the latest PSBR figures manifestly demonstrate. It is likely that the strategy will continue towards completion.

Could it have been done better? With the benefit of hindsight, it would be surprising if it could not. One obvious area is unemployment. I earlier suggested that one million was added cumulatively to unemployment by 1984 by the anti-inflation programme actually pursued from 1979. I have since calculated that inflation would have been more cheaply cured by shock tactics – as suggested by Hayek, for example – in 1979–80, rather than by the gradualism attempted. Such analysis as there was of breaking inflationary expectations favoured shock tactics (Sargent, 1986); and this tactic was, as we have seen, finally adopted on the ground. Yet it was not as fashionable in 1979 as gradualism.

Furthermore, Lord Young's idea of Restart was actually suggested long before – by Ralph Howell in 1981 and by me in the context of a full analysis of the incentives problem in 1983. American experiments with workfare were extant then, and the Swedish system was known about. There was an unconscionable delay in launching such ideas in a suitably British form.

These were two mistakes which could each have cost the programme its life. The reasons for them are surely in the time-lag between ideas and their acceptability in practice, whether to politicians or public opinion. Gradualism had been long in the public domain through the persuasive advocacy of Milton Friedman; the idea of shock tactics had not. It took the pressure of events to introduce them. Similarly with workfare/Restart: it was a new idea, as was the notion that unemployment could be substantially due to incentive problems. It took crucial time for this idea to hit the ground as strategy.

One could nitpick one's way through many *details* of the strategy, too. But that, to come back to my beginning, would be rather to miss the basic point about this whole operation.

Mrs Thatcher's reform odyssey has been, to repeat, a discovery process by a political entrepreneur of genius. And, like Odysseus,

Mrs Thatcher has had hair-raising adventures, made many mistakes, and enjoyed both good and bad fortune; the fact is she is still afloat with a following wind. No-one can tell when, how or whether she will reach the shores of her Schumpeterian vision. But the omens are, I believe, favourable.

Notes

1. £M3 is a very broad definition of money which includes high interest-bearing deposits; M0 is the narrow definition, consisting of cash in the hands of the public, and cash held by the banks at the Bank of England.

References

Ralph Howell (1981), 'Why Work? A Radical Solution', Conservative Political Centre.

Kent Matthews and Patrick Minford (1987), 'Mrs Thatcher's Economic Policies, 1979–87', *Economic Policy*, **5**, October, pp. 57–101.

Patrick Minford with David Davies, Michael Peel and Alison Sprague (1983), *Unemployment, Cause and Cure*, 1st edn, Martin Robertson, now Basil Blackwell, Oxford.

Patrick Minford and Anupam Rastogi (1988), 'A New Classical Policy Programme' in the proceedings of the NIESR Conference on Demand Management (published as *Policymaking with Macroeconomic Models*, ed. A. Britton, Gower 1989, pp. 83–97.)

Mancur Olson (1982), *The Rise and Decline of Nations*, Yale University Press, New Haven and London.

Thomas Sargent (1986), 'Stopping Moderate Inflations: the Methods of Poincare and Thatcher', ch. 4 of *Rational Expectations and Inflation*, Harper & Row, New York; an earlier version appeared as 'The Ends of Four Big Inflations', in R.E. Hall (ed.) (1982) *Inflation*, Chicago University Press, Chicago.

Cento Veljanovski, (1986), *Selling the State*, Weidenfeld and Nicholson, London.

Sir Alan Walters (1985), *Britain's Economic Renaissance – Margaret Thatcher's Economic Reforms, 1979–84*, Oxford University Press for American Enterprise Institute, Oxford.

George Yarrow (1986), 'Privatisation in Theory and Practice', *Economic Policy*, **2**, April, pp. 323–67.

Name Index

255

Subject Index